I0033660

Robustness
Anticipatory and Adaptive Human Systems

Volume 4
Exploring Organizational Complexity

Other volumes in the *Exploring Organizational Complexity* Series:

- Volume 1: *Complex Systems Leadership Theory: New Perspectives from Complexity Science on Social and Organizational Effectiveness*, Edited by James K. Hazy, Jeffrey A. Goldstein and Benyamin B. Lichtenstein, ISBN 9780979168864.

- Volume 2: *Complexity and Policy Analysis: Tools and Concepts for Designing Robust Policies in Complex World*, Edited by Linda Dennard, Kurt A. Richardson and Goktug Morcol, ISBN 9780981703220.

- Volume 3: *Complexity Science & Social Entrepreneurship: Adding Social Value Through Systems Thinking*, Edited by Jeffrey A. Goldstein, James K. Hazy and Joyce Silberstang, ISBN 9780984216406.

ROBUSTNESS
Anticipatory and Adaptive Human Systems

Written & Edited by

MIKA AALTONEN
Helsinki University of Technology

EMERGENT™
PUBLICATIONS

3810 N 188th Ave
Litchfield Park, AZ 85340

Robustness: Anticipatory and Adaptive Human Systems
Volume 4 of *Exploring Organizational Complexity* Series
Written and Edited by: Mika Aaltonen

Library of Congress Control Number: 2010928654

ISBN: 978-0-9842164-6-8

Copyright © 2010 Emergent Publications,
3810 N 188th Ave, Litchfield Park, AZ 85340, USA.

"The Perfect Storm" appears by permission of the
Research and Analysis Corporation of Finland.
© 2009 by Michael S. Loescher.

All rights reserved. No part of this publication may be
reproduced, stored on a retrieval system, or transmitted,
in any form or by any means, electronic, mechanical,
photocopying, microfilming, recording or otherwise,
without written permission from the publisher.

Printed in the United States of America

To my mother and father.

Author Biographies

Mika Aaltonen is a Ph.D. (Economics), Adjunct Professor (Foresight & Complexity), Editorial Board Member of the E:CO (Emergence: Complexity and Organizations) journal, Fellow of the Royal Society of Arts in London, Board Member of the European Regional Foresight College in Paris, and Member of the Millennium Project in Washington. He is also Head and Chairman of the Board of StraX (The Research Unit for Strategic Intelligence and Exploration of Futures) at Helsinki University of Technology and CEO of the Research and Analysis Corporation of Finland. Mika won the Emerald Literati Group's Highly Commended Award 2008.

Stefan Bergheim has been the Director of The Center for Progress since the beginning of 2009. Before launching the Center, he worked for leading international banks such as Merrill Lynch and JPMorgan in Frankfurt as an economist. Between 2002 and 2008, he worked for Deutsche Bank Research on topics such as growth, demographics, education and happiness. Stefan has a diploma in economics from Saarbrücken University, spent three years in the economics Ph.D. program at the University of Oregon (USA) and holds a doctoral degree from WHU in Koblenz/Vallendar, where he wrote the book "Long-run growth forecasting".

James Deegan is Professor in the Department of Learning, Society and Religious Education. He is also Director of Postgraduate Studies in Education at Mary Immaculate College in Limerick, Ireland and is a Fellow of the Royal Society of Arts in London. He is a former Associate Professor in Teacher Education at the University of Georgia, Athens, USA. He is a founding member of the Colleges of Education Research Consortium, Ireland and Immediate Past-Chair of the International Relations Committee, American Educational Research Association. His publications include Children's Friendships in Culturally Diverse Classrooms,

Routledge, 1996 and Primary Voices: Equality, Diversity and Childhood in Irish Primary Schools, Institute of Public Administration, 2004 (with D. Devine and A. Lodge). He has presented his ideas to the EU Ireland Presidency, the Royal Irish Academy, the American Educational Research Association and the American Anthropological Association.

Uffe Elbäk is Founder of The KaosPilots—International School of New Business Design & Social Innovation. Uffe Elbæk was born in 1954 and as he says himself has already managed to live several lives. Personally as well as professionally. From 1991 to 2006 he has been the principal of the KaosPilots in Denmark, but is also a regular contributor to a range of leading Danish and International newspapers and magazines. In November 2001 and again in 2005 Uffe Elbæk was elected to Aarhus City Council (Denmark's second city) for the Danish Social-Liberal Party. He is also on the board of several Danish and international organizations, and has received numerous honors and awards, ranging from his appointment as ambassador for the local premier league football club AGF to Knight of the Danneborg.

Rolf Jensen, M.Sc. (Political Science), Founder and Chief Imagination Officer of Dream Company A/S, former CEO of Copenhagen Institute of Future Studies, principal in the Ministry of Defence, then at the Ministry of Foreign Affairs, and also Ministry of Fisheries. He has written the bestsellers "The Dream Society" (translated into 10 languages), "Heartstorm" and "The Future Makers". Rolf is a frequently used advisor, author and lecturer on subjects within the future and corporate storytelling. He is currently on the Boards of Børnefonden (The Children's Foundation), Foreningen FAIR and Byprojekt Tordenskiold. Rolf is a Fellow at the Royal Geographical Society.

Chuan Lam Leong is Ambassador-at-Large with the Government of Singapore's Ministry of Foreign Affairs. He held the post of Permanent Secretary in the Ministry of Finance, Ministry of the Environment, the Ministry of National Development, the Ministry for Trade and Industry, and the Ministry of Communications and Information within the Government of Singapore.

Michael S. Loescher. During his 30 years of professional life Michael has become widely acknowledged as one of the foremost experts on government reform and strategic planning in the world. He has authored, or been contributing author to, five books on the subjects of intelligence, futures-forecasting and risk-management. He was twice selected one of the top 100 US employees, and held the first Admiral William A. Moffett Chair for Innovation in Naval Warfare at the US Naval Institute. He was a principal drafter of the present US Department of Defense Network-Centric Warfare doctrine. He is also a founding Director the Research and Analysis Corporation of Finland.

Riel Miller is a specialist in long-run strategic thinking, foresight theory and practice. As a global foresight design consultant he works closely with clients to develop and implement state-of-the-art action-research and strategic decision making processes. For over twenty-five years his work has concentrated on how to assess and direct the potential for socio-economic transformation in the private and public sectors. Between 1995 and 2005 Riel worked as a Principal Administrator in the International Futures Programme at the OECD. In 2005 he launched his own consulting company, xperidox futures consulting. His clients include governments and multi-national corporations around the world. He is also a faculty member at the Masters of Public Affairs, Sciences-Po, Paris and teaches regularly in leading business schools and universities.

Larry O'Connell was appointed Senior Economist to the National Economic and Social Council of Ireland (NESC) Secretariat in March 2007. His work to date has focused on industrial organization, innovation and the internationalization of Irish industry. Larry was formerly head of Research and Policy Development with the National Centre for Partnership and Performance and Greencore Newman Scholar in Competitive Advantage at University College Dublin. His work has produced an eclectic and customized account of Irish economic development. He has looked closely at the role of local and regional clustering, international networks and organizational structures and practices in key sectors of the Irish economy. In 2001 he received his PhD for his work in this area. Larry is currently working on the Futures Ireland project.

Rory O'Donnell is Director of the National Economic and Social Council of Ireland (NESC) and Chief Officer of the National Economic and Social Development Office (NESDO). In his work as Economist and later Director at NESC he has prepared the analysis that underpins Ireland's social partnership approach to economic and social policy and has written extensively on partnership. He was Jean Monet Professor of Business at the Smurfit Business School, University College Dublin; where he edited a review of Ireland's first 25 years in the EU, Europe—The Irish Experience (Institute of European Affairs, 2000) and coauthored Europe's Experimental Union: Rethinking Integration (Routledge, 2000).

Gerda Roeleveld is a landscape architect with Deltares, a Dutch independent research institute for water, soil and subsurface Issues. She has over 20 years experience in spatial planning and regional development issues in the Netherlands as well as at European level, acquired while working for the Spatial Planning Department of the Ministry of Housing, Spatial Planning and the Environment in The

Hague. The role of spatial design in participatory knowledge development and decision-making processes has been the focus of her interest throughout her professional career. Gerda is Member of the European Regional Foresight College in Paris and President of the Wageningen Landscape Architects Alumni Association.

Contents

Preface—The Foundations...1
    Discussing the Key Concepts...4
    Chapter by Chapter Outline...9

1. Emergence, Systems and Contexts 15

2. Colonizing Futures 37

3. Revisiting Histories.......................................51
    Conceptual and Relational Framework................................69
    Assuming a Responsibility for One's Identity 70
    Memoir as Design for Change..71
    Memoir as a Tool for Learning 72
    Contextual Data 72
    Discussing Findings 74
    Towards Elaborated Identities 74
    Conformity and Received Identities.................................78
    Conclusion 80

4. Building Intelligent and Flexible Systems...........85
    Time Horizon...88
    Alternative Futures 89
    Attitude Towards Risk and Probabilities............................89
    Lack of Synchronism between Performance and
    Reward...91
    A System of Risk Assessment and Anticipating
    Uncertainties...92
    Challenges to the Scenario Planning Process 95
    Induced Organizational Change......................................96
    Behavioral Implications..97
    Conclusion 98
    What Operations Analysis Yields 103
    Common Failures in Intelligence....................................105
    An Innovation Service 105
    And How to Build It..107
    The Perfect Storm—Transition in Global Logistics
    Lanes 111

5. Preparing for Futures 117
Dutch spatial planning system 131
Foresight 132
Randstad2040—The Case 134
Conclusions 143
Questions for Discussion................................ 145

6. Relationships as a Cause............................. 149
We are Embedded in Systems 151
From a Cognitive to an Affective Perspective 152
Empathic-Introspective Inquiry 152
Adapting a Process View 153
The Expansion of Subjective Worlds.................... 154
Preferring Common Sense Over Lots of Knowledge 154
Section 1—FuturesIreland: A Case Study in
Building Futures Literacy 155
Section 2—The Origins and the Focus of
FuturesIreland.. 160
The Distinctive Focus of FuturesIreland 161
Section 3—The Futures Literacy Approach 165
FuturesIreland: Organizational Attributes.............. 171
Section 4—FuturesIreland: Recounting the
Case Study.. 173
Mapping and Discussing the Evidence.................. 177
Box 3 179
Compliance Monitoring and Diagnostic Monitoring 179
Conclusion: What Does FuturesIreland Tell Us?.......... 182
Theories of Progress 185
Strong correlations across countries 189
Correlations, Factors, Clusters and Co-integration 191
Even More Variables of Possible Importance............ 193
Changes are Possible.................................... 194
A Robustness Check for Sweden and the USA 196
How to Foster Progress.................................. 197

7. Probing Futures 199
The Shocking.. 200
The Routine 201
The Jackpot 201
Time to Experiment 202

What to Experiment On 202
Resistance to Experimentation 204
Fear of Experimentalism 204
The Courage to Do It 205

8. Leadership—
Impact as Strategy 211
A "Business as Unusual" Event 214
Pockets of Intolerance 216
Success from the Point of View of the Program, the
Organization and the Finances 217
Upgrading the Infrastructure 219
Upgrading Organizations 220
Upgrading Businesses 220
Upgrading Knowledge 221
Upgrading Language 222
Upgrading Culture 222
Upgrading Identity 223
Sources of Anticipation and Adaptation 224
Impact as Strategy 229

Bibliography 235

Tables and Figures

Table 1 A Summary of Ontological Universals 5
Table 2 The Present Present 7
Figure 1 Chapter by Chapter Outline 10
Table 3 Aristotelian Causes and Manipulated Properties 17
Table 4 The Systemic Properties of Various Disciplines 18
Figure 2 System-Model Relationship 21
Figure 3 System-Model Relationship Detailing Feedback
and Feedforward Controllers 26
Figure 4 Different Systems Have Different Causal
Assumptions 29
Figure 5 Chronotope Space 32
Figure 6 The Steak Protocol 44
Figure 7 The Analytical Topology of the Production of
Steak 46
Figure 8 Traditional Historical Narratives 57
Figure 9 Narrative Networks 59
Figure 10 Dimensions of Identity Processes 75
Figure 11 The Two Track Approach of Horizon Scanning
and Scenario Planning 93
Figure 12 An Illustration of the High Consequence Risks
Facing the United Kingdom 94
Figure 13 From an OODA Loop to Decision-Wave 101
Figure 14 Melting of the Arctic Ice Gap 112
Figure 15 The Modernization of the Trans-Siberian
Railway 113
Figure 16 Petroleum and Gas Reserves in the Arctic 115
Table 5 Attitudes, Scenarios and Strategies 122
Figure 17 Ranstad2040 Structural Vision Map 132
Figure 18 Legend of Ranstad2040 Structural Vision Map .. 133
Figure 19 One of Three Thematic Development
Perspectives 139
Figure 20 One of three posters on the 'Outdoors city'
development perspective, used for exhibition 141
Table 6 The Three Phases of a Futures Literacy Process 170
Table 7 Framework for Mapping and Discussing the
Evidence 178
Figure 21 The Finnish Foresight System 212
Figure 22 Different Systems and Emergence of Futures 228
Table 8 Leader's role in Multiple Contexts 231

Preface—The Foundations

Time has passed quickly. It was four years ago when I started a dialogue with my sense-making colleagues around the world; some of them experts who share the mind set of critical thinking, and some of them decision-makers in various governments and governmental organizations trying to deal with the uncertainty they face. The discussions concerned the ideas, thinking, processes, projects and institutions we use to make sense of and to build our respective futures. The aim was not to rank or compare the countries between themselves, but rather to find out if there exits conditions for a novel, more robust sense-making and decision-making theory.

A lot has happened while writing this book. At the time of writing, in the spring of 2010, all the world is reeling from a financial crisis. At the top of the economic ladder, the rich are poorer. In the middle, decades of hard work by hundreds of millions of people has been lost to a sudden financial tsunami. And at the bottom, the poor have again been pushed aside.

The credit crunch has undermined faith in our economic and investment systems and raised difficult questions for policy-makers and private individuals alike. It has undermined or destroyed the credibility of many of the foresight, planning and investment theories and the reputations of the past generation.

For us, the issue is certainly not the preservation of any status quo, whether political, economic or societal. On the contrary, we are convinced that the world is undergoing an extraordinary complex and lengthy transformation. The signs of which are everywhere to anyone who will see them. We are all going somewhere new. None of us, the most or the least able, can plot a precise course. Nor will master plans see us through; they are the first to be jettisoned in a sea of complexity. We are all going to have to invent the new world, decision by decision, action by action, over the next several decades.

However *Robustness* is not about the horrors of the economic downturn that have appeared in almost all shapes and sizes, and have had dramatic effects upon most human activities. But *Robustness* hopes to represent a fundamental change in how sense-making and decision-making strategies can be achieved in a more conscious, responsible and sustainable way.

It seems to me that for those who participated in this research there is a consensus on the three major reasons of dissatisfaction with current dominant modes of thought and action practices. I shall state them explicitly:

Firstly, the legacy of the Western tradition of *efficient cause being the primary focus of science and economics,* is considered here erroneous and misleading. Its dominance in our thinking is also one of the reasons why many real-world problems appear intractable and are difficult to resolve. The difficulty arises when only single causes are sought, even though such problems arise from the interaction of multiple, underlying and interrelated causes.[1]

Secondly, our sense-making and decision-making *practices are set against an unchanging landscape,* where only a single element or few elements, if any, are extrapolated. Thus, is it any wonder that there is an inherent inability to deal with complex chains of causality and to take into consideration both top-down and bottom-up causes.

Thirdly, *the classical idea of a fixed, permanent and absolute, which is simultaneously an acontextual truth,* should be replaced with a spatio-temporal approach. This ought to be done because the explicit consideration of a spatio-temporal context will necessitate new ways of understanding epistemology, methodology and leadership and help produce better futures.

The theory emerging in this book has arisen in response to the limitations of our present modes of thinking. We hope we have a theory that builds a better understand-

---

1. C.f. Kaminska-Labbe & McKelvey 2006.

ing of the emerging landscape, and recognizes that there are multiple emerging cause and effect relationships on different levels. Furthermore, we emphasize the relevance of spatio-temporal context, which will be necessary in order to create more and better anticipatory and adaptive human systems.

For this research, a multiple case study approach[2] and in-depth thematic interviews[3] by individuals and groups were employed to investigate our ideas, thinking, processes, projects and institutions we use to make sense of and to build our futures.

Hundreds of people were interviewed. The interviews typically opened with a brief presentation of the research, after which the interviewees were guided by open-ended questions that were complemented by more specific ones. At the end interviewees were asked to name further contacts that could potentially be helpful in providing a deeper understanding of the research topics.

In addition to the interviews and confidential discussions, secondary documents and sources were consulted. These included a wide variety of material, from various relevant organizations to specific projects; some discussions merely pointed us in the direction of information contained in reports, news services and websites.

It would be naïve to believe that a theory could emerge solely from data. In every theory building research there is always a previously existing body of knowledge, and to claim ignorance of such existing literature will not benefit any research, vice versa it disguises the biases. This research builds on sense-making, decision-making, operational analysis, anticipation, foresight, prospective thinking and futures studies literature.

The results were achieved after iterating between the data, the relevant literature, and emerging ideas and

---

2. Eisenhardt 1989, Yin 1994.
3. Strauss & Corbin 1998.

constructs[4]. This process of iteration was repeated several times with different cases and people; in the end the new theory found its shape and form.

Discussing the Key Concepts

According to the Aristotelian idea of science, there are many different sciences and they are characterized according to their specific types of objects and their laws: physics is the field of natural movements and transformations; logic is the study of formal reasoning; politics is the analysis of public virtues; and rhetorics is the study of how to convince others[5].

Implicitly, Aristotle sets the basis for polynomial understanding of the world. By which I refer that certain names, terms, ideas and theories are supposed to work best, and sometimes only, within certain areas of, expertise and science, or certain professions.

Three questions arose from consideration of our polynomial understanding of the world: what is the nature of each science, what are the mutual connections and dependencies between the sciences; and what is the nature of the whole emerging from them.

To summarize briefly the long and colorful debates that have taken place in the science throughout the centuries, and to provide satisfactory answers that can be categorized and subsumed under distinguishable categories, i.e. to make ontological universals, we could claim that three positions can be identified in today's world: nominalism, conceptualism and realism. According to nominalists universals are linguistics expressions; to conceptualists universals result from our cognitive capabilities to conceptualize and categorize our experiences; and to realists universals exist independently of all forms of concrete existence.[6]

---

4. Miles & Huberman 1994.
5. Poli 2006.
6. Poli 2006.

	Ontological universals		
	Linguistic expressions	Concepts	Objects
Nominalism	Yes	No	No
Conceptualism	Yes	Yes	No
Realism	Yes	Yes	Yes

Table 1 *A summary of ontological universals*

One could say that nominalists only accept universal expressions, while conceptualists accept both universal expressions and universal concepts, and realists accept universal expressions, universal concepts and universal objects.[7]

For this research the previous categorization serves as a building block. It explicates elements that any serious new theory should be able to deal with. And indeed, after reconsidering the importance of time, living entities, and the spatio-temporal contexts in which we are engaged, we are able to evolve even some of the oldest ideas and most long-standing Western thinking.

There is an agreement that time is an essential element is social life and that it should be central to social theory, but most of the social theories are atemporal. In fact, the Newtonian description of change, and the approaches based on that, deal with non-temporal quantities without the need for a temporal context.

Most people assume that they share the same timeframe as other people. However, we often fail to recognize that time is considered in different ways by different people and is understood in different ways within a variety of contexts, for example, events, roles and organizations. Different things have different natural time scales. By matching the phenomena with their natural time scale the possibility to create more sensitivity regarding continuity and discontinuity is revealed. Thus, significant possibilities for chang-

7. Poli 2006.

es and interdependent events appear where previously we had assumed none.

We can find time in the life processes of growth; mechanical, biological and social interactions; natural and social rhythms; but also in identities, memories and social histories. An explicit focus on time reveals new ways of understanding and a different use of existing concepts[8]. Even the presentation of ontological universals in Table 1 has had to be reassessed and some of our longheld beliefs become invalidated, when time is given a focal role in our approach.

A significant question with huge practical implications for any anticipatory and adaptive human system is: Where is the future? If we think the future is somewhere out there, further in time and space, waiting for us in one form or another, we will have difficulties in taking the responsibility for it. If we place the future in our present decisions and actions then it is likely that more conscious, responsible and potentially sustainable solutions become achievable.

The second significant question concerns the way we comprehend the past, and in particular, how past events turn into a causal force that influence and determine our present and future social realities through communication, conceptualization and memory.

Here, the approach taken to *time is multileveled*, we understand time as "dendrochronology", literarly the dating of annual tree rings, according to which the levels of history and the different conceptions of futures are to be seen in the presence, and whether we refer to individuals, organizations or even nations our ideas of pasts as well as our conceptions of futures influence our ability to adapt with changing situations.

Traditionally human beings have used the concepts of past, present and future to make sense of their lives and to be able to comprehend it as continuum. In Table 2, I take

---

8. Adam 1990.

6

		Future future
	Present future	Future present
Past future	Present present	Future past
Past present	Present past	
Past past		

Table 2 *The present present*

St. Augustine's[9] considerations further. He concludes that the past and the future do not exist outside the mind, and argues that "the mind performs three functions; those of expectation, attention and memory. The future which it expects, passes through the present, to which it attends, is not the past which it remembers." The understanding of past, present and future as present past, present present and present future in the middle column is complemented in the left hand column by past past, past present and past future, and on the right by future past, future present and future future. Table 2 provides an explicit notional tool to discuss how the past future has moved to the present present, and how the present future will become the future present. If we want that the future present will be different from the present future, we need to have the elements that build a different future into it because continuing the way we always have makes the future predictable.

The second fundamental issue concerns *the nature of the living entities*—human beings, organisms, ecosystems and organizations are only ever partially determined and always partially open. The previous sentence applies to everyone and explicates our philosophy in *Robustness*. There is potentiality, even if hidden, which means that the potentiality is there, but waiting for a trigger to activate it, or latent, meaning elements that may not exist in the entity's current state, but which may emerge in time. For instance, a newborn baby cannot do most of the things adults

---

9. St. Augustine Book XI, quoted in Jaques 1982.

can, but in due time he will have the capacities to do them.[10] This necessitates a new approach to change, we cannot anymore comprehend and treat it like billiard balls in motion nor on the behavior of dead matter[11].

We are engaged in *spatio-temporal contexts*, our lives at home and in work happen within specific space-time environments. In everyday life these contexts are pretty far taken-for-granted. However, when our ontological framework becomes richer, it becomes more robust, and more anticipatory and adaptive. A richer framework enables us to see what we did not see before, and helps us to attain our hidden and latent potentialities, and benefit from the changes that take place in our environment.

Recent human history shows a preference for order and gradually we have come to the belief that order is or should be the basic state of affairs in our lives. Newtonian physics pervades our lives. Whenever we interact with a machine we interact with Newtonian physics in practice[12]. Using clocks, driving cars or having factories building them would be impossible without the knowledge of the physical principles involved and the full application of efficient cause. Nevertheless, we perceive physics not as a way of understanding but as being the fundamental reality of our existence.

Chemistry Nobel Prize Winner Ilya Prigogine would claim, human beings are dissipative beings and function "far from equilibrium". Sometimes our lives are in order and proceed linearily "as planned"; but sometimes we find ourselves in chaos, where the order is undone. It is probably likely that we are most often somewhere in between these states, in other words, we exist in a complex state. If we rethink and develop sensivity to the spatial contexts we work within, our behavior will begin to impact on its environment, because some interventions work best in linear

---

10. Poli 2009b.
11. Adam 1990.
12. Adam 1990.

contexts, some in disruptive ones, and some are appropriate interventions for complex contexts.

Naturally our approach is *polynomial*, but it is not organized according to professions, fields or sciences like in Aristotle's approach, but according to spatio-temporal contexts. I would like to argue that people use and are aware of various ontological, i.e. spatio-temporal, contexts and they have created specific terms, knowledge and approaches within them implicitly, and furthermore this book is the first one that explicitly brings them together into a coherent theory. The use of names, terms, concepts and theories is explicitly motivated in *Robustness*.

Chapter by Chapter Outline

The framework according to which also the chapters are organized represents the ontological basis in which the chapters best present relevant, insightful and contemporary observations. I claim that the framework is durable in time, and helpful in various contexts over and over again, because it captures something essential about our existence as human beings, because it is first of all an ontological framework, not a methodological or epistemological one.

Our employment of time and space reveals opportunities for changes, where we previously had detected none. As one of the contributors to *Robustness* states "there are always opportunities for an opportunist", and the spatio-temporal framework in Figure 1 gives an idea of where to look for them. I deploy the old Greek concept of a chronotope, literally a place in time, in order to discuss and make sense of the spatio-temporal quality of the situation and the spatio-temporal responses that are relevant to it. When we face a problem or require a change, it comes equipped with its own relevant family of chronotopes. A different problem or a different change is always accompanied with different famililies of chronotopes, places in times, each one with its own unique structure.

A change in a spatio-temporal context requires a change in epistemology, methodology and leadership. When we move in Figure 1 along horizontal axis, from left to right, we move from a linear context to a disruptive one, inbetween them the degrees of order vary. However, if we move along the vertical axis, from the bottom up, we move from relevant histories to long-term visionary time scale. Every chapter in *Robustness* represents a specific spatio-temporal context and is placed in Figure 1 in its approximate position to enable us to discuss appropriate knowledge, ways of acquiring it and effective leadership.

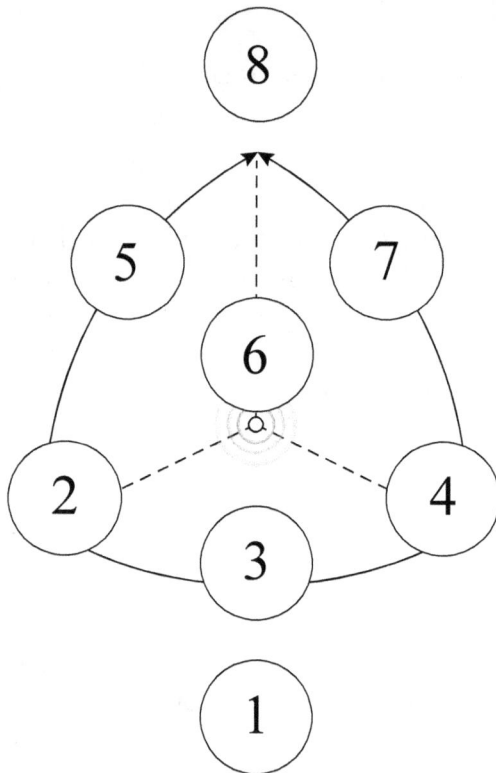

Figure 1 *Chapter by chapter outline*

In the introductory Chapter 1, I discuss how human beings have comprehended the *emergence* of things, and how our understanding of causality has evolved since the time of Aristotle. Robert Rosen's Metabolism-Repair (M, R) systems and Niklas Luhman's interpretation of auto-poesis systems lay the basis for an anticipatory and adaptive human *systems* theory in which the robustness of a system stems from the fact that past, present and futures states can influence the present sense-making and decision-making in the system. In the end of Chapter the mission of the *Robustness* is revealed—to reconnect the spatio-temporal *contexts* into formation of knowledge, use of methods and appropriate leadership—and is comprehensively stated.

The second Chapter—Colonizing Futures—is set mostly in linear context, and it explains how the Newtonian paradigm has become the most popular approach even outside the boundaries within which it was originally meant to work. It demonstrates why it is not applicable in all human contexts. *Michael Loescher* then explicates what *time compression* means for the American steak business and draws out what that means for sense-making and decision-making.

Chapter 3—Revisiting Histories—sees human history as being multileveled, a place where various historical levels and accounts work as a causal force in the determination of present and future social realities in their own right. I also place much attention on the relationship between language and history as well as to the narrative reasoning of our lives. *James Deegan* demonstrates how personal *memoirs* and *emotions* contribute to *teaching* and *learning*.

Set in the context of disruption Chapter 4 takes its headline from a statement by Singapore Vice Prime Minister in which the following idea was presented; because we cannot know the future, we should concentrate on something what we can do. It is entitled Building Intelligent and Flexible Systems. First, *Chuan Lam Leong* uses his notable experience to make sense of management under *complexity* and *uncertainty*, sometimes under *risks* and *crisis*, and then I write with *Michael Loescher* about *operations analysis* and *non-military intelligence*.

Chapter 5—Preparing for Futures—describes how the art of prognosis, developed in the 15th century Italy in order to help avoid the pitfalls governments had had difficulties in evading, and to enable their overall preparedness for possible futures. The idea started to flourish in European courts and has turned into thousands of contemporary foresight projects. *Gerda Roeleveld* reveals the latest Dutch spatial planning project *Randstad2040*, arguably the most important area of the Netherlands, and views the relevant issues with reference to climate change and to preparing the necessary long term investment decisions of national importance.

The sixth Chapter liberates us from Newtonian or Cartesian views that see human mind in isolation, separated from an external reality. Instead, we try to understand the human condition in terms of intersubjectivism and relatedness, that is why the chapter is called—Relationships as a Cause. *Larry O'Connell, Rory O'Donnell* and *Riel Miller* shed light on the recent *FuturesIreland* project that combined the intra-personal, inter-personal and institutional perspectives in the search for New Ireland. In the end of Chapter 6 *Stefan Bergheim* broadens the traditional economic approach to growth with his article *"The breadth of societal progress"*.

Chapter 7—Probing Futures—works within disruptive futures. If we describe what we know as a sphere which is continuously growing, we should also consider that the area of contact with the unknown is expanding even more rapidly. Often we cannot rely on the traditional scientific and industrial strategies to project, predict and program our futures by using our knowledge of the past as a base on which safety and innovation can be established. We need new theories and ideas to cultivate opportunities, facilitate experiments, and create a more open mindset. *Riel Miller* takes a critical look at the financial crisis and embraces experimentalism in his paper on whether *"to experiment or not to experiment"*. *Rolf Jensen* uses a narrative—*From the*

Few to the Many—and creates a notional world to discuss how the significant social markers that have constructed and constrained our lives have evolved, and also places people inside that world to learn more about possible developments.

For many policy-makers, the Nordic countries have served as a model for economically, socially and environmentally sustainable societies. The final Chapter 8 begins with the current Nordic debate about horizontal and shared leadership as an alternative for the traditional hierarchical leadership. *Uffe Elbäk* brings in the World Outgames 2009 organized in Copenhagen to present his ideas about *"an event as an entrepreneurial and attitude-forming strategy"*, He also demonstrates how leadership can be achieved in a multi-cultural and multi-organizational environment. At the end of the chapter, I focus on the mission of the *Robustness* by reconnecting the spatio-temporal contextuality to leadership. Out of this reconnection comes the title: Leadership—Impact as Strategy.

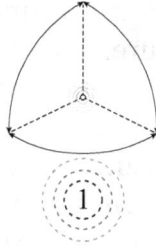

1. Emergence, Systems and Contexts

Lake Päijänne
Finland

Words, signs and concepts have an amazing capability. They can represent things that are spatially and temporally far away from our present situation. I am having a most pleasant morning cup of coffee in an island in the middle of Lake Päijänne. Still while I am thinking how things emerge in life, and how we think they emerge, I am using ideas created by some people a long time ago, and writing something for the future, for people who are not even born yet.

We start with our first challenge: the legacy of Western tradition, how efficient cause became the primary focus of science and economics, and why this should be considered erroneous and misleading.

There is an odd couple in Western philosophy that has immensely influenced, and still does, the way we comprehend causality. I refer to Aristotle and Isaac Newton. Despite them living 2000 years apart from each other; they are almost certainly the two major reference points in causality thinking.

The reason why causality, and I must be more precise—the way we comprehend causality—needs to be considered carefully, is because it has significant practical implications for the sciences as well as in business, and in our everyday lives when we try to understand and influence the *emergence* of the future.

Aristotle, a philosopher with origins of a biologist, offers a robust metrics for reflecting on the qualitative changes in Western causality thinking over the centuries. His explanation of how things emerge contains three basic entities: the material substance comprising physical objects, the abstract or geometric forms objects can assume, and the processes of change by which the substance or the form could be modified. Aristotle provides "because" results based on four causes or four different aspects, which taken together provide the answer to why the world is as it is. These causes are: 1) material, 2) efficient, 3) formal, and 4) final cause. They are presented in *Physics II* 3, and they can be found also in the dictionary of concepts in the *Metaphysics*:

> *Cause means 1) that form from which a thing comes into being,e.g., the bronze of the statue and the silver of the saucer, and the classes which include these. 2) The form or pattern, i.e., the formula or the essence, and the classes, which include this and the parts of the formula. 3) That form which that change or the freedom from change first begins,e.g., the adviser is a cause of the action, and father a cause of the child, and in general the maker of the thing made and the change-producing of the changing. 4) The end, i.e., that for the sake of which a thing,e.g., health is the cause of walking... all these are for the sake of the end, though they differ from one another in that some are instruments and others are actions... These then are practically all the sense in which causes are spoken of in several sense it follows that there are several causes of the same thing.[1]*

The overall scheme goes from material cause corresponding to substance, with efficient cause relating to the

---

1. Ross 1955.

processes used for changing a substance. In a similar fashion, formal cause explains the form of an entity, with final cause describing how one changes the form. The scheme explains why there are four cause, and not three or nine.[2] Even though Aristotle's guiding idea is that there are always several causes that together influence the emergence of the future, each of the four causes can be thought of being concerned with manipulating something specific as depicted in Table 3.

Cause	Manipulated Property
Material	Physical matter
Efficient	Energy
Formal	Information
Final	Desire

Table 3 *Aristotelian causes and manipulated properties*[3]

Physicist Isaac Newton's world consists of particles and forces. All properties of material systems can be expressed by identifying the particles constituting a system and the outside forces acting upon these particles. This is because everything knowable about a system is a function of the position and momenta of particles. The Newtonian framework can be thought of as an input/output system where the external forces are the input and the position and momenta of the particles are the outputs.[4]

Since its formulation, the Newtonian paradigm has been extremely successful. Already in the 17th century efficient cause gained predominance as Newtonian mechanics did not allow either objects or anticipated future-states to serve as intentional objects of desire and goals of action.[5]

2. Casti 1989.
3. Casti 1989.
4. Casti 1989.
5. Juarrero 1999.

This is a significant notion that explains why Newtonian systems are not anticipatory and adaptive.

In contrast to Newtonian systems, formal and final cause are emphasized in human systems. Table 3 indicates how much focus in a given discipline is upon material and efficient cause (on the left) and to what degree the questions and issues of a given discipline are concerned with formal and final cause. Generally speaking Newtonian – based modeling tends to work well for those disciplines on the left side of Table 3, but as we move towards the right, the Newtonian approaches become less competent at dealing with questions and issues of concern. In other words, Newtonian approaches were designed to address questions involving material and efficient cause, which dominate the hard sciences. The soft sciences concentrate on issues pertaining to formal and final cause.[6] It is not reasonable to expect models, concepts and tools based on the Newtonian paradigm to work well in such matters.

Newtonian principles work extremely well	Newtonian principles work well or can be applied	Newtonian principles are difficult to use
Physics	Engineering	Biology
Chemistry	Medicine	ICT
Material science	Environmental science	Economics
Meteorology	Linguistics	Political science

Table 4 *The systemic properties of various disciplines* [7]

Physics considers present states and present forces but biological and human systems often include also past states, in the form of memory and reflection, and even past

---

6. Casti 1989.
7. C.f. Casti 1989.

forces. This is the major difference between non-living and living systems, but the inclusion of memory is not sufficient for creating a precise distinction between Newtonian and anticipatory and adaptive systems. Besides memory, we need to add a second distinctive feature, namely futures states, i.e., we have to consider the changing or possibly changing futures landscape.[8]

Here we form our response to the second challenge we presented in the introduction—the sense-making and decision-making practices are set against an unchanging landscape, where only a single element or few elements, if any, are extrapolated—by presenting how more robust, anticipatory and adaptive human systems could be built.

In anticipatory and adaptive human systems robustness derives from the fact that past, present and futures states may affect and influence the present changes of state.

A natural point of departure for this research to discuss *systems* is Robert Rosen's[9] theory of Metabolism-Repair (M, R)-systems. Rosen was a relational biologist whose main idea was that organisms are something more than their material basis and in order to understand organisms one should throw away the matter and keep the underlying organization[10].

Let us consider the most quintessential living object, the cell. Living cells are engaged in three distinct activities:

1. Metabolic activity by which the cell carries on its primary function of transforming chemical compounds into others necessary for its existence;

2. Repair activity in which the cell attempts to counteract disturbances in its operating environment, and;

3. Reproductive activity in which the cell acts to preserve its functional activities by copying itself, e.g., The functional activities are understood pretty far to be indepen-

---

8. Poli 2009a.
9. Rosen 1972.
10. Rashevsky 1954.

dent of the particular physical substrate in which they are carried out. Thus, while a cell acts as a small chemical plant by transforming one sort of chemical into other, an economic system, e.g., a financial institute, may perform exactly the same functional activities but with no chemicals involved. With respect to our earlier discussion, we might argue that "systemness" consists of emphasizing the formal and final cause over the material and efficient.[11]

Robert Rosen presented (M, R)–systems as an abstract formal mathematical structure for capturing the essence of metabolic, repair and reproductive activities, and they are often seen as the simplest mathematical models mimicking autopoietic models.

By autopoeisis[12] we mean the capacity of a system to reproduce the components from which it is composed. By continuing the use of biological examples, a multi-cellular organism generates and regenerates the very cells of which it is composed; a unicellular organism generates and regenerates the components of the cell.

Autopoiesis modifies system theory. The Italian ontologist Roberto Poli[13] states that autopoietic systems do not start from pre-given elements, neither do they assemble them. Autopoeisis does not come in degrees—either a system is autopoietic or it is not. Furthermore, for an autopoietic system, the classical distinction between system and environment, and between an open and a closed system acquires new valence. Autopoietic systems are by their very nature self-referential systems, their relational self-production governs a system's capacity to have contacts with its environment. The relation between an autopoietic system and its environment is a reflexive one, mediated by the self-referential loops that constitute the system itself.

---

11. Casti 1989.
12. Maturana & Varela 1980, Maturana 1981.
13. Poli 2009b.

In autopoietic systems the guiding relation is not the system to environment, but the system to system interrelation. In a similar fashion the duality between open and closed systems, where the system's boundary is porous and allows both the system and the environment exchange matter and energy, acquires a new meaning: openness maintains the previous meaning of exchange with the environment, but closure means the generation of structure, and a set of constraints governing the system's internal processes. Closure, or structure, organizes the system as a integral whole.[14]

When considering the thinking on causality, the significant notion arises that self-referential systems are closed to efficient cause.

Now we are ready to present in a simplified way the connections between system S (any individual organism, ecosystem or social system) and model M of System S (Figure 2). By looking at M we are able to obtain information about a later state of S "because the trajectories of M are faster than those of S"[15]. In order for M to affect S, M must be equipped with a set of effectors E, which allow M to operate on S, or on the environmental inputs to S, to change the dynamics of S.[16]

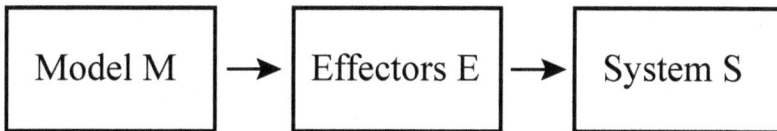

Model M → Effectors E → System S

Figure 2 *System-model relationship*

Making sense of the interactions between the observing system M and the observed system S is vital for robust decision-making. There are several reasons why this sense-making could fail: the model M can be based on an

14. Poli 2009b.
15. Rosen 1972.
16. Poli 2009b.

incorrect paradigm, its basic assumptions may not be helpful for dealing with the world, or it may be too linear and simple presentations may prevent us from anticipating and adapting to the changes; or there may exist an incorrect correspondence between the states of system S and the states of the model M. In essence, the effectors instead can be bad if they are unable to steer S or fail to manipulate the variables of S appropriately.

I think that our conception of human anticipatory and adaptive systems must first of all be human. We cannot exclude the perspective that sees a human being as a creature of "flesh and blood" at the expense of the "rational and logical" perspective. That exclusion would certainly limit our thinking and not result in a truly robust theory.

The German sociologist Niklas Luhmann[17] makes an important contribution generalizing autopoietic systems to social systems by seeing them as dynamical, autonomous and self-referential systems able to reproduce their own elements.

In my opinion, Luhmann's work should be understood as an extension to the main strand of sociological thought. Social systems are higher-order systems able to outlive their members—who are born and will die and sometimes move from one social system to another. Yet social systems have some kind of stability, which is at least partly independent of their individual members.[18] But obviously they are not reproduced in a similar fashion, for individuals reproduction is essentially a biological issue, even if it may be socially conditioned. Social reproduction is detached from material reproduction.[19] It is grounded in the reproduction of meaning, more specifically in roles or patterns of action which are points of reflections for perspectives, interests, values and senses. Therefore, the reproduc-

17. Luhmann 1995, 1997.
18. Poli 2009b.
19. Parson 1951.

tion of a higher order social system is not governed by its underlying material bases[20].

The units of meaning used for reproduction are understood to be communications, and for Luhmann[21] communication is based on information, utterance and understanding. Information refers to what is communicated, utterance refers to how it is communicated, and understanding refers to what the receiver grasps from the previous two aspects of a communication. Communications are the very beginning of social acts, they generate further communications. That is why a social system is an autopoietic system of communication; and communication is the unit of reproduction of it.[22]

The capacity for self-observation, the ability of a system to distinguish itself from its environment, is vital for an autopoietic system. And applying this ability leads to the fact that for a social system there are many subsystems, e.g., economy, law and science; and even further when the basic distinction between relevant and irrelevant communication is applied to subsystems, e.g., profit/non-profit, legal/illegal and true/untrue the subsystems can be further divided.

Naturally different systems are linked to each other, sometimes one of the systems becomes the environment of another system, eventually both systems can become the other's environment. When different systems are structurally coupled, the exchanges between them take the form of perturbations: the brain perturbs the mind, social systems perturb the psychological systems subsystems perturb one another and so on.

This leads us to consider levels. Immediately when we start to discuss different systems, systems and subsystems, and their relationships we can explicate upward forms of causality, from the lower level to the upper one,

---

20. Poli 2007.
21. Luhmann 1986, Buehler 1934.
22. Seidl 2005.

and also to address downward forms of causality, from the upper level to the lower level[23]. This notion entails recognition that a causal chain can be triggered at any level.

There is an additional dimension concerning levels. We may refer to levels as levels of reality, and distinguish between material, psychological and social types of interaction. Further distinctions can be made between causal dependence that occurs between items and actors, and categorical dependence that occurs between levels, which enables the development of an even stronger anti-reductionist vision[24]. But as Aloisio Louie[25] the former assistant of Robert Rosen, points out; a functional organization cuts across physical structures, and a physical structure is simultaneously involved in a variety of functional activities.

Perhaps a more modern way to discuss levels of realities, or the levels of influence that we use to influence others, and through which we can be influenced, is to refer to five separate levels:

- *Terrestrial.* The geopolitical domains of air, sea, undersea and land, as well as physical concentrations of wealth;
- *Space.* The world of satellites and future space platforms;
- *Spectral.* The electromagnetic spectrum, frequency management, and sensing;
- *Virtual.* The global world of networks and connectivity;
- *Psychological.* The media and conduits used to influence the hearts and minds of people.[26]

A reality can exist and can be uniquely created on one level, or as a combination of many levels. Time is also a vital concept here. We can communicate and cooperate with each other, only if we share the same time and space

---

23. Campbell 1990.
24. Poli 2009a.
25. Louie 2006.
26. Loescher *et al.* 2000.

dimension, or to use the previously presented terminology, we belong in the same chronotope.

At this point, we may conclude that anticipatory and adaptive systems differ from reactive systems because the former's choice of action depends on a system's anticipation of the evolution of itself and the environment in which it is embedded, the latter's choice of action depends instead on preceding states.[27]

Another significant notion follows, we can conceive anticipation in two ways: as a cognitive capacity and as coupling between the system and its environment.

For Niklas Luhmann[28] the value of autopoeisis, as a concept, lies in the fact that it introduces novel forces into adaptation. The first autopoietic cycle realizes the constitution of the system, while the second generates the system's identity. Robert Rosen's (M, R)-systems instead provide conceptually a very abstract framework for understanding the evolution of life, where the system is based on two relations—metabolism, the basic activity that constitutes the system, and repair, the modification of the system according to a norm. Whenever a system's metabolism, i.e., dynamics, go awry, the repair component intervenes.[29]

The two theories are complementary and allow us to present, in Figure 3, a basic form of anticipatory and adaptive human systems. Rosen[30] considers the regulatory structure of a system and distinguishes five different types of controllers:

1. System with feedback controllers;
2. System with feedforward controllers;
3. System with feedback controllers with memory;
4. System with feedforward controllers with memory, and;
5. System with general purpose controllers.

27. Rosen 1985, Poli 2009a.
28. Luhmann 2000.
29. Poli 2009.
30. Rosen 1985.

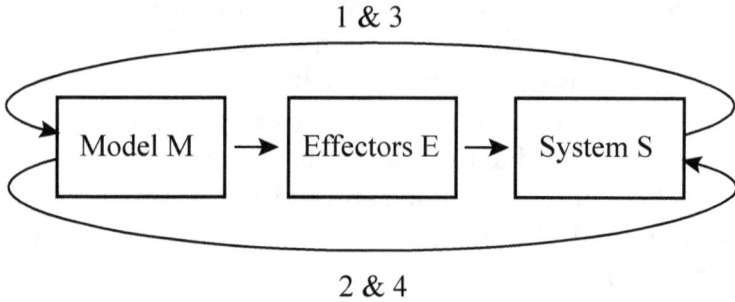

Figure 3 *System-model relationship detailing feedback and feedforward controllers*

Feedback controllers (1) perceive a system's environment. They are selective, and only some aspects of an environment are relevant for them. Their task is to steer the system in order to maintain a selected value. Feedback controllers are able, within limits, to neutralize environmental variations and keep the system stable. Their challenge is the delay between changes in the environment and a system's capability to adapt to them.

A feedforward controller (2) perceives the controlled system, not the environment. We could think of it as a model of the system, a material system with a feedforward controller is a system containing a material model of itself. To function it must run faster than the system, be able to distinguish positive states from the negative ones, and to modify a system's trajectories accordingly.

Feedback controllers (3) with memory are able to leave a trace of a system's experience that can be used to tune the system's behavior, and the system can learn from its past experience.

Feedforward controllers with memory (4) can also learn from the past experiences. Rosen notes with a sense of humour that these kinds of controllers must be able to work on deviations, i.e., they need error signals just like type 1 controllers.

General purpose controllers (5) can include all the above discussed controllers (in which 1 and 3 perceive the environment and 2 and 4 the system), but in an explicitly articulated way to exploit as many variables as possible. Despite Luhmann's insights he mainly relies on type 1 controllers, occasionally type 3 controllers, and misses the others.

Let us next move to our third challenge—*the fixed, permanent and absolute, and at the same time an acontextual truth.* I think there is one clearly identifiable reason for this situation.

It can be assumed that Immanuel Kant's decision to omit ontology from the second edition of his *Critique of Pure Reasons* was the beginning of a decline in interest in ontology. The first edition of the *Critique* presents three types of deductions subjective, metaphysical and objective based on the categories, whilst the second one considers only the problem of the validity of our knowledge.[31]

This means that the second edition views the categories only as logical functions operating independently. Kant radically modified the nature of the categories between the first and the second version, so that the categories no longer depend on the subjective deduction based on the intuitions of space and time. "Kant found himself trapped in a theoretical impasse—the nature of consciousness and its acts—which forced him to abandon part of his theory and to concentrate solely on the question of the categorical validity of empirical knowledge".[32]

Unlike Kant, I argue that the main source for increasing relevance and accuracy in sense-making and leadership derives from the reconnection of specific spatio-temporal contexts and knowledge. Furthermore, I demonstrate how the different systems can be recognized and show how this recognition, we could call it the ontological analysis, should influence the tools, techniques and methods we use in order to make sense of each situation and determine the leadership interventions we choose to make.

---

31. Albertrazzi 1996.
32. Albertrazzi 1996: 431.

Planning, management, leadership, strategy, sense-making and foresight are all disciplines for improving decision-making. We use these ways of thinking, and the practical tools that go along with them to manage our time, to allocate our resources, to launch projects, and to set targets and goals. These ways of thinking shape the decisions we take now and play a role in what happens next. And naturally, the quality of the life we live today is partly influenced by past and present decisions.[33]

The fundamental determinant of the quality of our sense-making and decision-making depends on whether we see the data, attend to what we see and if we act on what we see in appropriate manner. Additionally, both sense-making and leadership, gain their robustness not from tools, techniques and methods alone but from the fit between the tools, techniques and methods and the spatio-temporal context in question.

To start with, we need to take one step back and consider how, in Western societies, for hundreds of years, we have been taught to think, or we have been conditioned to think that order is good and something that must be maintained. The preference for order is accompanied by the assumption that the very nature of the strategic landscape is order. In brief, we assume a single ontology—that of order.[34] Consequently, if we assume something, it is only natural that we behave, i.e., make sense and lead accordingly.

The major issue that influences our sense-making and leadership is the way we think of relationships between cause and effect. *Robustness* suggests that instead of assuming a single ontology, that of order, we should be explicitly more sensitive towards the properties of the strategic landscape and assume multi-ontology, which means recognizing that there are different kinds of systems in which different causal assumptions apply.[35]

---

33. Miller 2006.
34. Aaltonen 2007b.
35. Aaltonen 2007b.

Visionary

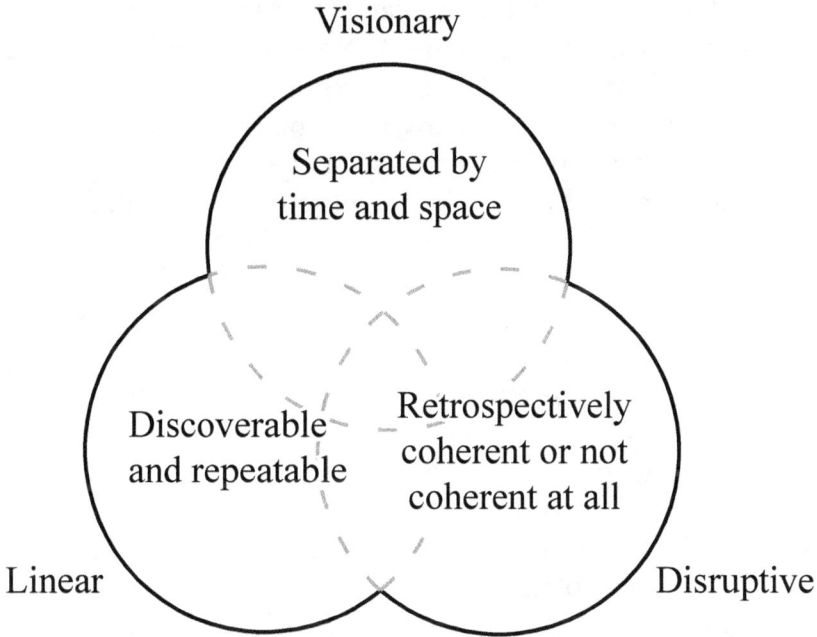

Separated by
time and space

Discoverable
and repeatable

Retrospectively
coherent or not
coherent at all

Linear

Disruptive

Figure 4 *Different systems have different causal assumptions*

In a linear system cause and effect relationships are discoverable and repeatable, in a disruptive system they are retrospectively coherent or not coherent at all, and in a visionary system they are separated by time and space from the present moment. This recognition should precede the selection of tools, techniques and methods in our sense-making and management decisions and choices[36].

When Figure 4 is presented to business people as a discussion point, they are perplexed. A significant minority claim that they do not understand what it means. However, a majority of managers and directors feel immediately, intuitively comfortable with the framework and are able to place themselves and aspects of their life inside of it in a natural way. In fact, they are able to explain and make sense of their lives in a comprehensive way, as well as to find a place for issues that have been difficult to deal within the linear system.

36. Aaltonen 2007a.

With a little effort we can move a step further from the ideas presented in Figure 4. Next we want to create a coherent model that takes into explicit consideration the two significant elements involved in the spatio-temporal context, obviously the nature of the phenomena under investigation, and time. The target is to present a relevant theory or a model that should be sufficiently generic so as not to express only part of the phenomena it claims to explain but all of it. It also has to be configured in a way that it expands our thinking, concerns, and planning so that we may see linear cause and effect processes that connect with other non-linear processes until we recognise a whole web of interconnections.

Time is considered to be historically and culturally specific. This means that situations are rooted in a particular moment and place and seen through the perspective of a certain set of lenses. Different historical periods, different cultures, and different stages of the life-cycle all display different relationships to time. The challenges people face have natural time-spans (days, weeks, months, years, decades, generations), which need to be taken into consideration. And if we are about to develop a temporal and situational awareness, we must also recall that when change happens over time, particular challenges can be situated in time according to people's values and expectations.[37]

Not only do specific events have their natural time-scales, also different organizations and even nations have their natural time-scales. These time-scales can range for example from Nokia's hectic three years rolling calendar, where everything from foresight to execution must take place inside a very short period of time to national security strategies where the time-frame from 2010 to 2015 can be for immediate consideration. The time-frame from 2010 to 2025 can represent the age of three technology life-cycles and a full demographic generation, while the time-frame from 2010 to 2035 is a distant horizon in which consider-

---

37. Miller 2007.

ations about global warming, energy and population make sense.[38]

Within a coherent model we can make explicit and understand the dependencies between different causal assumptions and spatio-temporal contexts. This transcends new perspectives and necessitates a different use of existing concepts.[39]

The notion of a strategic landscape simply refers to the nature of the environment where the work is carried out. It is considered that many things concerning our sense-making efforts and decision-making activities will change when we are more precise about the quality of the strategic landscape. The explicit recognition that there are different types of strategic landscapes where different causal assumptions apply—linear, disruptive and visionary—is the point of departure for increasing effectiveness in sense-making and decision-making.

Linear, disruptive and visionary systems are depicted in Figure 4. The spatio-temporal context is called the chronotope space for obvious reasons: It uses the ancient Greek concept of chronotope, a place in time, to reflect the strategic landscape and the time-frame in question. The reflection is socially and contextually constructed, it depends on people's perceptions (i.e., local information, logic, values, emotions, principles etc.) about the situation, not always their actual situation. The positioning made by each chronotope makes explicit our considerations about a situation, and our responses to it. If the positioning changes, the preferred tools and interventions need to change too.

Chronotope is a conceptual vehicle that gives space to socially constructed and spatially differentiated concepts of time and re-determines and re-presents causation. It is a place where the knots between items and actors, and between levels of reality are tied and untied.

---

38. Aaltonen 2009.
39. Adam 1990, Adam 2004, Aaltonen 2009.

In the chronotope space, the theoretical construction that enables us to reflect the qualities of a specific spatio-temporal context, in the bottom left corner is the linear system where cause and effect relationships are discoverable and repeatable. In the bottom right disruptive systems are found. There the cause and effect relationships can be found to be retrospectively coherent or not at all coherent. Above them is the visionary system, where the cause and effect relationships are separated by time and space from the present moment, which is an imaginary line drawn from the point where the arrows meet in the bottom left to an equivalent point on the right.[40]

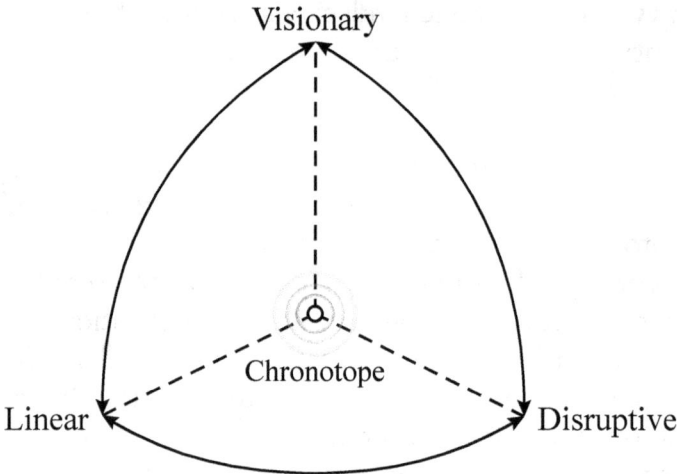

Figure 5 *Chronotope space*

The shape of the chronotope space in Figure 5, has a clear structure and is based on specific motivations. In the left corner where the arrows meet, there is the present moment in its most linear state; there the cause and effect relationships are clearly repeatable. If we go further in time, even in a very linear situation, the curve starts to bend to the right, because as we move further away from the present moment the amount of uncertainty increases. In the

---

40. Aaltonen 2009.

right hand corner where the arrows meet, there is the present moment in a state of chaos. The line bends to the left, because when the chaotic situation lies further away in the future, the likelihood of a future event or a condition coming into being can be changed by policy consideration—if work is begun on it in the present, and the policy consequences can be forecasted. The top corner presents the furthest relevant time horizon, and that varies according to the challenge.

Furthermore, the reason why the line below, from left to right, is not straight, like the imaginary line of the present moment would be, is because that there is, under the imaginary straight line is the history of the relevant events. This shape thus allows space for hindsight analysis. In both cases, the further we go into the future and the deeper we go back in the history, the more the abstraction increases, by this I mean that linguistically and conceptually built descriptions of situations which influence and shape our socially constructed present are produced.

On horizontal axis, our observations become more concrete the further we move from the center of the figure. Where the arrows meet on the left and on the right, the concreteness is tangible, though it is of a different kind, as on the left it is linear and on the right it is disruptive.

By using the terminology of the French philosophy of language, we might state that the relationship between signifier (the sign or the representation) and signified (the content or the meaning) changes with respect to the situation in chronotope space. When we are in linear context the signifier and signified relationship is fixed, it is taken as the truth; but when it is in a disruptive context the relationship is more open. In historical accounts, the choices that constitute the relationship have been made, but sometimes they change when history is rewritten, and if they change then the way we feel, think and act will change. This is what I mean when I refer to fact that our conceptions of historical events have a causal influence on the presence and future.

Turning our eyes into the future, we might consider that the signifier and signified relationship is somewhat loose and open to negotiation. However, as soon as the relationship is agreed on, it starts to influence our present choices and actions.

You may have immediately noticed the radicality of our approach, because the French philosophy of language like many other philosophies has been looking for an ideal scientific description of the signifier and signified relationships, while not considering that it might change according to the spatio-temporal context.

In the following chapters of *Robustness*, we will discuss the knowledge, leadership and projects relevant to various spatio-temporal contexts.

My claim is that in every situation there are specific issues in specific times and spaces. Traditionally, in problem-solving and change management, we have relied too heavily on efficient cause and looked for a single or few causes to resolve a problem or to manage a change, when real-world problems arise from the interaction of multiple, underlying and interrelated causes. A solution cannot stem from a single chronotope, even a very accurate one, but from a family of relevant chronotopes that do not operate independently, but merge into a coherent configuration to resolve a problem or manage a change.

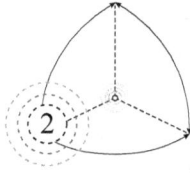

2. Colonizing Futures

Bundeskanslers Office
Berlin

Much of Germany's history, present and future is here. Bundeskansler's office, a huge monument sometimes called a washing machine due to its shape, is a few meters away from Brandenburger's Tor and the Parliament. I am having a relaxed, yet a very conscious and onwards going discussion with a few selected people about various anticipatory, foresight and intelligence systems, and their respective pros and cons. A major part of our discussions comes down to effectivity.

For Isaac Newton time and motion are inseparably linked. Motion cannot be described without time. In Newtonian science time is not studied in its own right, it is used operationally as the measure of things and events.[1]

So Newtonian physics deals with measurements and laws which pertain to the motion of things in time only and the absolute time within which a motion and its change take place. An important notion is that Newtonian mathematics is applied to calculate rates of change, not the change itself. The logic does not deal with change explicitly, it incorporates time implicitly in the description of events. Time is linked to the measurement of motion, duration, and rate.[2]

British social scientist Barbara Adam[3] states that the "Newtonian mathematical description of changing events

---

1. Adam 1990.
2. Adam 1990.
3. Adam 1990.

deals with non-temporal quantity which is generally applicable without the need for a temporal context or reference to past, present and future. There is change, but it is external and related to position. Rather than changing that which does the moving." A change in position is motion. It is understood as invariant with respect to time. It is also comprehended as being reversible, and as symmetrical with respect to the past and the future, because motion proceeds in non-temporal way.

When a system-model relationship, like in Figure 2, is built following the Newtonian logic and things remain discoverable and repeatable, the relationship works. However, with human systems events are time-independent, i.e. if it is true that "a sea-battle occurs at date D" it always was and it always will be true to utter this sentence concerning the events of this specific date. We should not confuse the causal necessitation of these events nor the causal process whereby we become informed of these events with it. Imagine one of admirals refusing to engage in the battle which had seemed imminent. As a result the sentence "a sea battle occurs at date D" would change the status of it to being timelessly false. Also timelessly true is valid counterfactual inference "if the admiral had not sailed away, there would have been a sea-battle" which pins the responsibility decisively on one person, the admiral, not the causal necessity nor causal process.[4]

Nevertheless, even today Newtonian physics is a sought after ideal in management. Process re-engineering, best practice and key performance indicators, to name just a few examples among contemporary management practices, tend to follow the absolute and the timeless ideal. But we seem to forget the fact that it is achievable on the basis of total abstraction. If it was possible to extract single units from interactive wholes, if we excluded friction, gravity and radiation, we would be left with a universe of perfect symmetry, single parts in motion, a non-temporal, and di-

---

4. Gell 1992.

rectionless time.[5]

Despite the fact that human systems hardly remind Newtonian physics, despite it describes only part of the physical reality, and despite its limited validity, Newtonian ideals and ideas have been applied widely beyond their original purposes.

Cognitive-Edge's popular blog[6] takes an ironic look at Henry Mintzberg's management principles:

1. Manage the bottom line (as if you make money by managing money);
2. Make a plan for every action: no spontaneity please, no learning;
3. Move managers around to be certain they never get to know anything but management well (and kick the boss upstairs as much it is better to manage a portfolio than a real business);
4. Always be objective, which means to treat people as objects (in particular, hire and fire employees the way you buy and sell machines because everything is a "portfolio"), and;
5. Do everything in five easy steps.

These principles might even be helpful in stable environments, but in more turbulent times... Well, any lucrative business would eventually suffer.

We might not be so surprised by the recent survey[7] conducted in Britain in which 70% of respondents considered the UK management industry to be more of a hindrance than a help for UK business!

Living systems hardly ever capture the Newtonian conditions that created repeatability, and that would not even be desirable, because without variation there will be

---

5. Prigogine & Stengers 1984.
6. Dave Snowden Spring 2009.
7. RSA Journal 2007.

no room for change, growth and development.

All machines can be understood according to Newtonian laws. While we are interacting with machines we are not merely relating to moving parts, but we are dealing and working with Newtonian concepts. Whenever we interact with a machine, for instance drive a car for instance, we are putting Newtonian physics in practice.[8] My idea is that we have been seduced by the pervasive experience of machines and technology, by the success of Newtonian physics which has become such an integral part of our lives in industrialized societies, so much so that we believe that it is or should be the very nature of our existence.

Our search for order is one thing; another thing is how we comprehend time. In any system where parts and subsystems are designed to interact in a repeatable and predictable way, time is considered as duration and rate. In mechanically organized systems time is implicated as duration and rate of change, speed or acceleration, but also as timing, sequence and periodicity. The car driver interacts with his car according to these principles; he wants that every engagement of the clutch involves them in duration and rate as well as the necessity of proper timing, sequence and periodicity.[9]

One of the greatest human endeavors has been to impose a cultural will on time whether it is to light the hours of darkness or to provide a stable food supply through periods of seasonal and climatic variation. Equally, to dance and make music, to write or to produce a documentary or a work of fiction involves an active engagement with time, whether through particular rhythms, texts or the technological means to edit events into new constellations.[10]

A tipping point was reached in 1884 when the International Meridian Conference met in Washington DC and members from twenty-five countries began to stan-

---

8. Pirsig 1979.
9. Adam 1990.
10. Adam 2004.

dardize time across the globe. This involved the establishment of time zones every 15 degrees of longitude. Time and longitude are connected because the earth rotates around its 360 degree axis over twenty-four hours, one hour being equivalent to 15 degrees longitude. Longitude and time can be expressed in terms of the other's measure, i.e. time in degrees and longitude in hours, or minutes and seconds. Greenwich was given the 0 meridian, with longitude one hour apart in each direction up to 180 degrees. Britain had adopted Greenwich Mean Time (GMT) in 1880, and a year before North America had instituted Standard Railway Time.[11]

Today the system is very much taken for granted, as we travel across time zones and reset our watches accordingly.

The globalization of clock time was completed when, at 10.00 am on 1 July 1913, the first time signal was transmitted across the globe from the Eiffel Tower. Wireless signals traveling at the speed of light displaced local times and established the world time.[12]

A Newtonian ideal of order became part of people's everyday life like never before when control over social time increased. A timed social life gives pupils little control over the time structuring the aspects of their lives that are connected to school: the sequencing of their learning, the pace of their studies, the choice over priorities of action, their starting and finishing times. In companies employers achieve this control by buying the time of their workers. The time structuring of work is bargained for, not the labor but labor time is being negotiated.[13]

Besides clock time also the creation of a calendar enables us to use and allocate time, make it a commodity that can be sold and exchanged.

---

11. Castells 1996.
12. Adam 2004.
13. Adam 1990.

Actually, according to a sociologist Eviator Zerubavel[14], the calendar is the first institution through which cultures established and maintained temporal regularity. Emile Durkheim[15] instead suggests that a calendar expresses the rhythm of the collective activities and simultaneously assures regularity. Obviously, social coordination, synchronization and temporal regulation need to be located in a temporal framework that transcends a specific society, organization or network, in something conceptually bigger than the entity that is employing know-how to organize its spatio-temporal life.

Our daily, weekly or monthly routines are imposed by social markers—opening and closing times in the factories, the beginning and end of the school days, weekdays and weekends, working days and holidays. In addition fiscal year and budgetary cycles define the economic year, municipal and national elections and other political activities.[16] These routines besides the fact that they construct a large part of our daily lives, produce socially important knowledge, sometimes used only implicitly, often searched for explicitly. The power to move these social markers is a significant source of adaptation, while the world we live in changes, these social markers should not remain unchanged.

I argue that the major lines on which competition between companies and nations occurs follow the Newtonian representation of time. Time compression has been achieved by a number of means by increasing the activity in the same unit of time, by reorganizing the sequence and ordering of activities, by using peaks and troughs more effectively, and by eliminating all unproductive times from the process[17].

---

14. Zerubavel 1985.
15. Durkheim 1971.
16. Adam 2004.
17. Adam 2004.

The futurist Jeromy Rifkin[18] paints the idea of compressing time as being stamped into the Western psyche, and recently much of the rest of the world. The French political theorist Paul Virilio[19] continues and suggests that we can read the history of modernity through time compressing innovations. For a long time the wealth and power has been associated with ownership of land, and having the capacity and speed to traverse it.

Since the nineteenth century, the invention of trains, cars and airplanes the relation of time and space has been continuously altered. The speed with which human beings could move across has increased significantly and the time involved has shortened dramatically.[20]

Other inventions like the wireless telegraph, telephone, radio, satellites and the Internet have compressed time even more. As a result duration has been compressed to zero and the present has become a global present at first for people in developed countries, but now this is true for the majority on the planet. A complementary view is offered by Manuel Castells[21] who contrasts the clock time with the network time of the network society in which the network time transforms social time into two distinct forms—simultaneity and timelessness. Simultaneity refers to the globally networked immediacy of satellite or cable television and the Internet which enable real-time exchanges irrespective of distances. Timelessness points to the loss of traditional chronological order and context-dependent rhythmicity, and is therefore "the dominant temporality of our society".

The Newtonian *colonization* of the future—measure time, create clock time, impose clock time and control the future—projects, predicts, plans and programmes the future. Simultaneously it pursues, procures and pollutes the future. Past knowledge becomes the basis of present

18. Rifkin 1987.
19. Virilio 1991, 1995, 2000.
20. Kern 1983.
21. Castells 1996.

decision-making, and the future is believed to be known, foretold and foreclosed on which innovation is justified and established and as a result the Newtonian scientific discounting attitude creeps into our reasoning.[22]

In Figure 6 Former US Intelligence Officer and Government Strategist *Michael Loescher* shows what *time compression* means for the steak business in the USA. It used to be that the steak business was about cows and acquiring the financing to buy more cows. Today, however, the key elements of that industry are the cost of reinsurance (against losing animals or a market drop) and the cost of antibiotics and supplements. Future innovation has very little to do with the actual product itself and much to do with making changes in the protocol.

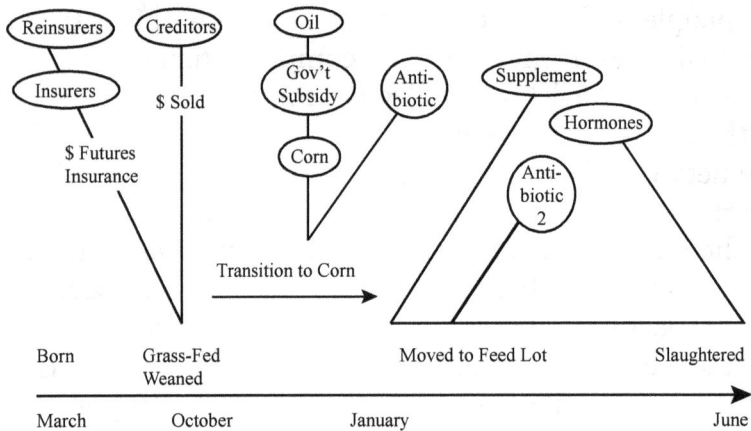

Figure 6 *The Steak Protocol*

The manifestations differ between people and ages, but the basic impulse is similar—imposing our will on time. Central heating has changed the design of houses, clothing habits in winter, the organization of family life and the layout of homes. Electricity brought along major changes in people's lives, it banished the darkness in houses and streets, allowed

22. C.f. Adam 2004.

for the division between day and night to become blurred, and facilitated the 24/7 non-stop society. Today, modern methods of preservation such as freezing, irradiation and genetic modification, the desire to arrest processes of ageing become dependent on more complex temporal relations and technologies, involving electricity, nuclear power and biotechnology. Here we have taken the genetic manipulation of food as our exemplar.[23]

Following Figure 6 Loescher insists that we can dissect the nature of innovation and model it deeply so that we can see the possibilities for innovation with more clarity. We can do that inside a "sector desk", an analytical node, focused on a specific field or segment consisting of:

- Professionally trained analysts;
- A tailored intelligence process specific to that field or segment, and;
- A topology of the main protocols of the field or segment (financial, technological etc.)

The result is a dynamic, analytical topology of a field (see Figure 7) out of which both strategic and tactical opportunities will become apparent—and potentially created—rapidly and methodically. Moreover, changes in the field over time will become visibly.

I believe that in a large scale the competition between people, organizations and nations takes place in three dimensions. Firstly, in finding new ways to organize our living and working. Secondly, in our sense-making and decision-making practices. As Microsoft's chief executive Steve Ballmer[24] pinpointed "probably the greatest source of economic value creation is choosing to be in the right business-

23. Adam 2004.
24. Waters 2009.

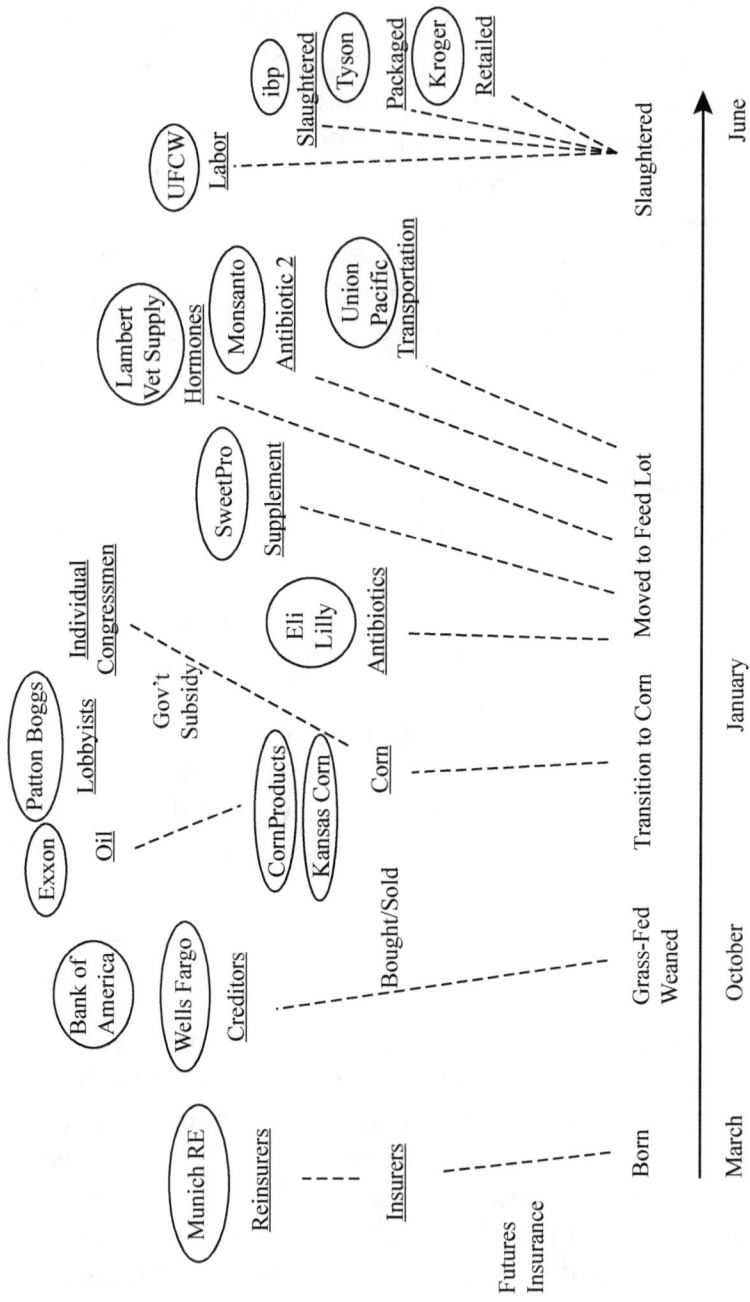

Figure 7 *The Analytical Topology of the Production of Steak*

es early enough. And when you don't choose to be in early enough, you have a problem." And thirdly, the competition is spread out to look for new operational realities to command and control.

In the USA this work is mostly organized through and around operations analysis organizations, some of them generally known, some of them not known publicly at all. Amongst such organizations the RAND Corporation is the most famous. "Our mission is to guarantee the American intellectual superiority" is a slogan that can be found on the wall of another important operations analysis organization, but because human beings are also "flesh and blood", not just "logic and rationality", the task remains difficult to maintain.

To put it simply, operations analysis looks beyond individual systems to try to yield new perspectives, opportunities, or to avoid potential catastrophes.

The beginnings of RAND are traced to the Commanding General of the U.S. Army Air Forces H.H. Arnold who saw engineers and scientists come up with vital inventions such as radar, the proximity fuse, and the atomic bomb. He thought that research and development would be even more important in the future. So before the World War II ended he made sure to create a flexible and innovative intellectual environment. The, at the time unique and advanced, feature of RAND emerged quickly after its creation first in 1946 and then in 1948 in the form of an independent nonprofit organization that has an interdisciplinary approach in identifying, evaluating and applying technology. The organization was structured along conventional lines of mathematics, physics, engineering, economics, psychology, chemistry and aerodynamics, but RAND sought to cross those lines at every opportunity.[25]
Today, RAND still looks to further and benefit society by using research and analysis to improve policy and decision-making.

---

25. Campbell 2004.

By considering the well-known example of the race to the moon from a fresh perspective we can clarify the point made here. The RAND analyst James Lipp remarked in 1950s: "The nation which first makes significant achievements in space travel will be acknowledged as the world leader in both military and scientific techniques. To visualize the impact on the world, one can imagine the consternation and admiration that would be felt here if the United States were to discover suddenly that some nation had already put up a successful satellite."[26]

Even if, at least from a strictly technological point of view, RAND's golden days are said to be over and have ended somewhere in the 1960s, it still plays an important role in the international arena. Testimonies for RAND come from people such as the former US President Gerard Ford who considers RAND as a precious national resource in formulating sound policy that clearly understands which courses of action are possible and what can be gained or lost by following them. An advantage of RAND is that it is singularly able to lay out the options and insure that decision-makers are not blind-sided, or Vaclav Havel, former President of Czeck Republic, has said that RAND influenced the outcome of the Cold War more than any other institution.

Other well-known operational analysis organizations are pushing the boundaries in their respective fields, for instance CNA's analysis and problem-solving practices; MITRE's work on the development command and control systems; and Aerospace's which commits itself to various satellite systems and programs.

The previous examples are based on and build on the traditional Newtonian thinking, and perhaps Darwinian ideas of evolution and competition. However, the new ways of living and working through the artifacts and technologies that shape our lives are also shaping our knowledge. It is time that we allow these changes to influence our understanding and develop a social theory that connects

---

26. Campbell 2004.

with the complexities, levels and different meanings in our lives.

As we go further, you are witnessing the emergence of a framework that aims at expanding our thinking, concerns, and planning. We aim to demonstrate that in any situation there are always opportunities, and we discuss chapter by chapter where these opportunities might be situated and what kinds of approaches, methods and leadership interventions might work within them.

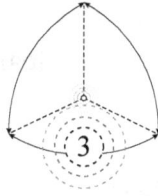

3. Revisiting Histories

Gregorian Foundation, Piazza della Pilotta
Rome

A few steps from the Fountain of Trevi, the President of the Gregorian Foundation Father Franco Imoda has one of the most beautiful offices I have ever seen. To begin our conversation he lays the manuscripts of the Gregorian Calendar, which was invented in the building next door, on the table. After that he brings in Matteo Ricci's paintings. Matteo Ricci was the Italian painter who introduced perspective painting to the Chinese.

Often when the name of the Catholic or the Gregorian Church comes up, it is associated with the passing on the tradition and maintaining the status quo. Father Franco Imoda emphasizes another aspect as our discussion turns into Jesuits and their role in Catholic Church. There is a reason why Ignatius Loyola founded Jesuits (in Latin Societas Jesu) in Rome, there was a need to be on the frontiers of intellectual, cultural and religious debate and Rome was the right place at the time. For hundreds of years the Jesuit doctrine that relied on "shaping minds and training people" was an easily recognizable feature. The sentences "he must be a Jesuit" and "he must come from the Gregorian" were linked to a high-level thinking, 7 to 10 years of education that took place in several different universities, and fluent speaking of three or four languages. There is also a distinctive philosophy of knowledge behind the reason why Jesuits were often referred to as the intellectuals of the Vatican:

- No thinking without reflection;
- What am I doing when I am learning?
- Criticality of thinking.

Father Imoda says that today's big issues are ethical ones; they are more about ethical principles, the basics, the roots. He states there is no economics without ethics, Eleonora Masini adds that in moral science, science and moral go hand in hand, and Cardinal Martini concludes that morality depends on the ends we pursuit, and the means we deploy.

From our discussions, I got the impression that postmodernism has left us floating without direction as there is lots of information and very little thinking. There is individualization and the pluralization of meaning, while at the same time when there is a feeling of lost meaning. This has led to identity related realities.

Father Imoda continues, people live on and live through tradition. Our tradition is to teach methodology. We do not truly understand our history if we cannot turn it into true vision. Cardinal Martini says that the primacy of the individual has been the guiding theme for a long time, but now history has opened up a new age which is again sensitive to spirituality and morality, and thus we need to make a clear vision of what it means to be a human being.

When we talk about the past, the historical knowledge or overall our ability to capture the past or a specific historical event we can turn to Reinhart Koselleck, professor of History at the University of Bielefeld, who has delivered some of the most recent and freshest ideas on the subject.

Firstly, he sees the human historical process as being characterized by a different kind of temporality from that found in nature. Human temporality is multi-leveled, it is subject to rates of acceleration and deceleration, and functions as a matrix within which historical events happen, as well as a causal force in the determination of social reality in its own right.[1]

Secondly, historical reality is social reality, a differentiated structure of functional relationships in which the rights and interests of one group collide with those of other groups and lead to the kinds of conflicts in which defeat is experienced as an ethical failure requiring reflection. For Reinhardt Koselleck historical knowledge is driven forward by the kind of theoretical reflection used to determine the historical significance of the conflict itself. The vanquished has a need to ask "What went wrong?" while the victorious have little reason to reflect. Thus the pattern of "rise and fall" is intrinsic to historical thinking, and another pattern is "progress" which is discernible to the historical consciousness that is capable of distinguishing a defeat and the new knowledge that becomes possible because of it.[2]

The third relevant notion concerns the relationship between language and history. There is a disparity between the historical events and the language used to represent them, both by people involved in these events and historians trying to reconstruct them. Awareness of this disparity is a basis of the recognition that every historical account is a construction in discourse rather than simply a translation of the facts contained in the history into contemporary language. This perspective converges with those of Roland Barthes, Michel Foucault and Jacques Derrida, who stress the staus of historiography as discourse rather than as discipline, and features the constitutive nature of historical discourse against the claims of historical truthfulness.[3]

The point I want to make here is that historical knowledge is not static by its nature, it is and should be a subject for evolution. It is grounded on spatio-temporal contexts, and on the social circumstances of its production. Therefore anticipatory and adaptive human systems need to be open to revision and aware of the provisionality of

---

1. White 2002.
2. White 2002.
3. White 2002.

history in order to more precisely assess and augment more precisely the space of experience upon which we build our ideas of human reality.

Historical time is around us. We can notice it in the wrinkles of our mothers or in the scars of our fathers. We notice it in ruins and rebuilt sites, noting the obvious shifts in styles and shapes. And there is distinctive coexistence, connectedness and hierarchy of successive generations—people and artifacts—in which different spaces of experience overlap and the perspectives of history and future intersect.[4]

Moreover, historical time is bound up with social actions, with people who act and suffer and their organizations and companies. All these actions have their definite forms of conduct, each with peculiar temporal rhythm. We only have to think of the examples given in Chapter 2 about how time is imposed through the working hours, annual holidays and festivals that punctuate social life. Consequently, it does not make sense to talk about one time or one history instead we should discuss many forms of time superimposed one upon other.[5]

The dates and duration of the life of a human being or an organization, the critical moments in political or business events, the acceleration or deceleration of production, the speed of the means of transport can be evaluated historically only when measured by naturalistic temporal divisions. However, the interpretation that arises from the relationship between these factors transcends temporal determinations derived from natural and physical sciences. Mutual interaction or dependence on several factors force the emergence of temporal determinations which are conditioned by nature and still defined as historical. Each survey of interconnections among events leads to the conclusion that eras and the doctrines of specific eras are sometimes entirely separate, although they can also overlap,

---

4. Koselleck 2004.
5. Koselleck 2004.

depending also upon the particular areas under consideration.[6]

I pinpoint two issues. Firstly, every mutable thing has within itself the measure of its time that persists even in the absence of any other, and no two human beings have the same measure of time.[7] Secondly, history made by others, no matter how well written and studied, seldom gives rise to reasonableness and wisdom: instead that is taught by experience.[8]

Nevertheless, in order to be able to learn that which we cannot ourselves experience, we have to follow the experience of others. For hundreds of years history has been comprehended as a reservoir of multiplied experiences that makes us free to repeat the successes and avoid the mistakes of the past.[9] For instance Cicero[10] makes use of history as a collection of examples, "history is full of examples" that can be employed instructively in a relatively straightforward manner or perhaps with more nuance "all that could be used again under the same conditions"[11].

For a long time this was the function of history for human beings. Although, the conditions when we can learn from history do not exist every time, i.e., when the cause and effect relationships do not repeat themselves, the lessons from the history were applied often and uncritically. To increase our adaptive ability, when our environment changes, we should be able to adjust our ideas and the assumptions upon which we have built our lives and businesses.

Since the middle of the 18th century ideas that have rejected the importance of historical examples in guiding the present day decision-making have started to appear.

---

6. Koselleck 2004.
7. Herder 1955.
8. Perthes 1872.
9. Zedler 1735.
10. Keuck 1934.
11. Schieder 1940.

The declared objective of Diderot's[12] Encyclopédie was to work through the past as quickly as possible so that a course towards a new future could be set. Sentences that gave rise to the new historical consciousness that still persists in the form of a collection of examples, but reduces and decreases their role in respect to what they used be, can be traced to that period of time, "One just learns history from history"[13], "to judge what happens according to what has already happened, it seems to me, to judge the familiar in terms of the unfamiliar"[14] and "as the past has ceased to throw light upon the future, the mind of man wanders in obscurity"[15].

This was also the lesson learnt by Chateaubriand[16] during the French revolution in 1797 when he drew up the conclusions between the new and the old revolution, from the past for the future, and was soon forced to realize that what he had written during the day was overtaken by events at night. He concluded that the revolution was leading towards an unparalleled future.

One does not find in history what is to be done is specific cases, because everything is ceaselessly altered by circumstances, everything in the world has its own time and space, or eras and nations.[17]

In 1748 the *German Lexicon of Art and Science* histories were perceived as a mirror for virtues and vices through which one can learn what is to be done or left undone; histories are a monument to evil as well as praiseworthy deeds. An important and characteristic notion here is that the definition of a history is bound up with a plurality of individual histories, of histories in the plural.[18]

---

12. Diderot 1791.
13. See Koselleck 2004.
14. See Koselleck 2004.
15. Tocqueville 1889.
16. Chateaubriand 1861.
17. C.f. Muller 1830.
18. Koselleck 2002.

Historical accounts tend to have a uniform appearance. In a conventional historical account the end determines the beginning and hence the elements to be organized in the narrative. In Figure 8 below, the nodes are specific events that took place, and the arrows links, causal or logical, between events in the narrative. Time moves from the left to the right. The pivotal events are those in the center of the figure that are bounded by the beginning and end of the narrative. The narrative is thin, it involves the selection of events needed for its inner and outer logic, and necessarily the identification of some events as salient and the denial of other events as not salient.[19]

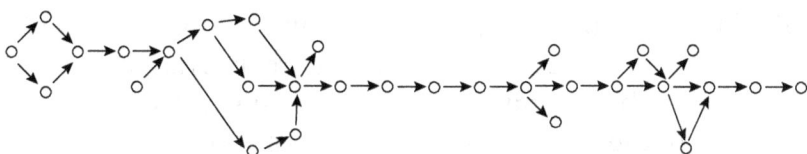

Figure 8 *Traditional Historical Narratives*

We could claim the stronger the story, the thinner the history.[20] American sociologists Peter Bearman, James Moody and Robert Faris[21] argue for the use of life stories that provide a thicker description of a history and deploy network imagery to describe the fragile contingent pathways through which complex historical outcomes occur. Like historical accounts, life stories presume an end. Relying on multiple stories provides a rich material, and placing people, places, things, events, and ideas into narrative sequences, towards that particular end, and in such a way as to create a plot, achieves that. Life stories are dense and more complex than conventional historical narratives, because ordinary people do not think like analysts who have trouble denying data. Even if the life stories are all different, because the narrators are standing in different places, still

19. Bearman, Moody & Faris 2003.
20. Aaltonen 2007c.
21. Bearman, Moody & Faris 2003.

some people, events and structures are shared by many narrators. These tangible social structures build on and depend on local fluidity. We can only observe social structures that are robust. Social structures that are not robust do not last long enough to make it into history.

The Figure 9 below *Report from a Chinese Village*[22] lends itself to our purposes. It illustrates the life stories of the people of Liu Ling village whose experiences encompassed agrarian revolt in the countryside, and the encoding of a revolutionary regime into an institutional framework. By deploying network imagery, by treating events as nodes and relations between events as arcs, narrative sequences can be transformed into networks, and a richer, more detailed history can be presented. In figure below, time moves from the top to the bottom of the figure. Narrative depth is represented by the number of arcs connecting events, i.e., the length, the number of steps from the bottom to a starting event at the top. The analysis can be extended further as there will be people, events and structures shared by most or many narrators. Those that remain are shared by few or only the narrator witnessed them.[23]

Whether we talk about history as it occurs or as it has occurred, there is always a difference between a history as it takes place, i.e., the social history between people and organizations, which forms the real social strata, and their linguistics and conceptual descriptions. However, there is no history without societal formations and the concepts they use to define their challenges reflexively or self-reflexively; without them it is impossible to experience and to interpret history, the present and the future and to represent or to recount it.[24]

Through the investigation of language and the concepts that have been used in certain times and by placing the in their correct contexts we have the basis for under-

---

22. Myrdal 1965.
23. See full presentation in Bearman, Moody & Faris 2003.
24. Koselleck 2002.

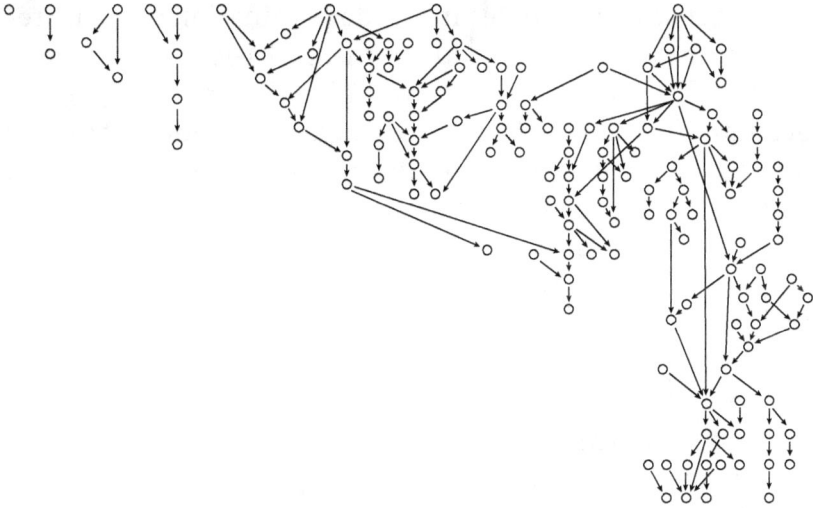

Figure 9 *Narrative Networks*

standing thinking, relationships and power structures of the specific situation.

People have always tried and are trying to adapt, modify and expand their language and concepts to anticipate, trigger or control events. Of course, no speech or written act is itself the action it helps to prepare or enact, but a history (or a future) does not happen without speaking. However, the account can never be identical to the act, it cannot be totally reduced to it. [25] There are two aspects I would like to pinpoint. Firstly, the more highly aggregated the human action is, e.g., the interconnections between actors and economies or the complexities of international politics, and secondly the further in the future or more distant in the past a communicated event is situated, the more important the linguistic and conceptual issues become. Or in other words, when we communicate commonly shared, ordered and present issues, there is less freedom to work with our expressions.

Even if the lessons from history ought to be applied with common sense, they have another kind of value - they turn into social reality. The historical events described be-

---

25. Koselleck 2002.

gin to act as causal forces in the determination of social reality in their own rights, due to the multi-leveled nature of temporality, i.e., the way we perceive histories that are relevant to us (our family's, city's, region's, nation's *et cetera*) influence how we feel, think and behave today, and the kind of decisions we make for our futures.

In the relation to communicating and acting in the enactment of events, it is difficult to separate synchrony and diachrony. The conditions and determinants reach from the past into the present to intervene in particular events as agents that simultaneously act on the basis of their respective outlines of the future. All temporal dimensions are always intertwined, and according to our philosophy it would contradict experience to perceive the present as only one of those moments that accumulate from the past into the future.[26]

What happens is always unique and new, but never too much so, because pre-given language and social conditions cannot enable each unique event. A new concept may be coined to articulate experiences and expectations, if it has, in some form, existed as a seed in the pre-given language or social context.

Not only are the temporal dimensions intertwined, so are the extral-inguistic and linguistic dimensions. The spoken and the written language intertwine in the topical performance of what has happened or what happens to form an event that is composed of extra-linguistic and linguistic elements of action. Even if the conversation ceases, the linguistic knowledge remains present, it is inherent in human beings and enables us to communicate with others and confronts them, be they other human beings or things.[27]

Karl Marx supposedly stressed this meaning into one sentence: "This cup of coffee contains within it the entire history of imperialism."

---

26. C.f. Koselleck 2002.
27. C.f. Koselleck 2002.

In this fusion of determinants, the extra-linguistic elements are also determined or influenced by the language that remains the primary instance of communication. Laws, customs, traditions, values and strategies each posit a framework of conditions for the concrete behavior a human being is expected to conduct.

I hope to have clarified by now that communicating history is not a neutral, objective reproduction of facts without consequences for today and tomorrow. It is more like mimesis, "a productive imagination", "a reactivation of human actions", or "an iconic augmentation".[28]

Having the facts and using the statistics, if available, has value, but I argue that building a convincing story whether we refer to a children's story, a historical narrative, a major scientific success or a religious myth has more to do with affective, emotional-moral plot structures.

In the Western world, the Jesus story has been an amazing success as spiritual guide, political propaganda and cultural idea. It is and it has been difficult for a long time to separate the extra-linguistic, linguistic and conceptual elements; they are fused together to give significance to both individual lives and to historical movements frequently, universally and lastingly. With modifications its influence has spanned at least four different modes of production: slavery, feudalism, early modern capitalism, and recent East European socialism.[29]

For me, the truly interesting topics lie beyond the religious and ideological aspects:

- What are the ways to ascertain specific meanings and feelings to build a convincing story?
- Where do the motivational power and the self-replicating qualities come from?
- Are there deeper narrative structures that could serve to rebuild other significant stories?

28. Alker 1996.
29. Alker 1996.

The epistemological and methodological choices in writing history form a deeper ontological entity that besides the usual descriptive functions becomes a causal force in the determination of social realities.

After years of following natural sciences, our fate has rejoined with that of anthropology, sociology, social psychology, the political sciences, and other theories that took a linguistic or cognitive turn. The narrative mode of knowing consists of organizing one's experience around the intentionality of human action. The plot is the basic means by which events are put into a meaningful whole; without the plot we will have only a list or a chronicle of things.[30] Not surprisingly, the moral philosopher Alasdair MacIntyre[31] claims that social life is best conceived of as an "enacted narrative" and calls human beings as "homo narrans".

In a good story, the events are the facts, and the point is the theory. A story without a point is meaningless. There are always one or several stories in the offing. Yet another story might offer a better, or more convincing explanation without ever challenging the truth of the elements in it.[32] And when the way we perceive ourselves, our history, present and future changes, also the way we feel, think and act changes; and therefore can be comprehended as a causal force in the determination of social reality.

How we build a convincing story has interested people throughout centuries. In ancient Greece, according to Aristotle a certain kind of structure produces a certain kind of emotionally positive feedback. In Russia, Vladimir Propp concluded that an appealing plot needs seven actors or dramatis personeas: hero, villain, donator, helper, princess, sender and false hero all of whom pursuit their own goals. In Paris, professor of semiotics A. J. Greimas knew his Aristotle, and Propp's and de Saussere's ideas as well,

---

30. Czarniawska 1999.
31. MacIntyre 1981.
32. Czarniawska 1997, 1998.

and presented the idea that a story is by its nature intentional and teleological, and based on the relationship between the subject and the object, and the driving force "désir" between them.[33]

An American literary theorist Kenneth Burke[34] instead suggests a dramatis analysis of human conduct based on the assumption that the rules of drama reflect, influence and shape the actual social life. He postulates the pervasive presence of the dramatistic pentad that consists of scene, agent, agency, purpose, and act. Burke's scheme is congruent with many well-known social scientist's insights, which emphasize how difficult it is to understand human conduct if we ignore its intentions, and it is difficult to understand human intentions if we ignore the settings in which they make sense.[35]

Reinhart Koselleck[36] notes that every history bears out how the actors perceive a certain duration: of inauguration, high points, peripeteia, crises, and termination. The credible narrative, the given distribution of possibilities, the number of adversaries, the redistricting or opening up of new possibilities determine the sequence of events and lend the narrative its diachronic structure. In addition to the narrative diachronic structures, there are also long-term social structures that are familiar to everyone. Such structures have names, constitutional forms and modes of rule that do not change in a day. We can also identify productive forces and the relationships of productions that later slowly and perhaps gradually, but without a doubt condition and shape social life. And constellations of friends and foes that can correspond to the interests of either party, and specific institutions or the characterizing of such institutions that will admit or limit the potentiality for experience and action. As do considerations of space and geography, out of which arise lasting possibilities for political, economic and

33. Aaltonen & Heikkilä 2003.
34. Burke 1968.
35. Schutz 1973.
36. Koselleck 2002.

social narratives and actions.

The structures define the space of experience which is available for specific subjects involved in the events. While events are caused or suffered by subjects, structures are supra-individual and inter-subjective. They cannot be reduced to the level of individuals, instead they have a processual character, they change in time, and can enter into the everyday experience of individuals.[37] Not only do structures change, so do the definitions of the existing ones, as well as the relationships between them. An analysis of one structure against another, on an individual, institutional or national level, is likely to reveal features that can explain why some actors are more anticipatory and adaptive than others.

Mary Immaculate College Professor *James Deegan*[38] writes how personal *memoirs* and *emotions* can contribute to *teaching* and *learning*. During the FuturesIreland process James raised a widely important question: where are the values in Irish education system?

This paper takes a "from-within" approach and examines student teachers experiences of writing emotionally through the lens of teacher-writer memoirs. The participants were ninety-nine postgraduate student teachers in a sociology of teaching module in an initial primary teacher education programme in the Republic of Ireland, but here we also consider how we can apply the philosophy in other contexts as well. The analysis of their responses indicated how people shaped and reshaped their emergent identities through discourse, memory, emotions, and personal biography and along a values-action continuum. Individual freedom was evidenced in moving towards danger and new ways of doing things. Conformity was

---

37. C.f. Koselleck 2004.
38. The complete original paper "Teacher-Writer Memoirs as Lens for Writing Emotionally in a Primary Teacher Education Programme" was published in Teaching Education, 19 (3), September 2008.

evidenced in maintaining the status quo and familiar ways of doing things. Contextual implications for teacher education renewal and reform are discussed at the end.

There is a long history of research on writing emotionally and identity in various social discourses[39] , and a comparatively more recent history in educational discourses[40] . One of the stories told in writer's lore is that Aldous Huxley[41], the English novelist, author of Brave New World once advised a budding writer that a white page and a sharp pencil were the pre-requisites for a good writer, which is a visceral metaphor for cutting the emotional vein, releasing memory, writing subjective, lived experiences, and building identity capital. This metaphor reminds us that all writing is a dialectical tick-tacking between notions of self, ideas and emotions at any given time in any particular milieu.

While there have been a number of positive developments in initial primary teacher education related to curriculum renewal and development in the last decade in the Republic of Ireland, the official discourse continues to privilege structural matters related to teacher quality, demand and supply.[42]

A recent positive initiative at the *Royal Society of Arts (RSA)* has been Opening Minds. It was born out of the RSA's examination of the way working patterns will develop by 2020 and of the policy agenda implied by the study in which education was a prime issue. The idea is quite simple: Due to the fact that jobs for life, state pension and paternalistic employers seem more and more to belong to the 19th or 20th century, the 21st century is going to require different skill sets that will enable people to change, adapt and innovate.

---

39. Barbalet 2002, Calhoun, Rojek & Turner 2005, Denzin 1992, 1989, 1984, Ellis & Flaherty 1992, Goleman 1995, Hochschild 1983, Kemper 1990, Lupton 1998, Rosengeil & Seymour 1999.
40. Clandinin 2005, Clark 2001, Florio-Ruane 2001, Hargreaves1992, 2002, Lyons & LaBoskey 2002, Loughran, Hamilton, LaBoskey, Russell 2004, Strong-Wilson 2006.
41. Huxley 1932.
42. OECD 2005.

We can imagine a puzzled Englishman asking himself what to teach to his children? "Should everyone know the date of the Battle of Waterloo? Should everyone be able to calculate the cosine of an angle and analyse The Whitsun Wedding?" Or is an understanding of global warming, how to open a bank account and foreign cultures more important?

Fortunately for us, the RSA has taken on this responsibility and taken the idea and the curriculum of Opening Minds further through research, experiment and consultation with teachers and students. As a result a list of five essential skills emerges:

- *Learning* pushes students to understand how they learn and how they manage their learning throughout life;
- *Citizenship* encourages students' understanding of ethics and values, and also examines how society operates and how different systems and structures impact on the individual;
- *Relating to people* focuses on managing and being managed by other people, managing personal and emotional relationships, stress and conflict;
- *Managing situations* gets students working out the importance of managing time, risk and uncertainty as well as establishing personal strategies for managing change, and;
- *Managing information* teaches the ability to access, evaluate, analyze and manipulate information by applying critical judgement.

In brief, Opening Minds accepts that schooling is not about teaching, but about learning and puts responsibility for learning and achievement in the hands of the individuals[43].

---

43. Four active age cohorts have been identified: baby boomers (born between 1946-1964), generation X (1965-1981) sometimes called also generation E for their entrepreneurial activities, millennials (1982-2000), and a tentative generation I which stands for internet (2000-). The silent generation (1925-1945) is considered to be less active.

Another point of reference related to curriculum renewal and development is the *Bureau of European Policy Advisers (BEPA) report*[44] "Investing in youth from childhood to adulthood" which begins by discussing the present and the future environment.

The discussion concerning the present highlights two topics: 1) improving young adults' situation in the labour markets, because their unemployment in almost every EU member country is twice that of adults[45] and the time gap between finishing studies and finding stable jobs is increasing the difficulties of young adults, and 2) while the labour market and the social inclusion of young adults is a major issue, the focus should shift to the general functioning of the labour market, a life long view of individuals and their learning from the very youngest to the oldest and on how to cope with new social realities.

Two topics that look even further forward into the future are: 1) the confrontation resulting from demographic trends and inter-generational imbalance. In the near future fewer people will have to provide for an increasing number of old people. The forthcoming demographic changes risk increasing the burden on present day youth because declining fertility, increasing life expectancy and the changed proportions of different age groups will probably call for a new inter-generational contract.[46] 2) Increasing our awareness of how the future is built on the present choices and the decisions that we make and how we should take responsibility for them. An investment in a more participative, inclusive and sustainable society is an investment in the future and is presented as such.

For such a future, five fields need special attention. The common rule seems to be that early investment is considered

---

44. http://ec.europa.eu/dgs/policy_advisers/publications/docs/ investing_in_youth_11_october_2006_final_en.pdf.
45. A lighter picture is given in Youth Employment in the EU, DG Empl., October 2006.
46. European Commission: The demographic challenge: an opportunity for Europe. Communication, October 2006.

crucial for all aspects of human capital formation. Making sense of and investing in early education is much more efficient than preparing things reactively. Early investments are also seen as an occasion to unite social and economic goals.

1. *Children's well-being and development* is required in order to avoid unfavourable socio-economic conditions and favour the full development of future adults;

2. *Health* education needs to be established early so that healthy habits can be induced and the growing number of people with mental illnesses and obesity can be reduced;

3. *Education* should place a greater importance on meta-skills, i.e., social skills and adaptation;

4. *Employment* should cater to the idea of education occurring alongside employment, plus working life transitions and improving the functioning of the labour market, and;

5. *Citizenship* is necessary for participation in social and political systems, active citizenship programmes, involvement in the use of new media and pathways into political arenas and monitoring.

In counterpoint to other leading scientific and knowledge-based economies, there have been no major debates and controversies about teaching and teacher education as a technical problem, a problem-solving problem, or a policy problem. There have been no paradigm wars about reflectivity, constructivism or diversity, notwithstanding their centrality in the Primary School Curriculum[47]. One of the outcomes is that little research exists on the ideological, moral and emotional dimensions of teaching and teacher education. What is especially missing is a significant corpus of research on teachers' "substantive, attitudes, values, beliefs, habits, assumptions, [and] ways of doing things".[48] We have distanced ourselves from some of the lessons we learned already during

---

47. Primary School Curriculum 1999.
48. Hargreaves 1992.

the time of Ignatius Loyola in Rome.

The research project reported here examined how, and in what ways student teachers bridged memories of their own childhood experiences through the prism of teacher-writer memoirs with scenes they are currently experiencing as student teachers in a primary teacher education program. In this way, the study is located in the research on autobiographical understanding and narrative inquiry as represented in Clandinin's[49] Handbook of Narrative Inquiry: Mapping a Methodology. Specifically, the study contributes to the narrative inquiry discourse and methodology by using teacher-writer memoirs to uncover some of the hidden everyday and aesthetic aspects of student teachers' lives in a particular sociology of education course in an initial primary teacher education program in the Republic of Ireland.

Conceptual and Relational Framework

The research on narrative, memory and identity contains a number of theoretical and conceptual tensions. While there are many elegant conceptualizations of emotions in terms of workplace realities, most notably Hochschild's[50] seminal work on the commercialization of feelings entitled The Managed Heart and Kemper's[51] sociological models in the explanation of emotions, there is an acute absence of research on writing emotionally in educational discourses. Writing emotionally is defined in this study as a way of coming to know, understand and act on the emotions through writing, including sympathy, imagination, intentions, feelings, and thoughts of self and others. Writing emotionally is a process of cutting the emotional vein and setting free feelings and ideas that have been silenced in everyday discourse. And only by cutting the emotional vein, as Lupton[52] stated, can "the emotional self as a dynamic project continually [be] shaped and reshaped via

---

49. Clandin 2005.
50. Hochschild 1983.
51. Kemper 1990.
52. Lupton 1998.

discourse, embodied sensations, memory, personal biography and interactions".

Assuming a Responsibility for One's Identity

Lupton's[53] writings on the emotional self beg an educational question: How is the emotional side of teaching shaped and reshaped in the lives of initial primary teacher education students. "Ironically, the emotional side of teaching that is ubiquitous in the [teacher's] work," as Rickert[54] states, "is seldom identified or discussed by people who talk about teaching". Evoking Deweys'[55] writings on teachers' thinking processes, Rickert states that writing emotionally provides essential insights into "the barometer that heralds the puzzles of practice". Yet, as Akin[56] points out, "too often novices' experience is written out of the teaching text by the plethora of programs and policies that neither ask what they think, nor care how they feel". These writers share a conviction in the importance of teachers "writing themselves back" into the texts of teaching and articulating a transformative vision for themselves and "[assuming] a responsibility for who I am as a teacher".

As a way of articulating a vision for teaching, Denzin[57] suggests Ulmer's[58] postmodern pedagogy described as mystory—which "brings into relation experience with three levels of discourse—personal (autobiography), popular (community stories, oral history, or popular culture), and expert (disciplines of knowledge)". In complement and counterpoint, Goodson[59] wrote that the life history of the individual should be located "within the history of his time" and by linking "personal troubles and public issues," a task which, as Wright Mills[60] pointed out many years ago, is the essence of the sociological enter-

---

53. Lupton 1998.
54. Rickert 2005.
55. Dewey 1933.
56. Akin 2005.
57. Denzin 1992.
58. Ulmer 1989.
59. Goodson 1988
60. Wright Mills 1959.

prise". These variants in the discourse on autobiographical understanding and narrative inquiry are represented through the lens of memoir, emotion and identity in the present study.

I discuss writing emotionally in one particular social foundations module. The module is part of a consecutive model of primary teacher education at graduate entry level in Ireland. The module entitled "The Sociology of Teaching" is theoretically and conceptually influenced by the American sociologist, Willard Waller's[61] "classic" writings on "closeness/distance" in teaching which date as far back as the 1930s and Andy Hargreaves[62] more recent postmodern writings on the "emotional geographies of teaching" in the early twenty-first century.

Memoir as Design for Change

What is innovative in the design used in the present study is the use of a clutch of intertextual themes about becoming a teacher and developing personal and professional possible selves—what Gitlin (2005) described as the "not yet" latent in the childhood and teaching memoirs of popular and critically-acclaimed "writer-teachers." The selected works were Bryan MacMahon's The Master (1992), and John McGahern's Memoir (2005). As Graham (1992) reminds us, "one approach for deconstructing mythologies is interstitial analysis [which] involves comparing several texts that hold some features in common, perhaps a set of representational techniques, a plot line, or a substantive topic." (pp. 32-33). What is especially innovative is the use of intertextual themes that have been circulating as "truths" for almost a century in the lore and language of becoming a primary teacher in Ireland but have not, heretofore, been used as sensitizing pedagogical tools of in educational inquiry, for example, the "call to teaching," "teacher as community leader," and "teacher as change agent." The use of teacher-writer memoirs has significant bridging capacity in straddling social, literary and educational domains of reality.

---

61. Waller 1932.
62. Hargreaves 2002.

I could imagine that the research design could be applicable in other contexts as well.

Memoir as a Tool for Learning

The memoirs of MacMahon and McGahern[63] represent two of the most popular and celebrated accounts of teaching and writing in Ireland. John McGahern challenged some of the sacred cows of his homeland's social, sexual, religious and nationalistic, and educational orthodoxies—what we might describe as "a portrait of the reluctant teacher as a young man." In complement and counterpoint, Bryan MacMahon is a self-proclaimed údar agus oide (writer and teacher) whose writings probed "the genius of the place (Hero Town as he described his native town of Listowel, Co. Kerry), the unusual, the bizarre, the estranged, as much as the more orthodox heroes and heroines of one's society"[64] and "turned it into "imagination"—what we might describe as "a portrait of the natural teacher as an older man." While feminist researchers could argue that these choices are restricted to the "silverback" variety, there is an absence of indigenous female "writer-teacher" memoirs, notwithstanding the existence of a wide range of novels, short stories and poetry references to being a teacher in Ireland.

Contextual Data

Data[65] was collected from the participants weekly journal entries. The journals were designed to contribute towards the unfolding of a self-narrative through a layered set of interrogatives/responses on the emotions in teaching and the cultures of teaching, and with implications for personal and public issues. The methodology was a simple question and response approach, using a series of questions derived from framed or excerpted sections in the selected memoirs. Sample questions included:

---

63. MacMahon 1992, McGahern 2005.
64. Fitzmaurice, 2005.
65. C.f. Deegan 2008.

- What lessons about teaching can I find in my past educational experiences?

- What lessons must I never forget?

- How am I beginning to think the same and differently about teaching from the teachers who taught me?

- In what ways do the fictional teaching accounts speak personally to me about the teacher I am becoming?

- When confronted by some of the cultures of teaching or emotions of teaching that I know get in the way of good teaching, how will I react?

- What will I do?

Response journals served as an integral component for generating conversation building, skill and technique development—"journaling on"—a thinly-veiled conceit for the personal and collective odyssey of thinking, talking and writing about becoming a teacher in class debate and outside class in quieter moments. Data was collected with student permission and consent and all names and places are disguised for the purposes of confidentiality.

Following speculative analysis[66] and the identification of themes and categories, I incorporated three forms of triangulation that helped to build confidence in the interpretation of the data: (a) data were compared for themes grounded in the selected teacher-writer memoirs; (b) data were compared for themes grounded in sociological writings on the emotions in teaching and cultures of teaching; and (3) data were compared for individual student teachers with other student teachers. Data were analyzed for central themes and recurring ideas. Using constant comparison method[67], I worked the data to build theoretical categories from relationships discovered among the data. In addition, discrepant examples were analyzed to consider their relevance to the categories and relationships that emerged.

---

66. Davies 1982.
67. Glaser & Strauss 1967.

Discussing Findings

The findings indicated that participants' identities were inter-related, dynamic and complex processes, defined by a values orientation and operationalized by corresponding actions. These processes are represented here in terms of a four-fold scheme, along a values orientation continuum with nodal points at individual freedom and conformity, and a corresponding actions continuum, with nodal points at received and elaborated identities. The four-fold-scheme included the following "couplets" or variables of analysis: (a) individual freedom/elaborated identities; (b) conformity/received identities; (c) individual freedom/received identities; and (d) conformity/elaborated identities. The four-fold conceptualization of identity processes is presented below in Figure 10.

The analysis yielded two branches in the data set with meaningful and useful data for variables (a) and (b) only. In this study received identities are operationalized as essentially given or inherited identities with nevertheless active and dynamic dimensions; elaborated identities are operationalized as essentially generative or re-fashioned identities which are always active and dynamic. The data overwhelmingly supported the recursive connections between a particular value's orientation and a set of corresponding actions, although there were some discrepant examples and non-synchronous patterns in a small number of student teachers' identities. The majority of responses supported a values orientation focused on individual freedom (70%), whereas a minority supported a value orientation focused on conformity (30%). While the data included useful and valuable insights on student teachers' social, cultural, political and educational convictions, there was no evidence to suggest that students experienced significant social or cognitive dissonance in writing emotionally about their own identity processes.

Towards Elaborated Identities

The first major theme in the findings is the dynamic between individual freedom and corresponding actions. Indicative di-

Individual Freedom
Liberating, generative, and transformative

Received Identities

Maintaining the
status quo,
distance, and
familiar ways of
doing things

Elaborated Identities

Moving towards
change, closeness,
and new ways of
doing things

Values

Actions

Conformity
Traditional, ascribed, and transmitted

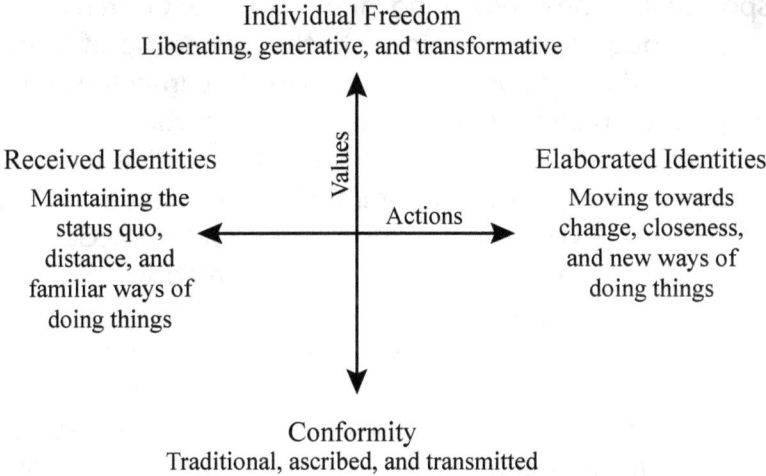

Figure 10 *Dimensions of Identity Processes*

mensions of individual freedom included a commitment to liberating, generative and transformative values, and indicative dimensions of elaborated identities included moving towards change, closeness and a welcoming response to new ways of doing things.

A number of student teacher used the resources of vicarious fictional accounts, their own biographies, and the wider dimensions of teachers' work to situate individual freedom at the heart of their identities. Their experiences in common with a number of their classmates show distinct resonances with Evans, Fraser and Taylor's[68] concept of "local feeling" which is rooted in the unique and contingent "mix" of emotions people hold for particular, people, places and things in their neighborhoods and localities. The place of "local feeling" in student teachers identities in the present study evidenced non-synchronous patterns with a range of consonant and dissonant dimensions. The following response is indicative of this non-synchronous pattern.

The writings of McGahern, MacMahon and McCourt painted a picture for me of a bygone era when teaching carried a different social perspective and a different form of social

_____

68. Evans, Fraser & Taylor 1996.

responsibility. The overbearing influence of the Church is now gone, although a link remains with the ownership of school property and the inclusion of religion in the curriculum. What has gone thankfully is the need for the teacher to be the priest's right-hand man in the parish and the obligation to be a highly visible aspect of the community. This is not to say that I would avoid involvement in my locality but like McGahern I would treasure my relative anonymity and freedom to choose how I live my life outside of work hours, just like any person in another profession. This would not necessarily be the same for everyone and I'm sure many would love the oneness and love of community that MacMahon writes about in The Master. It is the freedom element that goes with teaching, however, that I find most attractive.

One response indicates a new measure of involvement in the locality which is tied in the first instance to the postmodern notion of anonymity over oneness with community. The response does not suggest a turning away from the locality but relief that the stultifying presence and visibility that characterized the teacher until quite recently as a pillar of the local community and only third in line in the village and small town social hierarchy to the parish priest and the doctor has passed. The response interestingly is not predicated on managing avoidance or deflection from the inherent importance of community but in elaborating individual freedom as a values orientation with a corresponding set of actions. This perspective finds a prominent but not exclusive place for community in the set of a person's values orientation.

Several others situated the centrality of freedom in elaborating their identities. Elizabeth's response was typical of a number of other student teachers who described the quest for freedom as a moral endeavor and the antithesis of conformity. Her descriptions also point to a conviction in the centrality of a quest for freedom in combination with the brighter emotions of "empathy, generosity and kindness" in her teaching and behavior.

The willingness to conform seemed to be the main issue during McGahern's time in college, rather than any educational or moral purpose. The fictional accounts have helped me to dig deep and hit a raw nerve in my own practice. During my teaching practice, I naively believed that I could encourage the inquisitive nature of children in an environment of quietness. While I was inciting conformity, I began to see myself sitting in the desk quiet as a mouse and the teacher talking up a storm in my own primary school days. There was ciúnas everywhere. I do hope to have a classroom that promotes openness and freedom for me and my students, where all feel respected, where sociocultural distance is rejected in favor of acceptance and where the brighter emotions of empathy, generosity, and kindness will be harnessed to make change happen faster.

Another response provides interesting perspectives on what she sees as the power and controlling dimensions in "inciting conformity." Her response is recursively accomplished by bringing forward her school memories of teacher noise and children's silence. The culture of silence that she remembers was often issued in terms of the familiar word— "ciúnas"—which translates as silence in the Irish language. The phrase "ciúnas" is a loaded episteme that has been circulating in the lore and language of primary schooling for generations.

In the following response dimensions from both previous writings are brought together around the central notions of "conversation," "invitation/response" and "journey."

One of my teachers gave me confidence to learn beyond the school gate. From him I learned how to research and reference. I learned how to be an "independent learner." In truth, I learned how to be a teacher. In this way, being "vocational" is not "a call"; it is a conversation. It is about how I will relate to everyone in the educational sphere. It is not about teaching tricks but more about lifetime passions.

I would like to state that I do not like the question, "how are you the same and how are you different over the course of the program?" Emotionally and in every other way, I did not begin my journey the day I walked through the college gates. My experience is not the shortest distance between two points. I am not near the end of a journey. I am a work in progress. I like Hargreaves'[69] approach because it helps me articulate much of what I would understand myself to be a as teacher. The several forms of emotional distance he formulates such as sociocultural, moral, professional, political and physical distance resonated with my own approach to life and people—it is a matter of "invitation and response."

The response about "the call to teaching" emerged as a strong component for a number of students who wrote about the elaborating of identities as a project of choice. This theme is a variant of the writings on the emotions as "projects" or "endeavors" that need to be worked on continually and that never finish. One of the inherent features in the findings is that identity processes lie in the interstices between childhood memories and professional insights. It suggests that identities can be illuminated through simple and clear self-writing many years after they have been originally conceived.

Conformity and Received Identities

The second major theme in the findings is the dynamic between conformity and corresponding actions. Indicative dimensions of conformity included traditional, ascribed and transmitted values and indicative dimensions of received identities included maintaining the status quo, distancing, and adherence to familiar ways of doing things. In counterpoint to student teachers who used the resources of vicarious fictional accounts, their own biographies, and the wider dimensions of teachers work to situate individual freedom at the heart of their identities, other student teachers situated conformity at the heart of their identities. Aoife was typical of a number of student teachers who rooted received identities in traditional and ascribed values. She represents the broad swathe of students who modified as opposed to changed their identities in response to the fictional accounts of teaching and the readings on the emotions in teaching and the cultures of teaching.

69. Hargreaves 1992.

Her view of change is one of gradual and incremental steps and in response to pragmatic dimensions.

In terms of my thinking, I would have to say that I still believe in my own ability and I'm very much focused. I maybe a little cynical but I have a good awareness of things from my previous work experiences. I am realistic. I wouldn't say I've gone so far as to change the way I view things but I've taken a broader view of things and how to fit things into my plan.

Lena represented a small number of students who were impelled towards conformity, situating their responses in a psychological notion of identity. She rooted her perspectives in what she described as her "institutional nature." Her response also evidenced an incipient paralysis in her teaching values and actions, motivated by a fear of litigation.

In some cases, however, I feel that my identity will conform to my institutional nature. We all have to conform, if we want to be teachers. We all have to teach eleven subjects, including Religion which we do not get paid for. I know that by conforming to an institutionalized identity, there will be professional and political gaps in my life but I need to be aware that consciousness raising is coming under more scrutiny in schools. We need to be aware of out boundaries. Obviously, I have accepted that some things won't change. My concepts of teaching will always be rural rather than urban. Like McGahern's mother, I would rather be on the cart than the train.

Her response represents a variation on the theme of "oneness with community." It underscores a fusing of professional identity and place of origin. This is a significant finding given that it provides some evidence of the desire of student teachers to return home to teach in their home place. In MacMahon's terms she wants to become an "orthodox hero" of present times. Lena's views resonate with a number of students who wrote about how their emotional selves were tightly-braided into a locale of family, friends and community.

Another variant on the perspectives of students who were impelled towards conformity and familiar ways of doing things was given by Tricia who discussed conformity as a struggle of unequally matched forces where the student teacher will "break" in the end.

Professionally as a teacher I believe that I need to conform in my community. I believe that the teacher's role still has huge expectations. MacMahon suggests that teachers have a double identity with the "ringing of the bell signaling entry into the other part." MacMahon, however, makes a telling point that sticks with me. It is that personally and professionally if we are stuck in a struggle with individuality and conformity, essentially a power struggle with ourselves, we will break.

Tricia's views represent a heightened sense of sensibility combined with a sense of entrapment, captured in the phrase, "you can think but you can't act" in moral or political realms. Her experience has been fashioned in a dualistic encounter between powerful and vulnerable forces. She is resigned to conformity. Her statements collectively give strong evidence to the view that received identities are rooted in maintaining the status quo, keeping distance, and familiar ways of doing things.

Personally, I wouldn't describe my choice of becoming a teacher as "a call but rather, like McGahern, "the right thing to do"—the sensible option. In McGahern, I get a hint that you can be an individual on a personal level but that this doesn't extend to political or moral matters. It reminds me of the saying; "Think what you say, but don't say what you think." It is hard to move on because there is a fear that your own ideas might be against the grain of what is expected from you.

Conclusion

What the present study contributes to the research on teacher identity formation and development is support for the universality of student teachers' identities as contested terrain between individual freedom and conformity. This terrain is marked by a specific past that is evident in the present moment. Memoir is especially useful in illuminating signposts on this terrain. What makes these signposts interesting is that they exist very often in the subterranean world of becoming a teacher and rarely find expression in contemporary discourses on standards and competencies in becoming a teacher. These are the messy discourses of values and actions, the spiritual and moral dimensions, and the desire to make a difference by eschewing sameness and embracing difference.

The present moment is a critical one in the evolution of teaching and teacher education in Ireland, as it is elsewhere. The changing context in Ireland, however, has not yet produced a debate on the nature and value of scientific research in education[70]. This lacuna has stymied the cross-fertilization of ideas and practices across disciplinary boundaries and the near-absence of research on the aesthetic, emotional, moral, and political dimensions of teaching and learning in teacher education programs.[71] The present study raises serious theoretical and conceptual issues about how, and in what ways teacher knowledge is produced and reproduced. The emotions, cultures and politics in teaching are key parts of this answer and yet they rarely feature in official discourses on standards and competencies. So often official discourses dismiss the humanities as non-empirical and yet the humanities served as the spark for the high standards of dialectical tick-tacking evident in this paper.

What this paper attests to is that the value of teacher writing is not one of kind but one of degree. Few could argue, for example, with the potency of the selected teacher-writer memoirs above. These cut personally and professionally to the deep heart's core of what matters most in becoming a teacher for the participants in the present study. One of the key findings in this study is that student teachers' capacities and responsibilities lie along a values/actions continuum with conforming identities at one end and liberating identities at the other. This resonates closely with notions of authenticity and recognition in the discourse on the politics of identity where "authenticity connotes the idea that each of us should live in a

---

70. Shavelson, Phillips, Towne & Feuer 2002.
71. Deegan, Devine, Lodge 2004.

way that is true to himself, not conforming to a way of life simply because it is accepted by others"[72] and "recognition is the idea that others should be sensitive to my quest for authenticity". And this brings me to the net point of this paper—writing emotionally in search of self generates alternative kinds of teacher knowledge which can potentially yield alternative teacher capacities and teacher responsibilities. These fundamental challenges remind us of Dewey's[73] maxim that there can be no acquiring without first inquiring. If we truly want teachers with the capacities to think and the corresponding responsibilities to act, then freedom to inquire and not conformity to acquire needs to be reclaimed as a touchstone in teaching and teacher education renewal and reform.

---

72. Waldron 2000.
73. Dewey 1915.

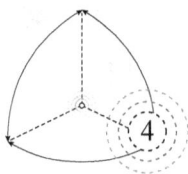

4. Building Intelligent and Flexible Systems

National Security Center
Singapore

For a man who comes from a country in which functionalism has ruled the architecture for decades, the atmosphere is familiar—clear lines, certain kind of coolness and spaces not filled up with things.

When the government of Singapore started its RAHS (Risk Assessment and Horizon Scanning) program about five years ago, there was a relatively short tradition in thinking about the future and using scenarios to do so. Nevertheless, as the sentiments and perceptions about the world were changing and becoming more complex, a feeling that something more needed to be done was born.

The guiding idea behind RAHS was that it is impossible to predict the future put it is possible to put in place systems and processes that can help to anticipate possible futures and help to prepare if something should happen. There is a recognized need to develop more intelligent and robust ways to think about the future. RAHS did not start as a project, there was not a masterplan behind it. It was, and has been since its beginning, a process of discovery that acknowledges that some of its concepts and technologies may work, some may not. More importantly, RAHS has provided for continuous learning to adopt a government level approach to strategic anticipation. In Singapore, the role of a small and active center which builds the organizational software to get people from different agencies to work together in order to foster vision, coordination and coherence, was comprehended necessary. If RAHS can connect silos, challenge mindsets and develop a collective analysis of possible futures, it may prove to be worth the effort.[1]

RAHS has multiple facets. It is linking various ministries and agencies across the government, and it is closely linked to Horizon Scanning Centre with a technology plan to map the rivers of the future, and with local universities which students provide feedback on the developed software and other ongoing issues.

This kind of structure derives quite naturally from the intellectual roots of RAHS. Permanent Secretary for national Security and Intelligence Coordination Peter Ho[2] recalls his discussions on projects like LISA (Large-scale Integrated Search and Analysis), DIANE (Digital Analysis Environment), NORA (Non-Obvious relationship Analysis), and TIA (Total Information Awareness), and the respective experts. The topics included rapid change, complexity, strategic surprises plus systems and technologies that connect databases to look for anomalous behavior or patterns of behavior.

In the next pages, the Singapore Government Ambassador at large *Chuan Leong Lam*[3] discusses management under conditions of *complexity* and *uncertainty*.

———————————

For much of the last 50 years or so, management has assumed that the world is linear. This is modeled after the very successful approach of the "scientific" method. This approach consists of the close observation of our environment and deducing the "laws" of behavior of people, corporations, markets and then

———————————

1. Read more in *Thinking about the Future—Strategic Anticipation and RAHS*.
2. Ho 2008.
3. Please note, the remarks reflect purely the views of the writer and do not represent view that may be taken by the Government of Singapore.

using these "laws" to predict and manage the future. Management is even referred to as a science.

During this period, within the hard sciences, the "scientific" method was undergoing tremendous changes. Classical physics was being displaced by theories of relativity, classical mechanics by Quantum Mechanics, simple systems theory by complex systems, linear systems by chaos theory and fractal systems.

The insights from these fields of sciences are beginning to be felt among management theorists and practitioners. The essence of these insights is that a system such as a country, an economy, let alone the global economy, is complex. A complex system is capable of periods of unexpected "turbulence". Complex systems are governed by non-linear effects that can produce very unexpected catastrophic events that cannot be predicted accurately or controlled by human study and interventions the way we can do so with simple mechanical systems.

Furthermore, the global system can go through long periods of quiescent behavior and then break out in multiple crises within a short time. Recent events point to a period of increased "turbulence", for example, the South East Asian Tsunami 2004, the September 11, 2001 World Trade Center attack, the Asian Financial Crisis 1998, the advent of the Severe Acute Respiratory Syndrome (SARS) 2003, the Financial Crisis 2008. Many organizations are asking why these severe crises are not detected sufficiently early by their risk management systems.

This paper argues that the reason for this is that such risk management systems are defined too narrowly. They are not also sufficiently forward-looking and are not integrated into the workflow and reward system of the organization. They fail to take into account our behavioral limitations in handling probabilities and also the nature of complex non-linear systems. Moreover, risk assessment programs are usually domain-specific, that is, those concerned with security threats look at security issues, those in financial sectors only look at economic risks etc.

It is necessary to differentiate risk from uncertainty. Risk is about known events for example an earthquake. The unknown is in the timing of its occurrence and its magnitude.

Uncertainties are events that are unknown or so rare that little is known about how the event would unfold let alone its likelihood distribution. The most severe crises that deserve our attention are precisely such unknown or emergent uncertain events.

This paper presents a framework with the four conceptual components that are needed when designing a system to assess both risks and uncertainties. The four components are: 1) Attitude towards the time horizon, 2) The meaning of Alternative Futures, 3) Attitude towards risk and probabilities, and 4) A lack of synchronism between performance and reward.

Time Horizon

Setting the relevant time horizon is very important. The evolution path of complex systems is critically dependent on even minute variations in the initial conditions. This is called the "butterfly effect", the idea that over a sufficiently long time, the flapping of a butterfly's wings in one part of the globe can cause a hurricane in another part. Over a short time, however, the evolution path of a complex system becomes more predictable. For example, weather forecasting is accurate up to 72 hours but forecasts beyond several weeks become highly unreliable.

Similarly, for complex systems like the economy, the financial markets, the spread of infectious disease or of human behavior in general, we may make reasonably useful forecasts for the short term say within 3 years or less. For the longer term, say, 5 or more years, past events and trends are no guide to what may happen in the future. Hence we need to think in terms of multiple possible outcomes which are usually termed "Alternative Futures". The bottom line of this observation is that we need to change our way of handling uncertainties according to the time horizon under discussion. Uncertainty increases exponentially with time and we need a more creative, visionary approach to "imagine" or "foresee" the future rather than depending on our own logic and deduction based on current trends to "predict" it.

Alternative Futures

This picture is again complicated by the fact that complex systems do not evolve smoothly along a linear path. At critical points, called bifurcations, it can undergo very sudden and sharp transitions towards a very different, unexpected outcome. Trend analysis looks back into the past for guidance for the future. Due to bifurcations, trend analysis can fail to detect the possibility of unexpected outcomes in the future.[4] However, most managers are accustomed to thinking in terms of trends because that is the predominant habit in work or life.

Thus a critical and sudden change due to this sort of non-linear bifurcation usually creates a crisis for which managers and organizations are ill prepared. However, we should not think of every crisis as a negative event to be avoided at all costs. Within a crisis, there are opportunities for some people if they can see them and adapt quickly enough to exploit the opportunities presented. A system that can prepare managers and organizations to detect sufficiently early emergent developments or events would be better prepared to avoid the downside and to exploit the upsides of future events. This is another reason to argue for the value of non-linear thinking and innovative thinking methods to conceptualize the future around multiple possible outcomes however improbable they may sound initially.

Attitude Towards Risk and Probabilities

Behavioral economists have studied how humans assess risk and probabilities. It turns out that the rules of thumb we use to assess risks and probabilities, while they serve us well in

---

4. Business Planning for Turbulent Times, Ch 5 by Mary Bernard, Edited by Rafael Ramirez, John W Selsky, Kees Van Der Heuden, Earthscan 2008

most situations, can give rise to systematic errors and bias-es.[5] Daniel Kahneman and Amos Tversky have identified three common heuristics. First, we tend to look at recent history when assessing probabilities. This is the availability heuristic. When something has not occurred recently, we underrate its likelihood of occurrence. On the other hand, if an event has occurred recently, we tend to overrate its recurrence. Thus events that have never occurred are even more likely to be underestimated.

Second, we make estimates from an initial starting point, or "anchor", and then adjust along the way, even when our anchors are irrelevant to the subject at hand. For example, people who move from an inexpensive city to a more expen-sive one tend to bring their housing budgets along with them, and squeeze themselves and their families into smaller houses rather than spend more on housing.[6]

Third we use the "representativeness" heuristic, we guess the probability that object A belongs to class B by the degree to which A resembles B. On reading a description of Steve as a quiet, bespectacled, tidy-minded chap, we think it highly probable that he is a librarian, because he fits our ste-reotypes of librarians. The representativeness heuristic is also manifest in our need to identify patterns where there may not be any, such as in the gambler's fallacy in thinking that black is "due" on the roulette wheel after a long spell of red.

This poor ability to estimate risks is not just limited to our intuitive nature. Some practitioners of risk assessments, for example, in the finance sector, have built elaborate mathe-matical model for risk assessments. Obviously any mathemati-

5. Daniel Kahneman and Amos Tversky, "Judgement under Uncertainty: Heuristics and Biases", Science, New Series, Vol. 185, No. 4157 (Sep. 27, 1974), pp. 1124-1131. See also the discussion of heuristics and biases in Richard H. Thaler and Cass R. Sunstein, Nudge, Yale University Press, New Haven, 2008 and of systematic biases and irrational behaviour in Dan Ariely, Predictably Irrational, Harper Collins, New York, 2008.
6. A study by Uri Simonsohn at the University of Pennsylvania and George Loewenstein at Carnegie Mellon University, cited in Dan Ariely, Predictably Irrational.

cal model has to be used with caution. Even mathematical models in the hard physical sciences have to be changed over time or when applied to a different domain. Classical physics gives way to relativistic equations at high speeds. Classical mechanics gives way to quantum theory at the sub-atomic scale. It is a mistake to be lulled into thinking that models are valid for all domains and times.

The recent financial crisis illustrates the danger of the use of quantitative models of risk without this caveat.[7] In particular, the common assumption that the variance of risks is normally distributed is flawed and grossly underestimates the likelihood of a large change in asset values. For example, a one-day fall of 7.7% in the Dow Jones index in 1987 was estimated to be one in 50 billion chance. The October 1987 one-day drop of 29.2% was according to standard finance theory one chance in 10^{50}. That would be an impossibility. Similarly, the fall of 7.9% in exchange rates between the dollar and yen was estimated to be an event with 10.7 standard deviation using Gaussian distribution. The normal odds against this event is enormous. According to them, it should have never occurred, not even if a bank has been trading these currencies every day since the Big Bang 15 billions years ago.[8] Although the danger of over dependence on mathematical models is apparent, it is quite possible to forget this limitation especially when the model appears to work for a time and bring in large profits. Yet, such models can fail spectacularly and very suddenly precisely because they fail to take into account the non-linearity or the impact of hitherto very small changes in the environment.

Lack of Synchronism between Performance and Reward

In principle it is good to link executive reward to the "performance" of the company as a form of performance incentive.

---

7. The formula that killed Wall Street, Felix Salmon, Wired Magazine, Feb 23, 2009.
8. (Mis)behaviour of markets, Benoit Mandelbrot and Richard L Hudson Profile Books 2005.

In practice, an important issue is how to take into account the impact of executive action over time. The more senior an executive, the longer the time it takes for the results of his actions to bear fruit, however, their bonuses are usually paid within a year and based on the previous year's results.

This time horizon issue has a great impact on an executive's attitude towards risk and his view of the possible risks facing himself and his company. There is a serious issue here if the executive is rewarded for the possible gains of his decision now but does not bear the negative consequences of the future risks that he may have helped bring about. Since risk assessment is resource intensive, with no reward or penalty forthcoming, it is not surprising that executives pay little attention to long-term risk assessment or avoidance systems. This phenomenon skews the whole risk assessment process towards under-rating the organization's future risks. This attitude will only change if the reward system puts more weight on longer term results and their associated risks. This lack of synchronism between performance and rewards underlies much of the overly-high leveraged risk-taking that led to the current financial crisis.

If such a long-term rewards or penalties system existed then entrepreneurs would be likely to assess their risk exposure better because they would then hold greater stakes in their future bets. Therefore, as long as they remain equity holders, they are rewarded for being right and are penalized for future losses.

A System of Risk Assessment and Anticipating Uncertainties

A system for both risk assessment and anticipating future uncertainties has to have a short-term horizon scanning system and a system that can explore multiple alternative futures. We will use the widely accepted scenario planning process as an example of such a system.

This relationship between horizon scanning, scenario planning and strategy is summarized below.

Risk Assessment   Scenario planning
Horizon Scanning

Foresign studies   Risk and Opportunity
Assessment

Corporate Strategic Plans

Figure 11 *The two track approach of horizon scanning and scenario planning*

Figure 11 shows a comprehensive risk assessment system with two tracks, namely a risk assessment horizon scanning track and a scenario planning track. This is the system employed by the Government of Singapore.

The horizon scanning track is used to identify the shorter-term risks typically those within three to five years. The exact demarcation of this time horizon depends on the nature of the business that the corporation is concerned with. There is some overlap between the horizon and scenario planning tracks once the time horizon exceeds one year. What is important is not the exact demarcation between the short and long-term but recognizing that the two tracks have their respective time horizon focus.

The outcome of horizon scanning is often expressed as a risk matrix showing the likelihood of each risk against its level of impact. An example of such a matrix is used by the Horizon Scanning Office of the UK is shown in Figure 12 below. Other tools include computer-aided software tools and cognitive tools for scanning for relations and patterns amongst published or collected data and methods for weak signal detection.

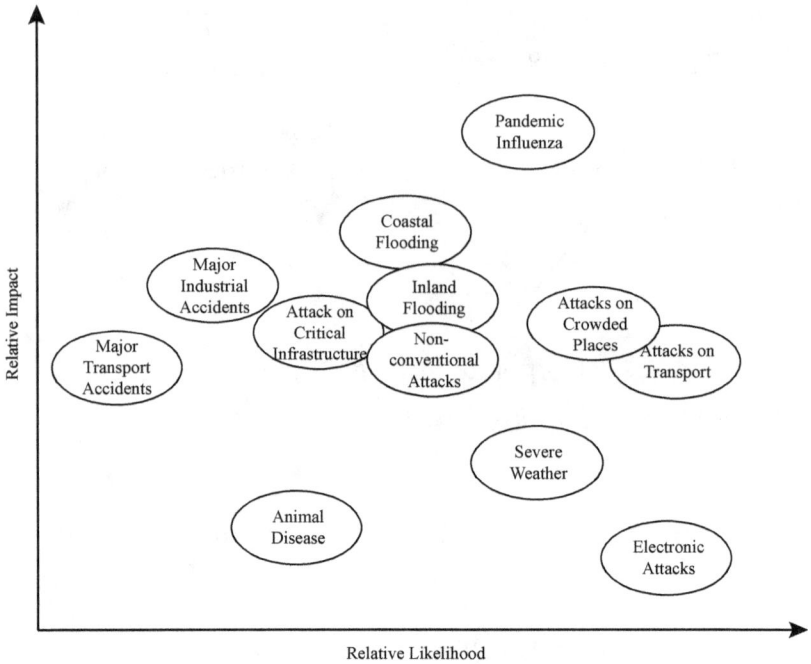

Figure 12 *An Illustration of the High Consequence Risks Facing the United Kingdom*

The horizon scanning assessment is based mainly on past trends and historical patterns. For the longer-term, uncertainties are more common than risks because of the complex bifurcation and self-organizing emergent properties of complex systems. To anticipate unexpected emergent threats or opportunities, it is necessary to think in terms of alternative futures.

Scenario planning is often used for this purpose. The objective is to generate "scenarios". Analysts then use these scenarios as "mental pictures" to make decisions and formulate strategies to cater for future uncertainties. The value of scenario planning is not entirely in the actual scenarios generated. Much of the value lies in the process leading up to the scenarios. Participation in this process heightens the sensitivity of the participants to the forces that may act on events and shape the future. Scenarios can also add value by allowing participants to identify the possible turning points and risks that they may be exposed to.

Challenges to the Scenario Planning Process

This description may give the impression that managing complexity can be reduced to a simple linear process. This is not the case. Complexity and uncertainty cannot be eliminated.

The challenge of handling future uncertainties is that humans have no choice but to rely on past experience and images to portray future possibilities. Soren Kierkegaard puts the dilemma this way: Life can only be understood backwards; but it must be lived forwards. The future is therefore always seen through the lens of the past. Complex adaptive systems such as humankind are capable of creating emergent behaviors that produce unexpected and unintended consequences. There is therefore a fundamental limitation in our ability to foresee future uncertainties.

One example is the current financial crisis. It is a form of emergent behavior resulting from the system parameters of the free market model. There is great debate now whether there should be greater regulation. In hindsight, there will always be a need for greater regulation. However, no matter what regulatory regime is chosen, it is a matter of time before the regulatory regime becomes too restrictive of growth. Then deregulation will set in. Eventually some unintended, emergent behavior will be created leading to another crisis. This is an inherent, inevitable cycle. However, it is also useful as a source of energy that propels the process of innovation forward. This is the source of the so-called "creative destruction" process. Any regulatory regime that can completely eliminate a crisis of future uncertainty will be so rigid that it will lead to a totally dysfunctional and non-innovative system.

Risk cannot therefore be eliminated because doing so will destroy its rewards as well. In this regard, greater attention should be paid to the detection of weak signals. Such signals can point to the emergence of risks and opportunities earlier and allow us to be better prepared to mitigate the unavoidable risks and to exploit the opportunities.

The second limitation of scenario planning is that it depends considerably on identifying important "driving forces". Driving forces are characterized by their importance and their degree of uncertainty. We have seen from behavioral studies that humans are quite unreliable in their ability to assess probabilities and uncertainties. It is even more problematic to assess the "importance" of a driving force. The fundamental assumption here is borrowed from that of classical linear dynamics, namely, that bigger forces create bigger outcomes. Smaller (less important) forces can be ignored for practical reasons. However, complex non-linear systems have precisely the property of very tiny forces eventually creating very high-impact outcomes. This "butterfly effect" is the very problem inherent in making good long-range weather or earth quake forecasts. Ignoring the "less important" forces in scenario planning may therefore miss some high impact outcomes in the future.

Nonetheless, scenario planning is still useful for managing in times of turbulence. It has been used for several decades for companies such as Shell or organizations like the Government of Singapore. However, we should not become complacent thinking that it will prepare us for all eventualities. Scenario planning should therefore be complemented by other methodologies to generate alternative futures. These include non-linear systems, the use of simulation, network analyses, data mining, dynamic systems modelling, sensitivity analysis, wild cards and morphological analysis.[9]

Induced Organizational Change

On the positive side, the benefit of doing horizon scanning and scenario planning is not limited to their direct outputs. Doing so can help bring about positive behavioral changes in the organizational culture. Some of these include:

---

9. See writings of Tom Ritchey on General Morphological Analysis and www.swemorph.com.

- Seeking multiple conflicting views especially from the out-side;
- Being aware of self-bias and blind spots;
- Seeking the planned and also the emergent future;
- Embracing risk taking, being flexible and not shell-shocked by the unexpected;
- Being opportunistic and not stuck on a single track, and;
- Constantly measuring assumptions and plans against changes and signals in an uncertain environment.

This new organizational culture is as valuable as the formal outputs of the planning process in preparing an organization to face future uncertainties.

Behavioral Implications

The risk and opportunities to an organization as a whole are not necessary the same as that for individuals or managers. This is the issue of goal congruence.

There are many factors for a lack of goal congruence. Attention has been drawn to the role played by the time horizon of the reward system in the lack of goal congruence. If managers are rewarded for the short-term, for example, for three years, then they have the incentive to optimize their risk exposure within that time period. They either underestimate future risks or they will apply a very high discount rate for risks that are beyond that three year horizon. They have little interest in making scenario or any risk planning beyond three years. In fact, the use of "golden parachutes" or large sign-on bonuses can increase the tendency to optimize short-term performance to the detriment of long-term performance. Therefore, managers would, most likely, strive to do things that promise short-term results even if these very things lead to longer-term risks. With the "golden parachutes", they need not fear that later, the fruits of their poor actions in the past will affect their longer-term appointment prospects. The reward system in the financial sector suffers from the ill effects of this lack of time and goal congruence. It is a major cause of the recent financial crisis. However, this same effect can be seen in other sectors. There are examples of executives being very richly rewarded for actions such as highly visible merger and acquisition activities. Some of these turn out later to be extremely damaging to the shareholders' value, but by that time either the executives are either no longer around or they are not accountable or penalized for their past actions.

It is no longer possible to simply base executive pay performance on short-term measures or the performance of the company's stock price. A part of their financial rewards must be measured against the time span effect of their decisions so that the overall performance of the corporation can be optimized. This time span will depend on the specific nature of the industry. It will be longer in some cases, for example, especially in the public sector, and shorter for others, for example, traders of commodities.

In standard project evaluation systems, it is usual to employ techniques such as discounted cash flows in capturing the future uncertainties of a long term project. A possible long term reward system can be pegged to the same discounted time period. A part of the executive's reward will be withheld. He will then be rewarded or has to give up his reward at key moments or critical success points during at least the initial part of the life cycle of the project. Such a system will focus his mind on the future risks that he is embracing now and restore a more balanced position into the risk assessment. No such system is perfect but the first steps to making such a system should be taken. This task should be considered as part of the challenge of managing modern corporations. Failure to do so will add to the existing risks of the global business and economic system.

Conclusion

There is increasing recognition that the global system, and especially its economic and financial sub-systems, is not merely becoming more complicated. It is also becoming more complex and therefore more volatile. With increased complexity, non-linear effects become more significant. These can produce unexpected, catastrophic events. Although such events are by definition rare, their high impact makes it worthwhile to invest in better methods of anticipating uncertainties for humans in order to be better prepared to face the impact of future shocks.

Future managers must be aware of the cognitive limitations that make foresight into future outcomes difficult. In some cases, the risks may be foreseen, but not reacted upon. This can be due to the fact that the reward systems are too much weighted on short-term performance. The challenge of corporate management is not only to create a forward-looking risk and uncertainty management system. They also need to create a tighter, more meaningful connection between future uncertainties, longer-term corporate performance and the executive reward system. The award of the bonus of executives needs to be linked to the achievement of key milestones over the life of major projects that he is responsible for.

———————————

Perhaps the most famous model designed to deal with complex situations that involve multiple levels of actors and different time-scales associated is the OODA loop[10]. OODA stands for Observe, Orient, Decide, Act. The decision-maker observes his environment and gathers relevant information; orients himself in the environment by making sense of it and by comparing the current state to the desired state decides on a course of action based on his sense-making; and finally implements this decision. Because the environment is constantly changing and the loop is rolling along a timeline, a decision wave is produced.[11]

———————————

10. The term was first coined to USAF colonel John Boyd. A copy of his original work "Patterns of Conflict" is available at http://www.d-n-i.net/boyd/pdf/poc.pdf.
11. Perla & Markowitz 2009.

Peter Perla and Michael Markowitz[12] elaborate in Figure 13 how the concepts of an OODA loop and decision wave interact. The figure is formed by the trajectory of a point lying on a circle of radius a rolling along an x-axis that represents time. The resulting wave has a wave length, here $2\pi a$, along the time axis and an amplitude along the y-axis. Which basically refers to the amount of information the decision-maker needs before making the decision. The high point of the curve is the point at which the decision-maker observes the outcomes of his action. The following downturn instead represents the orientation process to the new environment by processing maximum amount to information 2a. This leads to a decision point at the base of curve. In the end, the rising of the curve represents acting on the decision.

Different situations have different decision waves in frequency and amplitude. And so do different industries and different organizations.[13] Also within a single organization the time-scales vary.

In organizational life, much of the action is embodied in meetings and briefings, in dialogues and discussions. The different levels of decision and action (e.g., strategic, operational and tactical) have their distinctive time constraints, which drive from their information feedback loops, significant decisions that change an overall course that is not dependent on daily or even weekly decisions, although routine decisions take place daily. Generally, it is assumed that higher-levels use their processes to provide guidance and direction to the lower-levels, and the lower-levels feedback information to higher-levels on how situations are evolving.[14]

The interfaces between different organizational levels and processes occur almost everywhere, but the requirement for coordinated action is for people can meet and dia-

12. Perla & Markowitz 2009.
13. Aaltonen 2009.
14. C.f. Perla & Markowitz 2009.

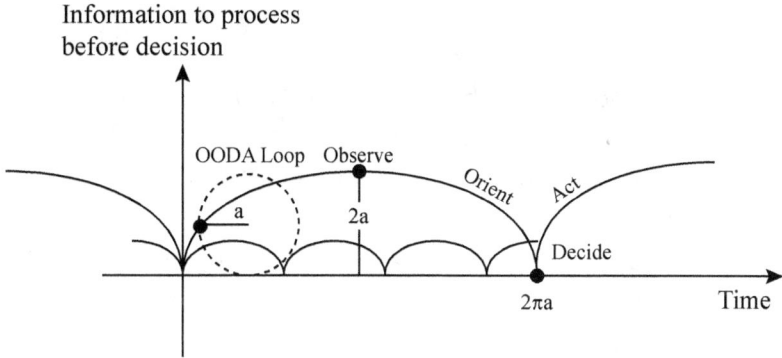

Figure 13 *From an OODA Loop to Decision-Wave*

logue in the same chronotope, whether it is a physical place or a digital address.

When a system is within these boundaries The Millennium Project senior fellow Theodore J. Gordon[15] suggests several appropriate means to influence it:

1. Slow things down, interfere with the feedback loops. If in the process of slowing down, the system passes from chaos to oscillation, then the cause or causes for the behavior of the system are proven and the right intervention strategy can be mediated;

2. Perturb the system. According to Ditto and Pecora[16] "the behavior of a chaotic system is a collection of many orderly behaviors, none of which dominates under ordinary circumstances, by perturbing a chaotic system in the right way, it can be encouraged to follow one of its many regular behaviors." The challenge of matching the system and the particular signal remains significant;

3. Control from the bottom up. As the science writer Kevin Kelley[17] describes it, if everything is connected to everything in a distributed network, everything happens at once, therefore overall governance must arise from

---

15. Gordon 2008.
16. Ditto & Pecora 1993.
17. Kelley 1994.

interdependent acts done locally and in parallel, and not from any central authority;

4. Accommodate it, which refers to "anticipating the outcome and defusing the tense situation by announcing the action that will be taken in view of arguments advanced by the crowd"[18];

5. Add capacity. For example in a rush hour the area which is crowded can be expanded so that the crowd density decreases;

6. Time the feedback. The means for control can be derived from providing feedback on the right frequency, phase, amplitude, and timing especially when dealing with physical systems, but also with human systems. For instance in a riot, the timing of the coverage of the crowd is extremely important,[19] and;

7. Add noise. There are number of ways, and today there are even more than before due to the Internet, e-mail and cell phones, to control, modify, or delay chaos by interfering with some aspect of the information that is fed to the system.

A concrete example of Theodor Gordon's work on above issues is the combination of a technology called ontology, capable of classifying spoken language, and the traditional Delphi analysis, i.e., looking for the best expert on each topic at stake, results in building a strategic decision-making system that enables "the best decision in 15 minutes".

The human systems differ from biological systems because *human beings are able to anticipate, are aware of time, and can have different attitudes towards the future.* While we can make sense of if the human systems as being in chaos, it is difficult to distinguish random and chaotic behavior—when humans and their organizations are involved new feedback loops and non-linearities will cer-

---

18. Gordon 2009.
19. Gordon 2009.

tainly be introduced as opposed to strictly mathematical analysis.

In the following pages I write with former US intelligence officer and government strategist *Michael Loescher* about the *criticality of operations analysis* in creating dynamic innovation organizations.[20]

What Operations Analysis Yields

For us operations analysis is similar to systems analysis, but transcends just the technology and engineering to include critical factors outside individual systems. While there are many research centers and think tanks all over the world, there are none that, that undertake our two major missions: non-military operations analysis and intelligence. In the US and the UK, there are operations analysis organizations, RAND perhaps being the most famous. But there are no centers that undertake to establish and maintain dynamic intelligence capabilities, which have largely been the domain of military organizations, and to some degree, banks and financial institutions. The type and nature of intelligence and analysis we undertake and the strategic purposes behind it are utterly different than anything in the past and are likely to be unique in the world for some time.

In simplest terms, RAC Finland analyzes and finds strategic opportunities for its customers that wish to develop new businesses and new products across the world. From an operations analysis perspective that means our job is to take apart business models, business processes, look for technology convergences, and market weaknesses and apply them against a set of criteria for feasibility, suitability and acceptability for the customer. So RAC Finland is moving operations analysis into an entirely new direction.

---

20. The article is excerpted from a forthcoming book to be called "The Perfect Storm", and it appears with the permission of RAC Finland LLC. Copyright 2009 Michael S. Loescher and Mika Aaltonen.

In terms of intelligence, it may seem a large task to build a large intelligence capability for commercial innovation, but in practice it is infinitely easier than the either the military versions or the financial versions of the art today. The reasons are straightforward:

Our findings need to be time-sensitive since timing matters in the marketplace. However, we don't require the kind of urgent early warning that military intelligence does, nor do we have to worry about short-term returns in the financial markets.

Once we enter into a partnership with a customer, in time and as a team we will be able to make priorities as to what is suitable, feasible, and acceptable for pursuit with their resources. Thus, we don't have to watch everything in the commercial sector all the time, everywhere in the world.

Most of the information we want is readily available, although not in the integrated form we want. For instance, a biotechnology-sector intelligence desk is not a vast enterprise, but is a relatively small group of experienced analysts and modelers working with collaborative software.

The value of what we produce has distinctive near, mid and long-term decision points. If a customer wants to explore nanotechnology, for example, we can have a nanotechnology desk set up with detailed cost-benefit criteria in 12 months for a fraction of the cost of a medium-sized R&D project. If there are opportunities found, then the cost of pursuing those opportunities specifically and the likelihood of success are vastly increased as those costs go down.

Finally, once the intelligence structure is in place, populating it with students within the university system provides a cheap source of highly educated future analysts.

We pride ourselves in passing on a process to the customer's innovation system. What this means is the likelihood of success is much higher than in other intelligence pursuits and the costs are far lower. RAC Finland will leverage the appropriate innovation system immediately.

Common Failures in Intelligence

Most of the failures in intelligence, whether in business or in national defense, come from four sources: over-reliance on theory, over-reliance on technology, a lack of flexible intelligence topology, and inexperience.

Over-reliance on theory is very common in financial sector intelligence, as the global hedge funds have just discovered. The search for the "golden algorithm" to capture the complexity in the world is a fascinating academic problem, but in the intelligence business, it is no substitute for the hard work of obtaining the level of detail necessary to gain insight.

Over-reliance on technology is a phenomenon usually associated with workstations where analysts use screening tools. It is very easy to come to completely incorrect conclusions when analysts become immersed in the screen and lose track of the context, or are not aware of the limits of the inputs.

The lack of a flexible topology means that at the outset of designing the overall intelligence system logic a dangerous assumption has been made about the total set of data that is relevant and its relationships. This usually arises when engineers can't resist the urge to begin everything with a top-down approach rather than accept the reality of uncertainty at the beginning.

Experience is the antidote to these problems. Intelligence is both an art and a science. Building an intelligence network without the benefit of experienced oversight is catastrophic.

An Innovation Service

This much is simple: knowledge is the fuel of innovation. Therefore, a knowledge-based economic strategy, such as Finland's new national innovation strategy, depends utterly on gaining a knowledge-based advantage over competitors. A global economy makes the globe a landscape of competitors. It follows that the knowledge needed must be global in nature, not only to produce innovations, but also to sustain the competitive advantage once produced and marketed.

Innovation has a time-space in the market. Because it does, the knowledge-base necessary for innovation takes on speciation. For example, some intelligence has to be accurate and timely, while other intelligence must be timely but can be approximated. Some knowledge is long-lasting, worthy of the time and expense of developing expertise. Other knowledge is perishable. However, because innovation can occur on the supply-side alone, or as an improved product or service development, or as an entirely new product or service, or through re-shaping or the development of a new market, or multiples of these, entrenched expertise can lead to disastrous choices. There are hundreds of examples.

Thus, the taxonomy of innovation is seemingly complex. But only seemingly so. If we were to compile the economic protocols of different commercial sectors of business, we would find that there are indeed recurring patterns of innovation. Compiled in detail, opportunities for innovation become methodically visible and can be gamed and explored for cost-benefits when placed against a set of strategic goals for the customer.

Any strategy of innovation in a global economy is only possible if a methodical approach to developing and sustaining a deep knowledge of the world's commercial sectors and emergent markets, in all of their manifestations, is put in place. Such knowledge must be dynamic, both anticipatory to and rapidly reactive to change across the global landscape of business. These are not the attributes of academic expertise. Nor can such knowledge be acquired in any single corporation.

Nor is such knowledge resident or dynamic in a traditional R&D organization. Nor should it be: when information has to be reacquired by each project, each corporation, and each R&D organization over and over, the need to do so places a drag on the process of innovation.

Rather, these three pools of expertise—universities, corporations, and other R&D entities, whether government or private—are the consumers of such knowledge, acting on it to create from it. None of these have, as their purpose an over-arching topology of the business-scape.

And How to Build It

Cost-benefit considerations, time to product or service, risk-mitigation, ability to predict and react to financial down-turns—all of these and more require an innovation system that is more leveraged, more networked, more integrated, and more agile than any other in the world. And, it must sustain that advantage above all others.

The question is *how to achieve such integration?* Long experience has taught us that success is best achieved by providing valuable services in practice, not theorizing from the top-down how to network. Instinctively organizations faced with such problems will jockey for position and embark on reorganization efforts, which are almost always difficult, combative, and expensive in time due to opportunities lost, frustration, and funds. The important thing is to plant the seed functionally and grow it over time with each passing project.

What works best is to begin with a multifunctional, shared system of services, overlaid across the organizations, providing a set of tools available to all. It should be non-threatening and shared. One can think of it as the mechanism for unifying and speeding up collaboration. It is the encircling Venn diagram that operationally overlays existing organizations, providing something that is non-threatening and value-added based on functions.

For the sake of illustration only, let us give it a name, the "Innovation Service." Ultimately, it incorporates five functions, each supporting the other and growing over a long period of time from the grass roots.

First, it will provide core staff services and residual information repositories for projects funded through the appropriate Innovation System. A small group of staff is assembled and trained in project methodology and becomes a common element of all projects funded by the private or government actor. The staff works to support that, so that more projects can be completed for less money, but makes no effort to manage the projects. Support, including virtual support, is the key. This is the enabling seed.

When a project is finished, the appropriate (i.e., non-patent) informational products are deposited at the service by the staff as a common service to all and to jump-start future projects in related areas. This becomes the next step, the beginning of a future intelligence system, which forms logically, simply and from the ground up—along the composite lines of a media news desk or analytic library.

To pick a Finnish example, a large ongoing project, such as TEKES' *Fuel Cell 2007-2013* would serve as the seed-basis to establish the "Energy Desk," which would endure beyond that project. The "Energy Desk" is then migrated to a sound analytical framework, which gradually comes to monitor and becomes available to support all research services in energy and is based, importantly, on the establishment of a modeled protocol.

Using networked analytical methods and an intranet, the "Energy Desk" begins to build virtually by acquiring the open-source tools, data resources, subscriptions and international human network to give Finland the deep intelligence it needs in that field.

Thus, the model is to "operationalize" research projects by migrating them through this mechanism into a set of Innovation Support Desks, with analytical frameworks and resources available to all. You may think of it as a combination of "Google, Morningstar, MI-5, and The Financial Times"—a desk that gradually becomes more and more operational and dynamic. Note that while a "desk function" needs a small staff of people, multiple desks can be managed by relatively few people when built correctly and professionally. It is important that the service does not interfere with or attempt to centralize research. Its purpose is the support and the growth of analytic technique and efficiency, and making previous work operationally available to new projects.

This brings us to a second function, often in a second stage: highly specialized education and training specifically in innovation techniques. This is best considered as a specialized 24-month full-time curriculum pathway, wherein the study of an innovation is undertaken in detail.

Students and faculty can be visiting from existing institutions, but the curriculum must be highly defined by the service. You cannot retread courses from a university. The first six months is deep immersion in business cases and the taxonomy of innovation. The second six months is immersion in analysis, in which (ultimately) students would sit as interns on one of the growing Innovation Support Desks. The final 12 months is spent, not in research, but on proposing specific innovations arising from their internship period and/or acting as staff for an ongoing project within the other agencies or companies.

Thus, the service acts as a pipeline for practical innovation through methodical analysis, which becomes shared and honed overtime. It is an engine by which the academic experience becomes augmented and transformed into an operational function, giving the customer, over time, a large number of practically trained innovators.

Third, such a service can give the innovation system at large a means to shape and meter the human capital requirements for the nation over long periods. For example, a national focus on ecological innovation ultimately demands systematically growing expertise in the area. We do this by having a specific approach to creating communities of expertise inside the appropriate innovation process.

Fourth, service functions as a gaming facility for appropriate companies and agencies that want to explore the cost-benefit of specific innovations before bringing them even into pre-design. To do this, a resident gaming staff is developed to support this function (with interns, so that the capability becomes embedded over time), devising specific risk-management games and other analytic scenarios for the proposed product or service to examine such issues as supply and demand suppositions, process prototypes, and market models.

It is important that this same gaming functionality be resident at levels higher than individual products, as well. In that way, service becomes a strategic test bed for the innovation system stakeholders to game broad funding decisions as the global marketplace changes. After all, opportunity costs are a part of the real world. Innovation in all sectors is neither possible nor desirable. Strategic gaming to identify which sectors pose best possibilities with the least risk should be a dynamic analytical process.

Fifth, the service is the glue that cements the innovation system into an operational whole, giving the customer the ability to manage a system without dampening initiative. It builds on the existing functions and agencies, slowly or rapidly as the situation allows, by connecting them without threatening them. It fosters rigorous analysis that yields consensus and common pride over time. In doing so, it provides through that dynamic consensus a way for the customer to facilitate its funding decisions beyond annual budgeting.

More, through its analytical tentacles, the service creates longer and deeper networks of expertise than the customer might otherwise be able to do. Foreign entrepreneurs can come to an agreement with the customer to use its test beds in innovation systems, further deepening the customer's involvement in worldwide innovation.

Today, to make good decisions, you must have deep intelligence—surfacing opportunities and be able to demonstrate why they are so. To defend your decisions, you must grow an operations analysis capability that extends beyond rhetoric and outside pressure.

To provide for this dilemma, in the UK and in the US, private companies have been established to undertake these two functions. They are restricted by agreement in what tasks they may undertake and are rigorous in the development of intelligence products.

The Perfect Storm—Transition in Global Logistics Lanes

Beginning in 2006, RAC Finland undertook a methodical two-year operational analysis of the strategic considerations Finland would face in implementing its new Innovation Strategy. We did it to demonstrate to the Finnish government agency, TEKES, how operations analysis and deep intelligence changes the game. The results were stunning to many in the Finnish Innovation System, which had conducted study after academic study of the future of their country. Neither the studies nor the policies reflected in government planning uncovered the three key developments that provide most opportunities and most threats to Finland. The reason they did not see them is because nearly all of the work involved Finnish academics and existing Finnish companies, which generally projected the past into the future. In doing so, they missed the developments, which are so obvious, one rigorous analysis is undertaken. The point is: these ideas did not come to us by an apple dropping on our head in the garden. They are supported by demonstrable logic and the factual research. We close this chapter with a truncated discussion of what we came to call "The Perfect Storm."

Figure 14 *Melting of the Arctic Ice Gap*

In the first quarter of the 21st Century a confluence of three otherwise unrelated developments is set to reposition Finland so that it lays precisely astride the largest communications and logistics lanes on the globe.

The first of these developments is the relentless melting of the Arctic Ice Cap, which is variously estimated to proceed at such a pace that by 2020, the circumpolar navigation of the globe will be possible year-round without icebreakers. This will mean that many types of goods can be moved to and from Finland to North America, South America, East Asia, and Australia at perhaps 60 percent of the cost of today's transit. From a Finnish point of shipment to the Arctic, either an easterly or a westerly Arctic transit, exiting by way of the Bering Straits opens up into the Pacific, which in turn leads to East Asia and, on the North American continent, the four principal rail lines that cross America.

The second development is the decision by the Russian government to continue the modernization of the Trans-Siberian Railway, which from St. Petersburg connects Europe to Vladivostok and the East China seaports. The TSR is presently a Russian Federal Corporation, but the govern-

Figure 15 *The modernization of the Trans-Siberian Railway*

ment has declared its intent to take the company public and the present collapse in the Russian economy almost certainly will require external capital. The first high-speed containerized freight moved from Moscow to Berlin in 2006. There are also many subordinate routes in development, the longest of which is the route through western China from her seaports (proceeding quickly with strong Chinese government backing.) Two other lines linking the Indian subcontinent and Indochina, respectively, have more significant funding and construction hurdles.

Almost all analysts agree that sometime during the decade from 2020-2030, these two vast communications lanes will reach sufficient maturity to create, in effect, three intersecting flows of transit, centered on the Arctic, and spinning into the transcontinental rail systems of Asia and North America. Finland, of course, is at the center of two key points, which presents both abundant opportunities and challenges. Cheap labor and cheap transportation lower the already low (relative to Europe) cost of China's supply-side logistics. Obviously, new markets for Europe in Asia, in the Americas and Australasia become much more accessible than they are now. Precision manufacturing come within closer reach when logistics costs are down and markets are, therefore, relatively, closer. The shipping industry, slowed because of the global financial crisis, will be forced to change. Much of the planned containerized shipping, tanking, and bulk carrier tonnage on the draft board today is for new ship types that can transit the smaller Panama Canal and Suez, which in turn are both planned to be widened and deepened at huge expense. Neither fits into the dynamics we illustrate below.

In effect, the northern hemisphere would become a kind of commercial "Pangaea", an economic super-continent linked by sophisticated rail/sea lanes.

Into this tumult we may throw the third development, which is the discovery and quantification of vast petroleum and gas reserves in the Arctic. The estimates of the new deposits are, at least, 90 billion barrels of oil (bbo), 1,670 trillion cubic feet of natural gas (tcf) and 44 billion barrels of natural gas liquids. This is roughly 40 percent of the now known world petroleum resources. If we add Canadian oil sands, 175 bbo, to the new Arctic discoveries, it is clear than the compass heading for the world's future petroleum energy resources points due north from everywhere.

Lastly, we have no doubt that the next two decades; at least, will make the battle between the Have's and the Have-Not's part of our daily news. As we write these words, 230 African indigents have been drowned trying to make an EU landfall off Italy, and from thence by way of the Schengen Agreement throughout Europe. The Canary Islands are similar stops, as are the Eastern European states. There is great pressure for migration north across the Mediterranean, and in the future, it seems clear that the economically promising shores of the Baltic will be a magnet for migrants.

These developments place the Baltic Sea Region in a unique position economically, politically and socially. The question is; can the Baltic Sea countries step up to the detailed planning necessary to move into the future. Studying

Figure 16 *Petroleum and gas reserves
in the Arctic*

technology is one thing: but what we describe here is a seismic event, with the Baltic at the center. Redrawing the map of the world hasn't been done since 1492. It is within these countries' power, over the next 10 years, to find an entirely new and self-supporting future with a thriving and sustainable economy.

The central obstacle, we predict, will be a well-meaning inertia. It is difficult for a small country or a group of countries to see the strategic crossroads in which time and chance have placed them. Yet like ancient Athens after its incredible defeat of the Persian Empire, Finland and Baltic Sea countries in 2024—at the center of two of the world's great trade routes—will be set in an extended geography they never expected. And, like Elizabethan England, they will see that their safety and prosperity must lie outside the border lines of their homelands. No amount of innovation study can bring sufficient industry onto Baltic soil to sustain its well-being in such a future. Nor is it necessary: next-generation in Baltic Sea Region has endless opportunities to choose its economic basis if the present generation can see the coming horizon.

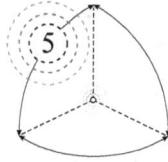

5. Preparing for Futures

The Office of the French Minister for the Prospective
and Public Policy
Paris

The setting is beautiful and the choice of wine is excellent, so I'm having lunch with Eric Besson, the French Minister for the Prospective and Public Policy.

The French enjoy two remarkable advantages, historical and linguistic, when it comes to preparing for futures. The French have long traditions in foresight, already Cardinal Richelieu[1] stated in his *Testament Politique* that nothing was more important for a government than foresight, only in this manner was one able to avoid evils that were difficult to evade. The second consequence was a preparedness for possible futures.

The roots of this kind of thinking—initially called the prognosis—were developed in the 15th and 16th century Italy as a counter-concept to contemporary prophecy. While prophecy transgressed the bounds of calculable experience, prognosis remains within the dimensions of a political situation. It is related to events whose novelty it releases. Hence time emanates from the prognosis in an unforeseeable, but predictable manner. Prognosis produces the time within which and out of which it weaves, whereas prophecy destroys time through its fixation on the end. For prophecy, events are merely symbols of something which is already known. A disappointed prophet does not doubt the

---

1. Richelieu

truth of his own predictions. Since they are variable, they can be renewed at any time. By contrast, an erroneous prognosis cannot be repeated, because it has been conditioned by specific assumptions.[2]

In Italy, Guicciardini[3] reintroduced Aristotle's phrase "de futuris contingentibus non est determinata veritas" or for future events the truth is indeterminate. From this insight a particular attitude followed. The future became a domain of finite possibilities, arranged according to their greater or lesser probability, and the art of political calculation started to flourish in the cabinets of the European courts. You can see this in places in modern France. For many years DATAR was located just few steps from the Eiffel Tower, and you could find a Charles de Gaulle slogan on the wall. It says: "Remember that we are making a project that will last a hundred years".

When discussing the future, it is important to refer to the various layers of time. Three different temporal planes can be distinguished, they are retriable in different ways that make prognoses possible.

First, there is a short-term succession of the before and after characterizing of our everyday actions. Always bound situationally; the prerequisites for the actors involved in a change are experienced either sooner or later in years, months, weeks or hours. In this kind of context, it is very difficult to make exact prognoses, because not all of the actions and reactions can, nor all cause and effect relationships can be grasped or recognized at the time they occur. Perhaps in some situations and only after a certain number of moves will a situation become clearer so that prognoses can be made with greater accuracy.[4]

Second, the plane of the middle-term trends is derived from the course of events beyond the control of acting subjects. Many intra-personal conditions exert an influ-

---

2. Koselleck 2004.
3. Guicciardini
4. C.f. Koselleck 2004.

ence on what is happening, but the conditions themselves change at a slower speed than that of the actions of the actors themselves. On this plane, we find economic crisis, the courses of a war, and also climate changes.[5]

Third, the plane of metahistorical duration, which is nevertheless timeless. On this plane, we can establish anthropological constants that elude the historical pressure of change. A wealth of principles, proverbs and anecdotes derived from experience stem from this sphere. They repeat themselves and are applied over and over gain, nevertheless their sometimes seemingly banal wisdom should not be underestimated. Thus these principles, which are derived from experience they possess hints of a prognostic truth.[6]

As the years passed by, it became accepted "that it is possible to forecast the approaching future, but one would not wish to prophesy individual events".[7] Lorenz von Stein's statement was formulated in 1850, and it can be perceived as a secularized version of the Christian prophets of doom whose lasting certainty always exceeded the accuracy of their individual short-term expectations. The long-term forecasts, such as those given by Bruno Bauer, Friedrich List or Donoso Cortes pointed towards the future and contained only the slightest attachment to the previous epoch they came from. Until that time it was universally accepted that one could learn lessons from the past for the future. In other words, knowledge of what had been and foreknowledge of what was yet to become remained connected, and nothing essentially new could occur. From then on, the new history became a long-term process which could be directed as it unfolded itself above the heads of participants. This being the case conclusions drawn from the past about the future appear not only out of place, but appear to be impossible. Nevertheless, this reasoning indicates the possibility of new experiences.[8]

---

5. C.f. Koselleck 2004.
6. C.f. Koselleck 2004.
7. Stein 1959.
8. C.f. Koselleck 2002.

We do not need to live in 2025 to think of a number of issues that will change as time passes; we can diagnose the present from the perspective of the future without actually being in the future. The long-term forecasts can affect medium-term and short-term planning in politics and economics, and have increasingly come to do so. Generally, also from the philosophical and ontological viewpoints, the argument that the future, when articulated, explicated and brought into present discussions, affects the present, can hardly be disputed[9]. This is a similar feature to that already expressed in Figure 2 when I discussed Robert Rosen's theory of anticipatory systems.

The ontological status of what is to come does not correspond to that what has already happened. Past events, or parts of them, are contained in our experience and can often be verified empirically. The future, what is yet to come, is beyond our experience and cannot be verified empirically. Nevertheless, there are predictions that can be transposed, from experience to expectation.[10]

Immanuel Kant[11] agrees with Cardinal Richelieu, and suggests that the faculty of foreseeing, or foresight, is of greater interest than anything else because it is "the condition of all possible practice and all possible purposes to which man can direct the use of his powers. All desire contains anticipation of what is possible through foresight. Recalling the past occurs only with the intention of making it possible to foresee the future; we look about us from the standpoint of the present in order to determine something, or to be prepared for something."

Of the three temporal dimensions—past, present and future—presented by Augustine, Kant is most interested in the future. Because *Robustness* is about human beings, our interest goes beyond foresight or foreknowledge, meaning rational planning processes, including calcula-

9. Koselleck 2004.
10. C.f. Koselleck 2004.
11. Kant in *Anthropology from a Pragmatic Point of View*.

tions and predictions, to all types of expectations—hopes, fears, wishes and apprehensions. They too play a significant role in the anticipatory and adaptive human systems that are necessary for us to exist, conduct our lives and survive.

This domain of the future, chapter 5, is not completely unknown, there are gradations of greater or lesser probability with which the future can be predicted. There are probabilities that individually and collectively indicate various chances of their realization. Furthermore, some of the approaches are better equipped to deal with great amounts, some with medium amounts, and some with little amounts of probability, and according to the art of foresight, they should be used aptly.

The further we distance ourselves from the future, the more difficult foresight becomes. The same applies when we distance ourselves from long-term naturally pre-given data, and become involved with complex political decision-making processes. Foresight takes place between dependable and relatively certain framework conditions and those that change procedurally.[12] In societies and organizations, there are structures and processes that persist. That is the reason why prognosis is possible, even if individual events remain unique.

Contemporary French foresight experts are aware of their role and history. Professor Remi Barré, the foresight advisor for the French Ministry of Higher Education and Research, informs us of three ongoing debates. Firstly, the issues what should be taught and how, and what a teacher should be are discussed. Also, the debate about whether the classroom should still be the place for learning or whether we should go beyond it is looked at. The idea for moving beyond the classroom is about not separating children from their everyday life. This also applies to teachers as they increasingly need to be able to discuss things that make sense in everyday life. Secondly, even if there is the habit in almost every research organization, in every important proj-

---

12. Koselleck 2004.

ect to prepare scenarios or at least to think about the future, there are also difficulties in engaging in meaningful discussions. And there is a debate if our future can be built on old and massive organizations. To cope with such challenges France is reorganizing and forming a strategy for research and innovation and reshifting her overall architecture with respect to relationship between science and society. Thirdly, as Barré is also a member of the European Research Area (ERA) vision team, he offers a ray of hope with the regard to the financial crisis by saying it may be a chance to reinvent good management, start to build upon open source idea and begin sharing national policies for certain challenges.

One of the best known French theorists and practitioners of prospective thinking is Conservatoire National des Arts et Métiers Professor Michel Godet[13]. In Table 5 in the spirit of Cardinal Richelieu's *Testament*, he explicates his philosophy of future and is able to illustrate how attitudes affect both scenarios and strategies.

Attitudes towards the future	Corresponding scenarios	Corresponding strategies
Passive	None	Go with
Reactive	None	Adaptive
Preactive	Trend-based	Preventive
Proactive	Desirable alternatives	Innovative

Table 5 *Attitudes, scenarios and strategies*

For a Frenchman, the DIV Director Adil Jazouli speaks exceptionally direct. He says that France has long traditions in technology foresight led by government and regions. He is concerned with the general process, "it is not acceptable to impose visions and strategies on people who have not been involved in the process of making them".

---

13. Godet 2006.

The DIV's mission has been to include people in decision-making processes, so that they can decide for themselves. The economic situation in numerous cities is difficult; their politics is focused on repairing, but shifting the focus towards proactivity does not seem to be happening.

Nevertheless, the European tradition of foresight is strong and long. Riel Miller[14] lists the most illustrative examples amongst the thousands of contemporary foresight studies[15]:

Scenarios for the poorest: the view from 2030: This exercise was conducted by the UK consultancy Outsights. It outlined four scenarios focusing on poverty in developed and developing countries. The project involved an international panel of 70 stakeholders and experts, collecting papers and interviews, and organizing workshops. The preparation of the scenarios was assisted by a UK research center.[16]

The world in 2025: A challenge to reason: This report was written at the request of the European Commission DG Research and BEPA. It was a foresight exercise aimed at analyzing the world situation from now to 2025 by involving an expert working group. Each member of the group delivered a report and there were two gatherings of the full group in order to exchange ideas and build scenarios.[17]

Scenarios for the future 2025: The scenarios developed by the European Patent Office, focused on how intellectual property rights regimes might have evolved by 2050 and on what global legitimacy such regimes might have. They are based on a vast interview survey of expert and stakeholders.[18]

---

14. Miller *et al.* 2010.
15. See http://www.efmn.eu amongst other sources, see bibliography.
16. See http://www.outsights.co.uk.
17. See http://www.2100.org/World2025.pdf.
18. See http://www.epo.org.

Foresight Futures 2020: This was sponsored by the UK Government's Department of Trade and Industry and realized by SPRU at the University of Sussex, the exercise attempts to identify social and economic trends in the UK, to explore the possible changes in the country over the next 20 to 30 years, and to develop alternative scenarios in consultation with stakeholders from business, government and academia.[19]

Four Scenarios for Europe Based on UNEP's third Global Environment Outlook: This was a study conducted on behalf of the United Nations Environment Programme and the Netherlands' Ministry of Housing, Spatial Planning and the Environment. This report presents a series of "what-if" scenarios that were produced using both qualitative scenarios, that explored the relationships and trends for which few or no numerical data are available. It included shocks and discontinuities, and quantitative sources, often generated by computer models in which assumptions are explicit and statistical uncertainty analysis can be applied by systematically changing assumptions.[20]

The Future of Manufacturing in Europe: A Survey of the Literature and a Modelling Approach: DG Enterprise sponsored this study which was undertaken by CPB, the Netherlands (Arjan Lejour) & TNO-IPG (Frans van der Zee). The scenarios in this study were developed in three consecutive stages, consisting of (i) a survey of existing futures studies, (ii) the drafting of qualitative scenarios, and (iii) a quantification of the scenarios using WorldScan, a dynamically applied general equilibrium model for the world economy. This approach was designed as a hybrid that combines traditional foresight studies with more quantitative oriented economic-scenario studies.[21]

---

19. See http://www.dti.gov.uk.
20. See http://www.unep.org/GEO/pdfs/four_scenarios_europe.pdf.
21. See http://ec.europa.eu/enterprise/enterprise_policy/industry/

Global Trends 2025: A Transformed World: This report was prepared by the US National Intelligence Council and published in November of 2008, Its purpose is to stimulate strategic thinking about the future by identifying key trends, the factors that drive them, where they seem to be headed, and how they might interact. It uses scenarios to illustrate some of the many ways in which the drivers examined in the study (e.g., globalization, demography, the rise of new powers, the decay of international institutions, climate change, and the geopolitics of energy) may interact to generate challenges and opportunities for future decision makers. The study as a whole is more a description of the factors likely to shape events than a prediction of what will actually happen.[22]

Anticipating Change for Europe's Industries 2020 to 2025: This Sector Futures project was undertaken by the European Monitoring Centre on Change, within The European Foundation for the Improvement of Living and Working Conditions. By 2005 this process had explored possible futures for eight sectors in Europe and created 24 separate articles covering trends and drivers, scenarios and policy implications.[23]

Horizons 2020: A thought-provoking looking at the future, which was sponsored by Siemens AG and implemented by TNS Infratest. This foresight exercise attempts to explore four societal dimensions (economy, politics, technology, society) framing life and life choices in the year 2020. The goal of the exercise is to place technological developments in a broader socio-economic framework. Based on a large expert survey, scenarios are discussed and elaborated in detail by a central research group.[24]

---

doc/future_manufacturing_europe_final_report.pdf.
22. See http://www.dni.gov/nic/NIC_2025_project.html.
23. See http://www.emcc.eurofound.eu.int/sector_futures.htm.
24. See http://www.tns-infratest.com.

The Rise of a Multi-polar World: This report authored by Accenture addresses the future of globalization. It is based on original research as well as our experience of working with organizations around the world to help them achieve and sustain high performance. It attempts to identify and understand the forces creating this new era of globalization. The analysis focuses on the fast-evolving economic geography of what we call 'the multi-polar world'.[25]

Global Scenarios 2025: The outstanding Royal Dutch/Shell series is an example of long-term scenarios addressing global developments and regional interdependencies. Focusing on structural trends, the Shell scenarios outline alternative business environments shaped by the diverse combinations of the three dimensions of market, state regulation, and aspirations to equity.[26]

This sample of works is only meant to be indicative of the kinds of studies that have recently been executed, and the kinds of problems, challenges and issues they have addressed.

Turning our eyes into the future, the French[27] are able to exploit the French language making a distinction between the future, "le futur", and the forthcoming, "l'avenir". The distinction does not come as naturally in English. L'avenir is the future of the long present, the pre-perceptive anticipation of the present, i.e., the protended future, as le futur is future time grasped from a standpoint not located in the present, but in advance of it, the future fantasized or modo futuri exacti[28]. The forthcoming is perceived and presented in the course of synthesis which establishes the present together with its temporal horizons, the future lies below this horizon, it is inaccessible except as a representation, an imaginary present defined in rela-

---

25. See http://www.accenture.com/forwardthinking.
26. See http://www.shell.com/scenarios/.
27. Bourdieu 1963.
28. Scutz 1967.

tion to the here and now. A further distinction between the forthcoming and the future can be explicated, it is the one between the possible and the potential. Possibilities can be explored in the activity of projecting, which is free and not constrained by data, potentialities on the other hand are perceived. To put it aptly, potentialities are inside the world, not beyond its boundaries, as are mere possibilities.

I have argued earlier that there exists a European intellectual heritage emphasizing the repeatable and predictable features of life. These features have been raised over and over again by several authorities. For instance, Macchiavelli stated that "he who wishes to foretell the future must look into the past, for all things on earth have at all times similarity with those of the past". Immanuel Kant summarized "things will remain as they were" and consequently one cannot forecast anything which was historically new.

Secondly, there exists a strong preference for order. In Western societies, we have been taught to think, or we have been conditioned to think that order is good and something that must be maintained. Eventually we have come into belief that the very nature of our lives is order.

These assumptions have guided the massive systems of compulsory schooling introduced in the 19th century and been extended to post-secondary education in the 20th century. First we invest in the various elements of a school system teachers, text books, classrooms, information technology etc. and then to expect, or to force, young people to attend schools. The creation of compulsory schooling is perhaps the greatest social innovation of recent times. It played and still plays a vital role in providing people with the specific cognitive, behavioral and social skills needed in our societies.[29]

However, even the new experiences gained from the exploration of lands overseas and from the developments of science and technology are still insufficient for making sense of the future, because all previous experience might

---

29. Miller 2006.

not count against the possible otherness of the future. The future will be different from the past, not just more of the same. Novelties and innovation detach the future from the past, inject something new into the present and create trajectories for novel futures.[30]

For The Millennium Project Director Jerome C. Glenn[31] to study the future means to study potential change, what is likely to make a systemic or fundamental difference over the next 10 to 25 years or more. Studying the future is not an economic projection or sociological analysis or technological forecasting, but a multi-disciplinary examination of change in all major areas of life to find the interacting dynamics that are creating the next age.

As historians tell us what happened and journalists what is happening, futurists tell us what could happen, and help us to think about what we might want to become. Futurists do not know what will happen, and most of them do not claim to prophesize. But they claim to know more about a range of possible and desirable futures, and how these futures might evolve. They also know about the methods and techniques that are used and have been used in their field. The knowledge that is achievable in this field differs from the Newtonian kind of knowledge presented in Chapter 2, it is not scientific, accurate or complete, but it helps to make sense of what is possible, identify policy choices and evaluate alternative actions.

According to Glenn there exists a consensus among the practitioners about the basic philosophical assumptions behind futures research:

- You cannot know the future, but a range of possible futures can be known;
- The likelihood of a future event or condition can be shaped by policy, and policy consequences can be forecasted;

---

30. Poli 2009b.
31. Glenn 2009.

- Gradations of foreknowledge and probabilities can be made; we can be more certain about the sunrise than about the rise of a stock market;
- No single method should be trusted; cross-referencing between the methods improves foresight, and;
- Human beings will have more influence on the future than they did in the past.

The ontological position this chapter takes differs significantly from those in the previous chapters, especially that of Chapter 2. Here we pinpoint the need to accept that reality is open. Something new can always happen. People, families, organizations and nations are not thoroughly established. All of them exhibit a tendency towards the future. However, what they can and will be is embedded in their presence. This openness means that the living entities are never more than partially determined. There are always, especially in turbulent times, opportunities waiting for us to activate them, but they remain open only for some time and then disappear when the context changes and time passes.

Unfortunately, we constantly miss them by taking a rationalist outlook.

On the other hand there are also latent properties that do not exist yet, which may imply that the internal structural determinations have not been formed. A newborn baby cannot do most of the things adults can, a new worker cannot perform at the top level straight away, and a new team will not work as a unified team immediately, but in due time they will have the capabilities to do so.[32]

Human systems can be comprehended through their boundaries. By virtue of possessing boundaries we can to distinguish what is internal to ourselves, our family or our organization from what is external. A boundary may be precise and rigid or vague and mobile, but as soon as it becomes established it starts to work at both separating and

32. Poli 2009b.

connecting the system to its environment.[33]

Moreover, it makes sense to discuss closed and open boundaries. The division between closed and open boundaries explains why some human systems stagnate and others develop. A closed boundary generates a gradually more homogeneous internal situation with limited differentiation, and more a distinct interior compared to the external environment. This is exactly what happens when history is used to guide us to the future and order is presumed and maintained. An open boundary allows and encourages greater internal differentiation, which in turn leads to a greater degree of development within systems than that which would happen in the presence of closed boundaries.[34]

Accepting openness means that the problem of missing information, imperfect knowledge or partially known subjects becomes less important, because life is perceived as ever emerging, amplifying and being formed, and what is knowable matters more than what is already known.[35]

Next *Gerda Roelevald* presents the *Randstad2040* example of the necessity of timely preparation for the future pretty much according to the updated and finest European tradition.

Before embarking on describing the actual case of 'Randstad2040' as an example of 'foresight' it seems appropriate to highlight some basic principles of the Dutch spatial planning system first and then to introduce how some fundamental characteristics of foresight are used in this paper to evaluate the case. The why, what and how of the Randstad2040 project are also presented and the paper concludes with some observations and questions for discussion.

---

33. Poli 2010.
34. Poli 2010.
35. C.f. Aaltonen 2007.

Dutch spatial planning system

In July 2008, a new Spatial Planning Act came into force in The Netherlands, replacing the first law in this field made in 1965. The new law substantially simplifies spatial planning procedures, clarifies the responsibilities of government authorities and provides all actors in spatial development processes with appropriate instruments, while at the same time leaving them much freedom on how to use them.

There are only two types of plans under the new law: the *land use plan* and the *structural vision*. In principle all three administrative levels in The Netherlands: national, regional (provinces) and local (communities) have the right to draw up and decide land use plans and structural visions[36]. All formerly existing plans such as Key Planning Decisions, Structure Schemes, Regional Plans and Local Structure Plans are to be abandoned and phased out under the new law.

Whereas the land use plan is a legally binding document for governments, citizens and enterprises alike, the structural vision only binds the authorities that signed for it (self binding). By means of general legal instruments, e.g. orders in council (state level) or by-laws (regional and local level), public authorities can pro-actively prescribe requirements regarding procedures or content of land use plans or structural visions that have to be met by lower level authorities. Such requirements need structural visions for a basis.

A structural vision is a strategic policy document on mid or long term spatial development in a certain area; the document should include an explicit implementation strategy (legal and voluntary instruments, financing, and time schedules). Ultimately, its policy objectives should materialize in land use plans. The structural vision 'Randstad2040' is one of

---

36. Here, the principle of subsidiarity is put into practice. Land use plans are primarily a community responsibility. Only if central or regional government consider a certain development (for example a railroad link of national interest) or a certain area (for example an urban network of regional interest) to be first and foremost their own responsibility, they can decide upon land use plans themselves, overruling the authorities at local level in doing so.

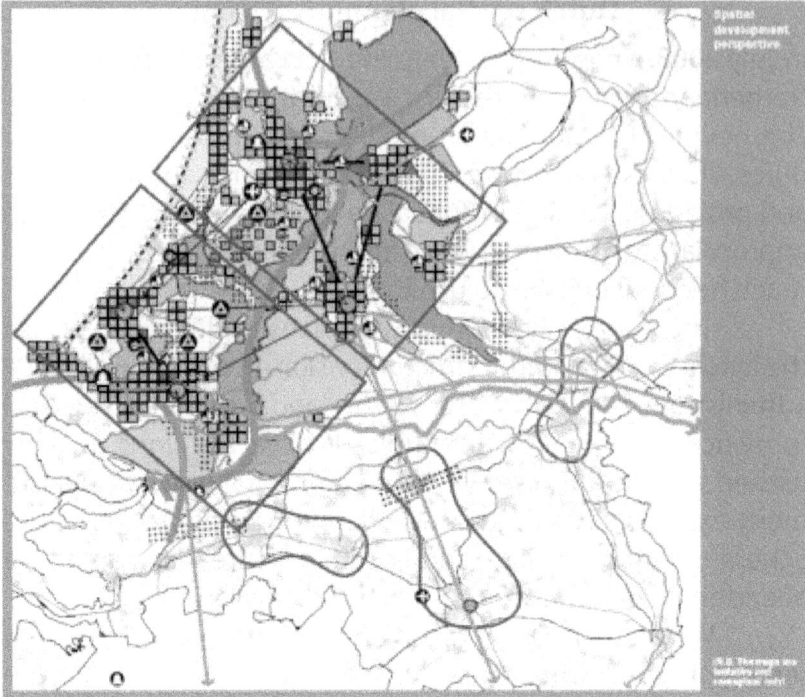

Figure 17 *Ranstad2040 structural vision map*

the first structural visions adopted by the Dutch Parliament under the new law and is integrated of nature, covering all spatial aspects of the area[37].

Foresight

From the several definitions of 'Foresight' given in the recently published Glossary[38] by DIACT, some basic characteristics can be identified. Thus, if a spatial planning process is to be considered an example of 'foresight', it will contain:

- The anticipation on possible and/or desirable futures guides current decision-making;

---

37. Structural visions can also be thematic of nature, e.g. the National Water Plan, adopted by the Cabinet of Ministers in December 2008.
38. p. 43; 'Les mots clés de la prospective territoriale', sous la direction de Ph. Destatte et Ph. Durance; DIACT, 2009

Figure 18 *Legend of Ranstad2040 structural vision map*

- Rational research and analysis is paired with intuitive visioning and imagination;
- Policy objectives are translated into concrete actions, and;
- The following of an integrated (holistic) and trans disciplinary approach.

In the following description the 'foresight' character of the Randstad2040 project is illustrated by focusing on these characteristics, although less attention is paid to the actual nature of problems and solutions for the Randstad region.

Randstad2040—The Case

Context: why a long term vision for the Randstad?

In their article[39] for the 44th ISOCARP Congress in 2008, Van der Burg and Vink mention that, already in 2006, the Dutch parliament requested a long term vision to be drawn up for the Randstad area, which is the long standing economic and cultural center of the Netherlands, comprised by the so called 'Big 4': the cities of Amsterdam, Rotterdam, The Hague and Utrecht and the green area these cities more or less encircle, usually referred to as the Green Heart. The population of the Randstad adds up to 7 million people, i.e., 45% of the total Dutch population, living on 26% of the country's land area, generating about 50% of the country's GDP.

The reason for the interest of parliament in a long term vision for the Randstad, Van der Burg and Vink recall is that when the Dutch Parliament approved of the national Spatial Planning Policy Document ('Nota Ruimte'[40], 2006) they felt that this document did not provide with enough detailed policy measures for the future development of this most important area of The Netherlands, especially so in relation to issues relevant to climate change as its time horizon was 'only' 2020. This time the horizon was thought to be too short to prepare necessary long-term investment decisions of national importance, such as the development of the Schiphol Airport or the major housing development projects, not to mention the adaptation of the water management system that is required to cope with climate change. Major investments in those physical realms require a long time to prepare; hence it was considered sensible to start preparing now, for beyond 2020.

---

39. 'Randstad Holland towards 2040—perspectives from national government', Arjen J. van der Burg and Bart L. Vink, 2008.
40. The fifth such document since the Spatial Planning Act came into force (1965).

134

Process

Kick-off: critical issues and parallel tracks.

The Randstad2040 project started in September 2007, with a Starting Memorandum, agreed by the Cabinet of ministers. The Starting Memorandum put forward seven critical questions for debate:

How can we ensure a climate proof Delta in the future?

What are considered strategic spatial investments in the area?

What kind of green-blue framework could act as a means to structure further urban development?

What balance between the concentration within the boundaries of existing cities (including high-rise options) and green field development should an urban strategy aim in order to be considered sustainable?

What would a sustainable transportation concept for the area look like?

How can existing strong economic functions like harbors, airports and related industries, that place stress on the environment, be reconciled with the demand for attractive living and working space corresponding with further development of the knowledge economy, in an area where competition for scarce space is fierce?

Can Schiphol Airport, as the fourth most important airport in Europe, continue to grow in a sustainable way?

Inspired by a strong belief in the necessity of a participatory approach in drawing up a structural vision for the Randstad, the government parties involved chose to launch an intensive consultation campaign based on these critical questions, consisting of four parallel tracks: a dialogue with the public; research and advisory contributions, either requested or unsolicited; visioning exercises, and an inventory of strategic implementation alliances.

Dialogue

In order to obtain reactions from the public[41], a special website was created from which the Starting Memorandum and other relevant documents could be downloaded. Four interactive on-line discussions with citizens were organized, in which some 400 citizens participated. Advertisements were put in newspapers and a random selection of citizens received a letter, inviting them to join the debate and react to the questions raised. International professionals in the field filled a special Randstad2040 issue of Nova Terra, an expert magazine on spatial planning matters, with articles. A total of seven 'Randstad tables' were organized in the cities of Amsterdam, Rotterdam and The Hague, where stakeholders, citizens and professional planners exchanged views, helped by three visions of the future Randstad (in 2040), that were obtained from the visioning exercises (see below). An on-line questionnaire attracted 13.500 participants, who gave quantitative scores to what they deemed to be the major issues for the structural vision. The outcome showed that improvements in physical and mental health are considered top-priority issues, with accessibility, attractive living and working environments with sufficient, accessible green areas and multi-purpose utilization of water were ranked second. At a conference in May 2008, the results of the dialogue were presented as an advisory paper, which was given to the minister of VROM, responsible for spatial planning[42].

---

41. Focusing not only at inhabitants of the Randstad area, but nationwide.

42. Responsibilities of the ministry of VROM comprise Housing, Social Integration, Spatial Planning, and the Environment. At this occasion the minister of VROM represented three other ministries responsible for policy fields with major impacts on spatial planning: Agriculture, Nature and Food safety (LNV), Transport and Water management (V&W) and Economic Affairs.

Research and Advice

To provide a solid scientific base for policy making, the government bodies involved[43] ordered reports on a wide variety of subjects from scientist employed within their own organizations as well as from policy-independent, state funded science institutes such as the Spatial Planning Bureau[44]; Nature and Environment Planning Bureau[45]; Central Planning Bureau[46], independent consultants, advisory councils to the government[47] and from the OECD[48]. From those contacted they also received unsolicited advice, which they also took into account.

From the reports and advice the following was obtained: scenarios on the standard of life and the environment; an inventory of implementation strategies in other European regions; long term perspectives on water management, on spatial development, on mobility and on the structure of economic sectors; reports on spatial development policy in general and on governance issues in the realm of spatial planning; ex-ante evaluation- and environmental effect reports on the eventual structural vision.

In addition to the above, a temporary platform of experts was installed, who procured advice on the strategic position of the structural vision and its implementation; this platform also developed a definition of the concept 'sustainable top-region', using the 'people, planet, profit'[49] paradigm as a framework.

---

43. Including the ministers mentioned in footnote 7 as well as provincial and local authorities.
44. Ruimtelijk Planbureau (RPB).
45. Natuur en Milieu Planbureau (NMP).
46. Centraal Planbureau (CPB).
47. Social Economic Council (SER); Transport and Water management Council; Rural Areas Council; Housing, Spatial Planning and Environment (VROM)-Council; Scientific Council for Policy making (WRR).
48. OECD Territorial Review of the Randstad (2007).
49. Standing for three aspects widely associated with sustainability: (respectively) social, ecological and economic aspects.

To enhance the political status of consultation activities and to facilitate necessary negotiations in a later phase of the process, a group of national and regional politicians was formed. This group consisted of one minister representing the Cabinet of ministers, two county council members and two community aldermen representing regional and local level government. In addition, a so called Randstad ambassador was appointed to facilitate cooperation amongst different levels of government. During the process the group of government representatives received four different advice reports, respectively from the four provinces that make up a large part of the Randstad area, from (the four largest) communities and city-regions within the area, and from parties (public and private) cooperating within two sub area's separately, the so called North wing- and South wing parties.

Visioning Exercises: Research by Design

The drawing up of the structural vision for the Randstad sets an example when it comes to involvement of experts from the architectural domain e.g. landscape architects and urban designers in spatial planning processes. Although this procedure has been considered good practice since the early twentieth century, the Dutch Cabinet of ministers recently committed itself by means of a new architectural policy[50] to explicit regulations and protocols to ensure an even wider and more consistent involvement of design experts during all phases of spatial planning procedures, from the very start till the end of the implementation phase. The role of design during a spatial planning process can be described in the first place as imagining, 'visioning', or the forward casting of possible and/or desirable futures for the area at hand. The images or drawings that result from such visioning exercises communicate comprehensive pictures of possible futures that integrate different aspects of complex questions in one view and in doing so facilitate discussions with stakeholders and other actors. By

---

50. Vision on Architecture and Spatial Design, Design as part of Dutch Culture, The Hague, 2008.

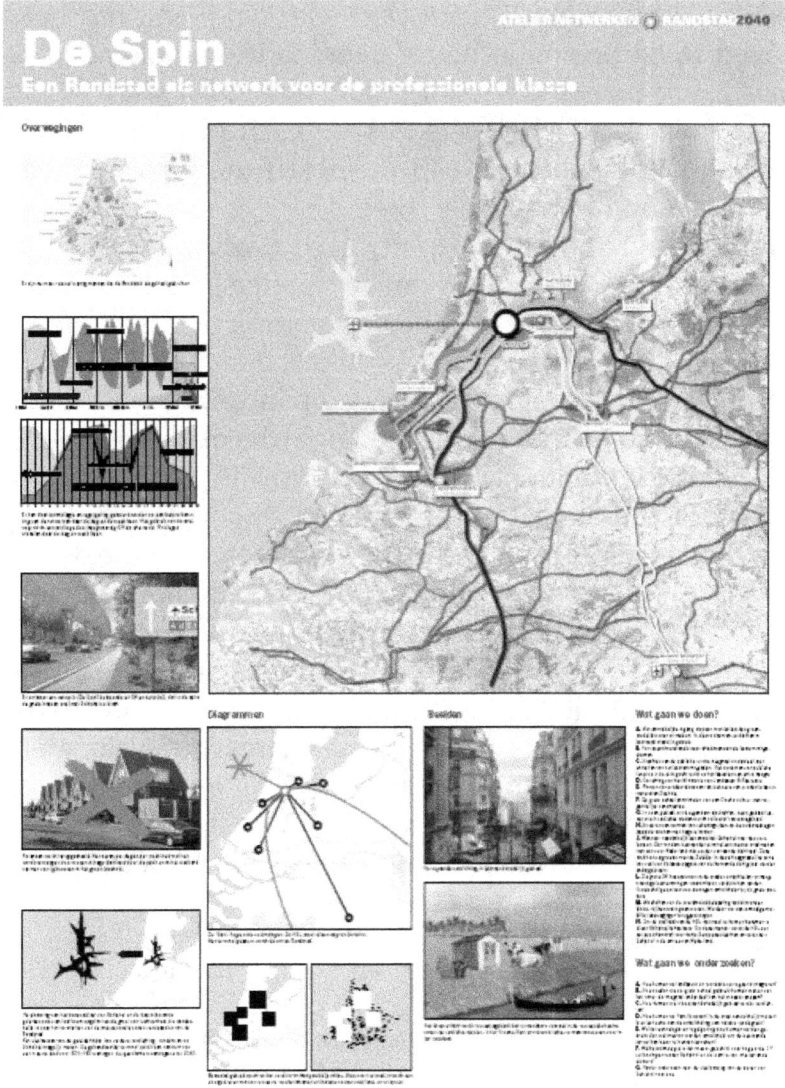

Figure 19 *One of three thematic development perspectives (Networking atelier); due to drastic measures like outplacement of Schiphol Airport into the North Sea, this alternative was widely discussed in national newspapers.*

providing integrated solutions to complex, interrelated questions, spatial designs offer a starting point for further scientific and technical research (backward reasoning) and has been proved to be helpful in better defining the problems to be solved.

This approach, labeled as 'research by design'[51], was applied in the Randstad2040 project in the following way. Over a period of one week, three design ateliers took place with teams of some ten experts each[52], which were led by renowned spatial designers (atelier masters). Each team departed from a different set of given starting points, the focus of each set being on a different theme: green/blue development, network development and urban development. The sets of starting points were derived from the many documents and other contributions (e.g. interviews with experts), which were collected as part of the research and advice trajectory (see above), which served as terms of reference for the design teams. Each team was asked to come up with three different spatial development perspectives with their given theme as primary focus (Figure 19). A fourth atelier, supervised by a member of the atelier of the Chief Government Architect[53] was dedicated to integrating those thematic development perspectives and this resulted into three future images of the Randstad area: Wereldstad (Global city), Kuststad (Coastal city) and Buitenstad (Outer city; Figure 20). The results of all ateliers (thematic as well as integrated) served as input into the dialogue trajectory (mentioned above). They were published on

---

51. So far no widely recognized definition of this term has been established. Recently Deltares started a reconnaissance study into this phenomenon, together with Wageningen University Research centre (WUR) and Technical University Delft (TUD).
52. Urban designers, landscape architects, national and regional goverment officials from the area and experts in fields such as water management, housing, environment, transport etc.
53. This atelier serves as the working bureau of the Chief Government Architect and three other Government Advisors: on Landscape, on Infrastructure and on Cultural Heritage; together they advise the government on design and policy issues regarding architecture in the broadest sense of the word.

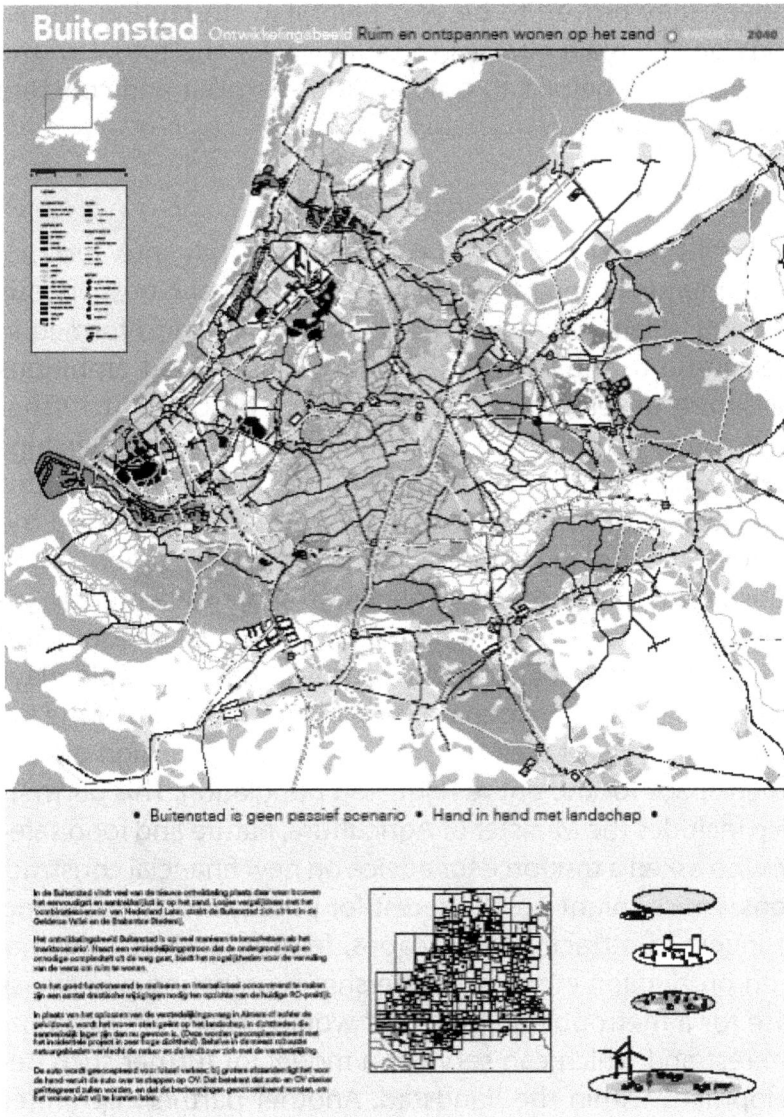

Figure 20 *One of three posters on the 'Outdoors city' development perspective, used for exhibition*

the aforementioned website and shown to the public in simultaneous expositions in six different cities within the Randstad area. During the 'Randstad table' discussions (see Dialogue, above), they proved to be very helpful in structuring discussions on the main choices to be made for the future of the Randstad and helped to omulate more explicit and concrete conclusions.

Strategic Alliances

Inspired by the results of a comparative study into successful implementation strategies in other global cities, various strategic alliances or implementation partnerships formed in the run-up to the structural vision to ensure that ambitions for future development would actually be brought further once the structural vision was published. These partnerships include public authorities, market parties, social organizations and citizens. So far, five partnerships are active, covering the establishment of metropolitan parks, port cooperation, urban transformation processes, city-center and sub-center development and The Hague—city of human rights, freedom and safety. The Metropolitan Parks partnership for example plays an important part in opening up the huge potential of the so-called Green Heart area for providing accessible, high quality green space for the entire Randstad population. This partnership includes the Minister of Agriculture, nature and food safety, who asked a taskforce for advice on new financial constructions, which might be of interest for private investors hoping to invest in attractive landscapes, leisure facilities, regional food production etc. The partnership is preparing a business case for a metropolitan park that would attract international interest and which can serve as a model for further such development within the Randstad. Another partnership unites the Amsterdam and Rotterdam harbor authorities and the Ministry of Water Management and Transport. Coordinated international profiling of both harbors—which are fierce competitors, is one objective under discussion, as is cooperation that would allow them to be more effective in innovation and sustainable development. The formation of a national harbor holding on the longer run is an option currently studied.

Bottom up initiatives for new implementation partnerships on other issues have been stimulated and can count on support from government authorities as long as they match with the ambitions laid out in the structural vision. Additionally, the possibilities for a new series of key-projects of national importance, funded largely by national government, are being explored.

Conclusions

The Randstad2040 structural vision process and its trajectory provided ample food for thought for the discussions organized with the stakeholders. In total twelve 'possible futures' were created and presented to audiences at meetings and made available on the website and the results of these consultations were valued as important input for decision-making. So it seems appropriate to conclude that the Randstad2040 project meets the first criterion of foresight because it incorporates anticipation on possible and/or desirable futures in a prominent way. However, it is not easy to establish a clear relationship between the final, politically agreed choices laid down in the structural vision on the one hand and the content of the possible futures and discussion results on the other hand. How the latter actually gave guidance to the decision-making process remains an interesting question for further research.

When combined both the visioning and the research and advice tracks fulfill the second criterion for foresight as it can be seen that rational research was paired with intuitive imagination during the process. Again, it would be interesting to know how both tracks influenced each other and how the decision-making process benefited from this interaction.

From the start, all parties involved emphasized the importance of an implementation strategy, taken up parallel to the structural vision. As a result, five strategic partnerships had been formed by the time the structural vision was agreed

(September 2008) and an additional project, researching new national key projects within the Randstad area, was launched as a follow up to the structural vision. In relation to hoped for developments after 2020, the most important concrete actions to be taken at this moment may be to create funding for globally defined long term investments. It would be correct to state that the structural vision helped create the sense of urgency needed for the type of action that is now taking place in the partnerships. The Randstad2040 project therefore meets the third criterion of foresight: the translation into concrete actions.

As for the fourth foresight criterion: an integrated and trans disciplinary approach, it is clear that the range of critical questions raised in the Starting Memorandum have already give evidence of a ambitious holistic approach. Also the research and advice track show a wide variety of topics covered by scientific research reports as well as specialists advice. The visioning exercises are particularly interesting, because they show different ways of integrated approaches. To start with, the series of the three thematic design ateliers, focused on finding solutions for one specific problem, whilst taking into account the effects of these solutions on other themes. This was followed by a fourth integration atelier, in which particular combinations of 'thematic' solutions were integrated in three different designs for the future. Finally the structural vision itself, showing the twelve choices made, was presented and demonstrated how they are clearly interrelated. Most of the choices contained answers to several questions at the same time. In addition, the participants of the ateliers were comprised of experts from different fields, ensuring a broad range of complementary knowledge found its way into the various designs.

Yet, the emphasis on the physical spatial system seems to have overshadowed somewhat the economic, social and cultural aspects that cannot easily be mapped or designed.

Questions for Discussion

The time horizon chosen for the Randstad structural vision is 2040. This seems far enough and yet not too far into the future, to raise interest for long term investments, which was a main driver for the vision. However, the impacts of climate change largely extend this period and thus 2040 would seem to be rather close. In addition, some of the future perspectives developed in the ateliers seem to have chosen a later time horizon than 2040.

The above raise the following questions: How can we define the right time horizon when practicing foresight? How can we deal with different time horizons for different trends, when imagining a situation at one point in the future?

The term 'foresight' is difficult to translate into Dutch. Maybe in general the word 'toekomstverkenning', literally: investigation into the future comes close. In the field of spatial policy making in the Netherlands 'research by design', as explained in this paper has been formally adopted as part of the process. Research by design seems to have a lot in common with the foresight approach.

Questions: To what extent can foresight, when applied in spatial planning, be considered synonymous with a 'research by design' approach? If not, what are the crucial differences?

One of the important characteristics of the Randstad2040 project is the effort taken to involve as many participants as possible during the process. Images and maps of possible futures, a key ingredient of foresight played an important role in this regard, facilitating discussions and providing a clearer picture of problems as well as solutions.

Questions: To what extent is foresight conditional for a participatory approach, or vice versa: can foresight benefit from a participatory approach? If this were the case for foresight as part of a spatial planning process such as Randstad2040, is it equally true for foresight in general? Or is a participatory ap-

proach a precondition dictated by the nature of spatial planning processes only, whether or not foresight is practiced?

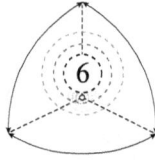

6. Relationships as a Cause

Farmleigh
Dublin

Farmleigh is a truly beautiful mansion in Dublin's Phoenix Park. It used to belong to the Guinness family. In 1999 it was purchased by the Irish government to work as the premier accommodation for visiting guests and for high level government meetings such as when FuturesIreland meet there. In the Nobel Room, that celebrates the achievements of the Irish Nobel Laureates for literature, you will also find James Joyce's works and a black and white painting of him which says "Never mind my immortal soul, but get the tie right". The tie is red. And despite his tremendous talent, James Joyce never won a Nobel Prize.

It is often a pleasure to spend time with colleagues, and it can be very useful if they happen to be experts with clear ideas like Helsinki University of Technology professors Raimo Hämäläinen and Esa Saarinen[1] who operate on the assumption that social encounters can be meaningfully conceptualized as systems.

Being sensitive to the instinctual awareness of a situation and utilizing common sense in our daily decision-making practices is systems intelligence. It is intelligence embedded in action and with respect to the spatio-temporal context in which in many respects the uncertainty is more or less present. We have to act and make decisions without knowing the external forces at play, when influences move hither and thither, and within social systems as

---

1. Hämäläinen & Saarinen 2007.

they emerge.[2]

We refer to the ability to act meaningfully in the systems we are embedded in. The focus is on us and the system,i.e., the everyday encounters between two or more human beings. Here the earlier presented inter-subjective systems theory makes a distinction between Rosen's MR systems and becomes valuable for the discussion of anticipatory and adaptive human systems. Inter-subjective systems theory is most of all a human theory, a theory about human beings with limited horizons of understanding and with the world interpreted by their own subjectivity, and the life lived between interacting subjectivities.

The two distinctive features of the inter-subjective systems theory, the perspectivism that gives up on the idea of an absolute truth and intersubjectivity lead to a systems view on human encounters. Whenever two or more people meet, there is a reciprocal, mutual influence between them to which the participants make ongoing, co-determining contributions.[3] The human systems are mutually created and unfolding and we need our sensibilities and our multi-faceted skills that enable us to be responsive to the subtle aspects of situations.[4]

This chapter represents some of greatest challenges to our thinking: How can we liberate from the given, taken for granted approaches whether they are called Cartesian, objectivist, positivist or Newtonian?, as we have called them in Chapter 1. From the Cartesian perspective the human mind is seen "in isolation, radically separated from an external reality that either accurately apprehends or distorts"[5]. The mind of a human being comprehended as an essentially self-closed entity detached from the world by the subject-object division. The human mind has an inside and it causally interacts with other things outside it. In other words, the external world and the mind are two separate

---

2. Hämäläinen & Saatinen 2006.
3. Orange *et al.* 1997.
4. Martela & Saarinen 2008.
5. Orange *et al.* 1997.

and independent entities that are able to interact with each other.[6]

Inter-subjective systems theory provides an alternative to often implicit "Myth of the Isolated Mind" approaches[7]. In contrast, inter-subjective systems theory builds on the insights of Heidegger[8] in attempt to understand the human condition on a post-Cartesian contextualism of the constitutive role of relatedness in the making of all experience. Furthermore, the inspiration stems from Husserl's[9] lifeworld, Merleau-Ponty's[10] being-toward-the-world and by Wittgenstein's[11] ideas about the contextuality of meaning, language games and forms of life.[12]

Here the Cartesian dualism between internal and external is challenged. Inter-subjective systems theory delivers a rationale for contextually sensitive and at the same time non-subjective approach for formulating a comprehension of the inter-subjective context in which human being act and conduct their lives. It can be presented through six main features.[13]

We are Embedded in Systems

The principle notion is that human beings are embedded in the inter-subjective systems they live in, they can never step outside their own experimental world. This means that our horizon of experience is defined and redefined by the inter-subjective systems we are currently embedded in. Thus, what you comprehend to be the system, will be the system for you, and intersubjectivity largely defines what you believe the system to be.[14] The approach breaks

---

6. Storolow 2002.
7. Stolorow & Atwood 1992.
8. Heidegger 1962.
9. Husserl 1970.
10. Merleau-Ponty 1962.
11. Wittgenstein 1953, 1958, 1961.
12. Martela & Saarinen 2008.
13. Martela & Saarinen 2008.
14. Hämäläinen & Saarinen 2007.

free from the assumption that an encounter between two human beings could be viewed from an objective perspective, because as we meet our colleague or a customer we are always interwoven in a inter-subjective system which operates by a within—perspective rather than from any external or objective perspective.[15] Awareness of our own embeddedness and our own participation in the process is the point of departure. It means ongoing sensitivity and attention to a multiplicity of contexts whether they are developmental, relational or cultural.[16]

From a Cognitive to an Affective Perspective

The inter-subjective systems theory emphasizes the affective and emotional perspective of any social encounter; it should not be ignored instead it should be addressed and utilized. For instance, in organizations all the actions of the superior contribute to the affective nature of the system and therefore open up new options for development, but often we tend to focus on the cognitive side of our interaction. In doing so we overlook the rich affective elements that are always at play under the seemingly neutral surface level, and that are potentially very useful.[17] Often it is more important how you say something than what you say, because the human life is immensely rich with emotions, inner subtleties and is sensitive to relational issue, giving them a priority instead of cognitive and measurable parameters. Thus, it releases energy in an organization.[18]

Empathic-Introspective Inquiry

Given the impossibility of an objective opinion, we should perhaps not be so eager to evaluate, classify and judge the other. Instead our emphasis should be on understanding

15. Shotter 2006.
16. Stolorow *et al.* 2002.
17. Martela & Saarinen 2008.
18. Hämäläinen & Saarinen 2007.

the other person.[19] Therefore, we should not ask what is wrong with a person, but rather what her personal world is like, to seek to comprehend the meaning of her expressions, behavior, and what affects her states from a perspective within the inter-subjective system. That process can be called a sustained empathic-introspective inquiry.[20] Arguably the key to flourishing social encounters is the distinction between inquiry and advocacy mode for parallel developments. Empathic inquiry tends to be rather open- and does not foreclose conversation. Understanding other person is not about analysis and reports, it is about giving up our own perspective and immersing ourselves for a moment into the perspective of another, it is about a dialogue between people in which the personal worlds of experience interplay.[21]

Adapting a Process View

Most of the encounters between people can be seen as processes. A social encounter is a mutually constitutive process in which our own perspective also evolves. The way we make sense of a situation depends on ourselves, other people and their opinions. The process view opposes any snapshot views of social encounters and also emphasizes the temporal perspective of people who have their own histories as well as their own ideas about their futures. Thus, the present moment cannot be separated from personal, historical, developmental and substantive contexts. In organizations, we can be pretty sure that achieving almost anything important requires more than one meeting. And when we need more meetings they form an even more complex ever-evolving process.

---

19. Martela & Saarinen 2008.
20. Stolorow & Atwood 1992, Stolorow *et al.* 2002.
21. Gadamer 1994, Solorow *et al.* 2002.

The Expansion of Subjective Worlds

A positive change can occur if we alter people's mind sets, mental models and basic ideas how they think about their work or futures. Another approach would be to create new relational experiences and enhance their capability for reflective self-awareness. An important source of change can be addressed as an expansion of one's theoretical and experimental horizons. As a rule, the expansion of the subjective world is worth pursuing in our everyday encounters in order to enrich them. An enriched, more complex, and more flexible emotional life will provide a better basis for anticipatory and adaptive action.[22]

Preferring Common Sense Over Lots of Knowledge

If we accept as a starting point that the human realm is thoroughly incomplete, indefinite and open, then it is easy to accept Aristotelian reasoning which says it is impossible to know in advance the right means to any end. The ends emerge in the acting situation in all of its complexities. Taking these complexities seriously means giving up any hope of controlling events fully, even with the available analysis or technique. Instead the emphasis should be placed on common sense, on the human ability to make sense in situations that are too complex to be covered by any one technique.[23]

Previously we have considered the importance of relationships in daily social encounters within a short time horizon. Now we take a medium-distance time horizon and return to *FuturesIreland*, the latest significant effort to join forces for Ireland. Often when I talked with the participants, the time horizons they mentioned were between one to three years. Over the following pages the project is presented by *Riel Miller* who played a key role as the consultant helping with the design and implementation of the

---

22. Martela & Saarinen 2008.
23. Martela & Saarinen 2008.

process, *Larry O'Connell* who served as the lead staff person at the National Economic and Social Development Office (NESDO), and *Rory O'Donnell* who as Chair of NESDO and Vice-Chair of the Steering Committee played a central leadership role throughout the process.

Section 1—FuturesIreland: A Case Study in Building Futures Literacy

When an explorer seeks to discover "uncharted" territory or an innovator to invent something so far unknown, they do not know what they will find—otherwise it would not be exploration. But what they do have are tools and methods, ways of guiding their efforts so that they do not wander in circles or "reinvent the wheel". When thinking about the future, foresight techniques are the equivalent of the explorer's Mercator projection and innovator's good research methods. The following case study of the FuturesIreland project offers an example of an ambitious, cutting edge approach to applying the techniques of foresight to thinking about the future of Ireland.

At the heart of this exercise in strategic foresight was a collaborative learning process that combined the insights of people throughout Ireland—from government, business and civil society. These people worked together in a participatory, action research process that revealed both the current and emergent anticipatory assumptions—images of the future— that play a critical role in formulating and making policy for Ireland. The future of Ireland project (FuturesIreland) generated new knowledge using effective and familiar scientific methods for accumulating and testing insights into our complex emergent reality.

In particular, FuturesIreland was designed as a strategic policy research project that integrated into the core of its analytical processes three important hypotheses about the nature of the changes occurring in the present.

The first, perhaps least evident transformation is in the theory of knowledge underlying social science. Recent developments in the theories of complexity, evolution and even physics open up new ways of thinking about social change. Research (including by authors in this volume) bringing together methodologies from the social and natural sciences has sparked new insights regarding the properties of complex systems. Like the Copernican and Newtonian "revolutions" that transformed the way people looked at the world and tried to understand it, the current change may (or may not) take centuries before it completely alters everyday perceptions of causality and choice. The main point for the design of FuturesIreland was to embrace from the outset and consistently throughout the process the recognition of the fundamental indeterminacy of complex system. As Prigogine expressed it: "the present does not determine the future."[24] Serendipity, discovery, inspiration and creative imagination all conspire to render each moment distinct and, in many of its attributes, fundamentally indeterminate until it happens. Creativity is part of our universe.

The second transformation is in the socio-economic context. The financial crisis of 2008/2009 signaled more than the collapse of a series of speculative bubbles; it can be seen as symptomatic of the difficult process of breaking away from the industrial era. Nations, regions, even the planet as a whole are beginning to function in new ways. Traditional boundaries are blurring as the birth, death, entry and exit of networks—communities of actors—becomes significantly more fluid. There is also greater emphasis on strategic experimentation, flexibility and the capacity to both inspire and use our creativity. There are many signs of new and emergent systems, although the overarching patterns may not have coalesced yet. One of the primary challenges for FuturesIreland was to offer new ways of making sense of the present by exploring what and how people imagine the future. FuturesIreland aimed to

---

24. I. Prigogine, The End of Certainty: Time, Chaos and the New Laws of Nature, Free Press, 1997

discover the words, stories and new ways of understanding systemic coherence in order to identify choices based on a deeper understanding of the transformations occurring in today's socio-economic context.

The third transformation, shaped by the two preceding ones, is about changes in the way we think about change. This is a shift from predictive, planning based anticipatory systems to ones that are more pluralistic (or multi-ontological)—capable of integrating both deterministic and non-deterministic decision making. In part FuturesIreland was designed to detect and gain a deeper understanding of emergent "post-industrial" decision-making systems, many of which take a heterarchical and creative form that depends on imagination and spontaneity. This means that one of the main analytical challenges for FuturesIreland was to seek throughout Irish society for evidence of experimentation, spontaneity and the use of complexity. Planning to entice the unplanned, FuturesIreland was designed to "walk the talk" of new approaches to discovery and creative deliberation.

Rooted in an awareness of this threefold transformation, FuturesIreland was also about building new capacities and skills for thinking about the future by producing original, rigorously sourced research results that provide Ireland with a richer understanding of its context—locally and globally. FuturesIreland was designed as an innovative process meant to enhance the capacity of Ireland to both create the conditions, in terms of new knowledge and new skills, and make the appropriate decisions, that take full advantage of the history, resources and aspirations of Ireland. As an action-research and experimentalist endeavor FuturesIreland was an inherently ambitious and risky project. To succeed it had to create a process that met four targets with respect to: legitimacy, rigor, communications, and capacity-building:

Legitimacy. FuturesIreland could only succeed if it was deeply rooted in the creation of "collective intelligence"[25]—not just the collection of data or a survey of the impressive acquired know-how of its diverse participants—but a living conversation that produced new sense-making and invention. FuturesIreland had to be able to tap into and genuinely reflect or represent the practices and experiments, for instance in heterarchical decision-making, that are signs of emergence. To find resonance and sustain confidence Futures Ireland had to 'walk-the-talk' by being open in the creation of its role, seeking new and unfamiliar ways of engaging in its work. FuturesIreland needed to be as fluid and ready to embrace complexity and spontaneity as the open learning networks it was creating. FuturesIreland addressed this challenge from the outset, ensuring that in its basic design there was a careful matching between the appropriate tool (engagement, analytical reflection, debate, formalization, etc.) and the well-defined tasks ("rigorous imagining"[26] and research based strategic conversations) at each stage of the process.

---

25. See Wikipedia: George Pór, author of The Quest for Collective Intelligence (1995), defined this phenomenon in his Blog of Collective Intelligence as "the capacity of a human community to evolve toward higher order complexity thought, problem-solving and integration through collaboration and innovation."

26. See Annex 3, "Futures Literacy: A Hybrid Strategic Scenario Method, Version 1.3, May 2006: "Level 2 FL futures literacy is the capacity to overcome the limitations imposed by values and expectations on thinking about the future. It is a technique for conducting the potentially paradoxical task of "rigorous imagining". This is a crucial and challenging step in opening up new insights into the nature and determinants of today's potential. Rigorous imagining depends on carefully and consistently distinguishing possible, probable and preferable. Such distinctions are necessary for rigorous imagining because the task of imagining possible futures is logically and practically prior to the assessment of probabilities and preferences. Prior from a logical perspective because preferable and probable futures are subsets of the possible. Prior from a practical perspective since as already pointed out consideration of preferences and probabilities constrain the imagining of possibilities."

Rigor. In order to effectively imagine the unexplored potential and patterns of emergent social orders—FuturesIreland needed to use the latest developments in social science methodology. Realizing the overall objective of knowledge creation required a combination of elements. On one side there was an important place of for probabilistic methodologies that when specified on the basis of clear theoretical assumptions and hypothesis,can use historical data series offer one (extrapolative) way of imagining the future. On the other side there were creative methods that helped to address the dual challenge that arises when trying to imagine the potential of the present: first overcoming the constraints on imagination set by the language, patterns and assumptions of the past, and second finding ways to develop novel frames that liberate the imagination without falling into fantasy or extrapolation. FuturesIreland used a series of creative techniques for facilitating strategic discussions. Careful attention was paid to sense making processes using methods like "rigorous imagining" that enrich participant's cognitive landscape step by step.

Communication. Humans comprehend the world, in part, by telling stories. These are the narratives told, more or less explicitly, when we wake up in the morning and set out on our daily routine or when we decide to undertake a course of study or purchase shares on the stock market or run up debt to buy a house. These stories, told and acted out in the present, often contain anticipatory assumptions—specific imagined futures. Sometimes this is a private or idiosyncratic future, but most often the people of a community share common stories, weaving together the same protagonists and plots. From this perspective one of the keys to the success of FuturesIreland was generating the research foundations for new stories that speak to people's lives. This could not be a single vision or map that imposed one story or terrain (stage/context for the story). Rather the approach adopted by FuturesIreland was about producing knowledge, creating the shared elements, the components of many stories, told at many levels (personal, local, national, regional, global) that could intertwine and continuously evolve. The stories need to be varied and fluid. They must also integrate imagination, complexity and, critically, the depth of knowledge of the variety of communities participating in FuturesIreland.

Capacity building. FuturesIreland, in order to meet its ambitious terms of reference, had to address the concrete choices faced by Ireland and the world today in the context of global transformation. These choices were, from the point of view of potential collective action by a nation like Ireland, largely about building shared capabilities across organizations and communities (the codes and roads that connect people in Ireland). Like the diffusion of alpha-numeric literacy throughout society during the 19th and 20th centuries the existence of individuals with such underlying capabilities alter what is possible, imaginable and doable. Similarly FuturesIreland was designed to help build foresight capacity within Ireland by detecting the emergent meanings of the economic, social, governance, ecological, technological, scientific and organizational challenges. The process was designed to make sense of phenomena not only at the centre and periphery of current frames but crucially to discover through invention, creative becoming, novel ways of making sense of the world around us (exploratory futures, as opposed to contingent or optimization futures).

Section 2—The Origins and the Focus of FuturesIreland

FuturesIreland had its origin in the final report of the Information Society Commission (ISC). In that report the Commission proposed that, following its work on information technology, a wider foresight exercise on the 'knowledge society' should be undertaken. It identified a number of factors that should inform such an exercise and a number of themes that might be explored. These are summarized in Box 2. In the 2006 national agreement, Towards 2016, the Irish Government stated that a knowledge society foresight initiative, focusing on Ireland's advance to the innovation-driven stage of socio-economic development, would be undertaken by the National Economic and Social Development Office (NESDO). NESDO began work on this in 2007.

The Distinctive Focus of FuturesIreland

A significant number of 'futures' studies have taken place in Ireland over the last 10 years. Some of these are listed in Box

---

Box 1

Shaping the Knowledge Foresight Exercise:

Information Society Commission

The Information Society Commission made a number of suggestions on factors which should be taken into account or explored in wider knowledge society foresight exercise. These included:

- Adopt a holistic perspective: The need for a small country like Ireland to view its role in a holistic way, and to take the longer-term perspective necessary to mobilize and concentrate resources effectively around a sustainable path of development.

- Focus on the capacity to deal with uncertainty: Referring to the work of the German sociologist Ulrich Beck, it suggested that people and organizations in the twenty-first century will increasingly require the capacity and confidence to navigate an environment characterized by ambiguity, uncertainty, unpredictability and unreliability.

- Find new or novel solutions: It argued that many of the more complex issues presented by the digital era can be understood as problem situations for which solutions lie largely outside current ways of operating.

- Learn continuously: The ISC argued that the challeng-

---

es of the digital era the development of new know-how, and new models of organization and ways of learning. It noted that thriving in a changing environment demands experimentation, learning about what is effective, and dispensing with the expendable.

- Develop full potential: The report pointed to the broader societal implications associated with the digital era and information technology and the need to develop the full potential of our human resources as the crucial issue.

- Support user-centered learning: It suggested that the challenge of bringing about the comprehensive availability of personalized (or user-centered) lifelong learning opportunities is one that will require new ways of thinking and operating, system-wide innovation, and a wider acceptance of responsibility by all stakeholders.

- Capture the changing network relationship between Government, society and economy: Governments and citizens are increasingly operating in a network society in which they are becoming more and more equal and in which the strength of government is determined by the delivery of quality and by the joint creation and sharing of policy. Indeed policy can be said to be a coproduction" (Ref).

Source: Derived from Learning to Innovate—Reperceiving the Global Information Society, pp. 54-55, Information Society Commission, 2005.

2. Most such studies identify existing and possible trends and drivers of change and then use these to generate a number of scenarios. The scenarios shape debate among a range of stakeholders about future possibilities and policy challenges. A notable feature of many futures studies is that, while they identify three or four scenarios, they conclude by observing that the actual outcome, and whether it is a good or bad one for Ireland, will depend on how business, the state and society interact.

Will business be able to draw on individual and collective capabilities formed in society and the public education system? Will both business and society be able to rely on the public system to provide order, high-quality infrastructure, good regulation and responsive policy? Will the democratic and administrative system find individuals, social groups and economic interests willing to participate and cooperate in making public choices and producing public goods? Most of the existing scenarios studies finish by noting the important connections between these three, but were not or are not in a position to explore them to any great degree.

Rather than replicate existing futures work, FuturesIreland sought to build on and complement these studies in four ways.

The point of departure was not particular trends and drivers, instead FuturesIreland focused explicitly on how people and organizations respond to change and uncertainty. In particular, the project focused on innovation and learning and how they occur in the context of uncertainty and ambiguity.

In particular FuturesIreland was concerned with the interaction between wealth creation, society and public governance—a theme on which other futures studies tend to finish.

Two other, methodological, features also distinguished this project from existing futures and scenarios work:

Network thinking and analysis were used, reflecting our sense that networks are increasingly prevalent in efforts to address new and complex problems in a context of uncertainty and ambiguity;

Mika Aaltonen, Riel Miller, Larry O'Connell,
Rory O'Donnell & Stefan Bergheim

Box 2

Foresight Work In Ireland

A number of futures studies have been undertaken in recent years. These studies provide insight into key trends and drivers of change:

- Socio-economic scenarios 2025 (Forfás, forthcoming 2009)
- Public Service 2022 (IPA, 2008)
- Scenarios for Ireland 2030 (DIT Futures Academy, 2008)
- Marine Foresight Exercise (Marine Institute, 2006)
- Imagineering Ireland: Future Scenarios for 2030 (DIT Futures Academy, 2005)
- Rural Ireland 2025 (Teagasc, UCD & NUI Maynooth, 2005)
- Engineering a Knowledge Island 2020 (Engineers Ireland, 2005)
- Borders, Midland and Western Regional Foresight 2025 (BMW Regional Assembly, 2005)
- Dublin City Foresight 2015 (DIT Futures Academy, 2003)
- Technology Foresight (Forfás, 1999).

Some of these studies have led to important policy decisions. In particular, the Knowledge Society Foresight, undertaken by Forfas in 1999, led to the creation of Science Foundation Ireland, which has been a conduit for dramatically increased funding for scientific research in Irish third level institutions.

It was decided to base much of the work on people's experience of innovation and learning in current Irish conditions. This reflected our belief that experience of problem solving and innovation, and of the challenges involved, would help reveal the conditions of learning. The idea is that cutting-edge existing practices can provide what futures analysts call 'weak signals' of patterns that may become widespread in future years and decades. This approach is based on the belief that, in many respects, the future is here already in the practices and patterns of those actors most attuned to emerging possibilities.

This overall approach reflected an intuition that the way we typically describe the challenges facing Ireland's public governance, and maybe even the way they are analyzed and understood, might be refreshed and reframed by taking more account of what is happening in society and business.

Section 3—The Futures Literacy Approach

As already noted both FutureIreland's focus and its approach to foresight were built on the foundation of past practices, in Ireland and elsewhere[27], as well as several recent advances in methodology and project design. The Futures Literacy approach that was adopted to guide design and implementation of FuturesIreland was based on a successful and recognized track record for the "hybrid strategic scenario" method[28]. The HSS method builds Futures Literacy by mixing learning-by-doing with intensive use of cutting edge social science. The HSS method is "hybrid" because the specific way of engaging in strategic foresight conversations or bringing research into the process is adapted to the specific context, the specific

---

27. E.g., Norway and New Zealand.
28. Riel Miller, "Futures Literacy: A Hybrid Strategic Scenario Method", Futures: the journal of policy, planning and future studies, 39, Elsevier, Pp. 341-362, May 2007 and "From Trends to Futures Literacy: Reclaiming the Future", Centre for Strategic Education, Seminar Series Papers, No. 160, Melbourne, Australia, December 2006.

Mika Aaltonen, Riel Miller, Larry O'Connell,
Rory O'Donnell & Stefan Bergheim

participants and tasks. One of the reasons for using a Futures Literacy approach was that it addressed the limitations, particularly for policy making, of foresight processes built around divergent probabilistic and/or normative scenarios.

The trouble with stories about the future, based either on trends or a range of good to bad normative outcomes, is generally twofold. First stories of "likely futures" often take existing sense making frames or models as given and use them to produce extrapolations of the past and present. Typically the future is a "better", more efficient version of the present. For instance a future that is "green" because CO_2 emitting technologies have been replaced by non-CO_2 emitting technologies—everything else remains pretty much the same. This can be useful for a number of planning or optimization purposes, but tends to either obscure or simply miss the challenge of reframing or providing a different basis for making sense of the present. Little explicit consideration is given to the one thing we know for certain: that there will be changes in the conditions of change (i.e., in the frames/models we use to make sense of the world around us).

The second problem, compounded by the first, is that divergent probabilistic and/or normative scenarios are usually built, more or less explicitly, using a variety of models or disciplinary perspectives. This is considered appropriate because it offers a more "realistic" story of the "highly complex" future. Unfortunately what this often translates into in practice is a confused narrative, where different, at times incompatible models, assumptions and levels of analysis are assembled into an intriguingly rich set of scenarios. Only the result is frequently unintelligible for decision making or policy analysis. Here again the failure to explicitly address the challenge of changes in the conditions of change,i.e., the invention of new sense-making models/frames, impoverishes the foresight exercise and makes it more difficult to build explicit bridges to the discourse of policy and the imperatives of decision making.

166

FuturesIreland was designed from the outset as a rigorous exploratory research exercise based on the Futures Literacy (FL) approach and HSS method noted earlier. FL is an overarching design framework that helps to guide customization at each step in the process in order to construct and then connect imaginative, analytically coherent strategic scenarios to policy discourse and decision making processes in the present. The findings and methods of scientific research are the source of both the design principles and content of a FL approach. Table 1 outlines, very succinctly, the general framework of a FL process, one that is simultaneously an action-research methodology and a capacity building exercise.

By taking a carefully selected, diverse set of participants through an FL learning process FuturesIreland used the in-depth knowledge of participants to coproduce a clearer picture of both current and alternative anticipatory assumptions about Ireland. As leading researchers and decision makers worked their way through the challenges posed by FuturesIreland using an FL approach they at first expose and then coproduce the way they both think about and use the future in order to understand and make choices in the present. Jointly they construct a shared understanding, a way of making sense of the future that respects their knowledge of specific subjects and places while also finding common threads and systemic coherence across disciplines[29]. Such sense making, or mapping, is a technique for detecting emergent and systemic changes in complex evolutionary organizations like Ireland and the society in which it operates.

However, this cognitive developmental process, even when able to capture a wide range of phenomena and generate highly creative/imaginative conversations, is not suffi-

---

29. Riel Miller, "Connecting Policy and Research in a Period of Transition Scale Change: A Role for Future Studies?" in the proceedings of the Cambridge-MIT Institute conference, hosted by the Oxford Internet Institute, on: *New Approaches to Research on the Social Implications of Emerging Technologies*, Oxford, UK, 15-16 April 2005, http://www.oii.ox.ac.uk/collaboration/?rq=specialevents/20050415

Mika Aaltonen, Riel Miller, Larry O'Connell, Rory O'Donnell & Stefan Bergheim

cient. Two critical ingredients are missing. The first is the need in the context of a foresight exercise for more explicit treatment of the future as a multidimensional reality (multi-ontology) and of the distinct anticipatory systems (epistemologies) used to generate inevitably imaginary futures. The second is the construction of non-ergodic sense-making frames—or ways of thinking that take the point-of-view of a world already changed by changes in the conditions of change. This latter challenge is about thinking in terms of systemic discontinuity. Yet doing so in ways that remain comprehensible to the policy and decision making realities of the sponsors and participants in the foresight exercise. This was one of the foremost design challenges for FuturesIreland. A challenge that the Futures Literacy approach addresses explicitly and which FuturesIreland successfully tackled with, as discussed below, the formulation of a specific theoretical framework for making sense of the result of the cognitive processes.

The FL action-research process goes through three phases of jointly produced learning-by-doing. FuturesIreland was designed to move participants through these different phases.

Level 1 FL activities build awareness using custom-built catalysts that summarize the latest research assessments (horizon scans) of key phenomena as well as the absence of phenomena (what does not happen is often as important as what does). Participants in FuturesIreland shared their expectations and aspirations by projecting themselves into Ireland's future.

Level 2 shifts the process of sense making into a more explicitly creative but still rigorously structured phase. In Level 2 participants deepen their Futures Literacy by combining inputs that summarize leading edge policy analysis/goals with social science theories/evidence to create the parameters for imagining distinctive and operationally detailed scenarios of future outcomes. These models use technically exacting, research-based specifications of key descriptive variables and metrics. The models are produced in an iterative manner, on parallel and inter-acting tracks, that include a broad cross-section of innovators, researchers and practitioners. Out of this process participants developed stories, imaginative outcome scenarios[30] of Ireland, that move beyond extrapolative anticipatory assumptions to explore emergent alternative systems. These rich strategic scenarios set the stage for the policy debates of the next phase of the "futures literacy" process.

Level 3 builds directly on the insights of Levels 1 and 2 to bring forward the similarities and differences across the range of anticipatory models being used to make decisions in the present. In this phase, once again, the refinement of ideas and insights through structured deliberative processes is a critical part of the action-research methodology and the development of Futures Literacy. Thinking through the implications for policy at this stage in the process calls for a consideration of the nature of collective choices outside the existing systemic anticipatory assumptions. This means, in part, that FuturesIreland considers aspects of governance that go beyond what has historically been considered the means and jurisdiction of "the state" or "the individual".

Level 3 research is also designed to evoke innovative propositions about the ways in which the questions "what do you expect" and "what do you desire" influence what is imaginable and doable. This allows for a reconsideration of the dis-

---

30. These scenarios avoid the pitfalls experienced by many such exercises by subjecting the analysis to stringent analytical parameters that exclude futures that take the forms of: good versus bad versus muddling through; high versus medium versus low rates of growth in key or dominant variables; and path a, path b, path c, etc.. These Level 2 strategic scenarios are descriptive (not causal), comparative static, iso-probable and iso-desirable; hence they are on a common basis of comparison and are solely differentiated on the basis of operational (institutional, behavioural, cultural) grounds. Subjecting the scenario exercise to these analytical constraints is critical for ensuring a tight connection to both the findings and methods of social science as well as the technically sophisticated discourse of policy making.

Mika Aaltonen, Riel Miller, Larry O'Connell,
Rory O'Donnell & Stefan Bergheim

Futures Literacy:	Task	Technique(s)
Level 1 Catalytic Awareness	Temporal awareness, shifting both values and expectations from tacit to explicit—builds the capacity of teams and leaders to define and re-fine the specific topics for FuturesIreland	A wide range of catalysts (existing scenarios) and processes (group work) generate the discussions and sharing of stories that define the values, ex-pectations and topics for FuturesIreland
Level 2 Imaginative Discovery	Rigorous Imagining (RI) involves two distinct challenges—imagination and rigor, the former in order to push the bound-aries and the latter so that what is imagined is "sci-entific" and intelligible	Escaping from the prob-able and preferable to imagine the possible demands systematic creativity and creating systematically, non-discursive reflection and social science are essential ingredients
Level 3 Strategic Choice	Strategic scenarios aimed at questioning the as-sumptions used to make decisions in the present, not as targets to plan by but to provide new insights into actions that might alter the potential of the present	Strategic scenarios are constructed using the capacities and stories acquired in developing Levels 1 and 2 FL, by combining values, expec-tations and possibilities into scenarios that follow clear narrative rules

Table 6 *The Three Phases of a Futures Literacy Process*

cussions that occurred at Level 1 and helps set the stage for a debate about what is policy relevant. Level 3 closes by devel-oping more than an imaginative set of scenarios, it offers ways of distinguishing initiatives (policies) that address change in its intra-, inter- and extra-systemic dimensions. This put Fu-turesIreland in a good position, in its final report, to present robust and innovative findings that address the question of the future of Ireland with a greater awareness of both the an-ticipatory assumptions that set many of the parameters for choice and the range of potential initiatives that serve as the menu for action.

FuturesIreland: Organizational Attributes

FuturesIreland was a learning-by-doing process, made up of series of structured and cumulative research steps. FuturesIreland created a community of researchers and decision makers, who took a voyage of discovery together. This means that as an exploratory process FuturesIreland could not pre-judge its findings. Rather, the participants discovered the attributes of systemic change and the features of complex, evolutionary emergence that are pertinent to Ireland.

FuturesIreland had a three part organizational structure—two types of deliberative bodies (the National Advisory Panel and the Consultative Panel), a panel of international experts, and an analytical and logistical team that provided the inputs, collected findings, authored papers, and attended to the organizational parts of the process. The Steering Committee's role was to ensure: a) the integrity of the process with respect to scientific standards and methods; b) the effective representation of the views of Irish society; and c) the diffusion of the findings. The Consultative Panel undertook an action-research Futures Literacy process. The panel of international experts contributed the key aspects of the (re)framing for the different stages of the process. The Analytical and Logistical Team pulled it all together, an ambitious process like FuturesIreland required a clear, efficient and managerially effective organizational structure and secretariat.

National Advisory Panel. The 23-member Advisory Panel consisted of high-level actors and leaders drawn from across the Irish economy, society and the public sector. It was chaired by Peter Cassells, Chairman of the National Centre for Partnership and Performance (NCPP) and former General Secretary of the Irish Congress of Trade Unions. Reflecting its composition, it focused on the national dimension of the work and possible implications for national policy and development. On several occasions, it discussed the evidence generated in the Consultative Panel and the ideas emerging from the work of the international experts.

The Consultative Panel. The 170 members in the Consultative Panel. Members were chosen because of their track-record and creative ideas about life and work in Ireland. They were selected from all areas of Irish society: business and technology, education, health, environment, community groups, the arts and young people. Members of the Advisory Panel helped to identify innovative actors who might participate and others were identified through desk-research. Each of the 170 people on the Consultative Panel contributed three days to the project.

International Experts. Four international experts worked on the project at various times. Dr Riel Miller, an economist and consultant in the design of strategic foresight, served as an independent consultant throughout the project. Professor Carlota Perez, of the Judge Business School in Cambridge University, and Professor Yochai Benkler, of Harvard Law School, advised the project team on technological trends and the associated changes in organization, regulation and public policy. Professor Perez's contribution included a public lecture in April 2007, held in Trinity College Dublin, and a workshop with the project team and a number of members of the Advisory Panel. The fourth international contributor was Professor Charles Sabel, of Columbia Law School. Professor Sabel advised on the design of our third round of inquiry with the Consultative Panel (described below) and participated in the four days of data gathering, discussion and analysis.

Clearly the selection process for each of the key bodies in the FuturesIreland played a fundamental role in the kinds of knowledge and interaction that occurred. This is where the role of the key initiators of the process was central: Peter Cassells, Chair of the National Advisory Panel and major player on the Irish political field; Rory O'Donnell, Chair of the National Economic and Development Office, a powerful thought leader and the head of the secretariat; Maureen Gaffney, Chair of the National Economic and Social Forum and a leading thinker in Ireland, she led the input from the international expert panel; and Paula Carey, who played a critical role in seeking out members for the consultative panel, connecting them to the process, analyzing the results of the conversations and sustaining the learning process throughout.

Beyond the diffusion of process and content knowledge that was integral to FuturesIreland as action-research there were a number of ways in which FuturesIreland was designed to disseminate and encourage the use of the project's results. One was by including a certain number of opinion leaders, journalists, artists and other communicators within the process. Naturally they contributed to the deliberations but were also able to help craft the messages and carry the stories that emerged from FuturesIreland. Another was that FuturesIreland was conceived from the outset as a social networking process and used internet based mechanisms to enhance communication and deliberation, as well as providing content and examples for both specialist and more general audiences.

This also meant that FuturesIreland had to be designed with effective knowledge management principles from the outset. At each stage in the process the questions, debates, hypotheses, contradictions, and insights had to be accumulated, refined and given a sense that made the created knowledge useful both for the process and for dissemination. This type of careful knowledge management put FuturesIreland in the position to spark some "viral" communication, giving rise to memes that flow through the noosphere. Finally, of course, there are the manifold meetings and documents that were generated by FuturesIreland and serve as direct vehicles for the dissemination of research findings and policy conclusions.

Section 4—FuturesIreland: Recounting the Case Study

In its early meetings the Advisory Panel identified a range of economic, social, cultural and political challenges likely to confront Ireland in the years ahead. It highlighted the need to both draw on past Irish experience of managing change and to develop new thinking to cope with greater levels of complexity and ambiguity. Among these was the need to combine democratic decision making and accountability with the effective governance of complex policy spheres and services in which expertise is a key factor. Members suggested that Ireland was at a turning point, moving from a familiar economic, social and policy context to a much more uncertain, and possibly less benign, combination of economic, social and political factors. In our final chapter we discuss the idea that Ireland is at a turning point and consider what the findings of the project imply for our understanding of the crisis and likely turning point.

In the first round of work with the Consultative Panel, in December 2007 and January 2008, participants in the process were asked to describe in detail their experience of innovating and achieving change in an uncertain environment. The approach was based on an appreciative enquiry technique (Elliot 1999). The discussions took place in small groups that were professionally facilitated. The evidence generated by these sessions was used extensively for developing the frames and analysis throughout FuturesIreland. However, two features are important for understanding the work process. First, in telling their stories, the participants in the Consultative Panel frequently made reference not only to the institutional or organizational context in which they worked, but also to the nature and quality of inter-personal and professional relations, and to 'self-knowledge', 'self-development' and personal identity. Second, in many of the cases reported, innovation and problem solving involved seeking alliances, resources and ideas from individuals and organizations in surprisingly different spheres of work. These two features of the early evidence led the NESDO secretariat, at the next meeting of the Advisory Panel, to propose an analytical framework for making sense of the findings of the FuturesIreland action research processes (described in more detail below).

In the second round of work, the members of the Consultative Panel were asked, first, to describe their connections and networks in greater detail and, second, to imagine how Ireland might be different in 2030. Participants were set the challenge of thinking about three particular aspects of an imaginary Ireland in 2030: health and well-being, enterprise and wealth creation, and education and learning. To support this, a case study was created based loosely on the proposed Grangegorman regeneration project in Dublin. The result was a picture of Ireland in 2030 which emphasized prosperity more centered on the quality of life and well-being, widely available information technology more local decision making, new forms of community involvement, preventative medicine, tailored services available to all who need them, and experiential learning. It was notable that this vision of a desirable future differed little from that envisaged by the members of the Advisory Panel.

But the evidence gathered revealed a major disjuncture between the widespread disposition to be flexible and to learn from experience, on the one hand, and the near despair about the limits of learning in our collective endeavors, on the other. Indeed, this disjuncture was a thread that ran through much of the evidence heard in the Consultative Panel and became a central subject of discussion in the Advisory Panel, as we discuss below.

In May 2008, the Advisor Panel discussed this disjuncture and explored in some detail what it would look like to have a system that, on the one hand, allowed actors working in concrete contexts to identify opportunities and threats and, at the same time, find a way of learning from, and generalizing, what actors close to problems are doing. Drawing on their extensive experience at high levels in business, public policy and administration, social organizations, the arts and academic life, the members of the Advisory Panel acknowledged the limits of traditional command and control, but also that alternatives are poorly defined. They emphasized the need to think deeply about the nature of leadership, better forms of accountability and real responsibility. The members also discussed the importance of emotional competency and the personal motivations behind decisions.

In order for senior actors to work out a new approach at the 'center' they required a clearer view on what is needed to achieve more learning and innovation at the 'local' level. Higher levels of innovation and learning seem to require greater discretion and flexibility at the level of delivery and implementation. They also seem to be associated with an anxiety about how to ensure compliance with legitimate standards and resources constraints. Much discussion of how to balance the requirements for discretion with the need for compliance proceeds from the top down: beginning with high level policy and accountability, moving to organizational structuring and, finally, the considering of local delivery and learning. For a number of reasons, the NESDO Secretariat proposed that we should work *in reverse order*: explore first and foremost what local innovation and learning look like in business, society and the public system and only then considering what this might imply for organizational structures and accountability, and touching only lightly on the implications for broader policy, participation and democratic legitimacy.

This led the Advisory Panel to discuss the challenge of quality, standards and accountability in systems that might empower local decision making and learning. A recurring theme was how local learning and experimentation might be made accountable to others. For this reason, the Secretariat decided that learning and accountability and the related sets of routines, arrangements, norms and practices would be the central focus of inquiry in the third round of the Consultative Panel meetings.

Given these orientations, the approach was to design a set of instruments and a procedure which would gather evidence to throw light on the subject of innovation and learning in the context of ambiguity, which was at the heart of the project, and, in particular, the questions posed by members of the Advisory Panel. In designing the third day of Consultative Panel work, the secretariat was informed by recent international thinking and evidence on learning and the settings which support it. Important bodies of research in business, public administration, regulation, law, European integration and economic development draw attention to new approaches in which organizations of diverse kinds handle the limitations of their own knowledge and their need to cooperate with others in contexts of pervasive ambiguity (Gunningham, Grabosky and Sinclair 1998; Sabel 2004; Power 2007; Sabel and Zeitlin 2008).

The aspect of this work that was of most immediate relevance in designing our work with the Consultative Panel was the distinction between 'compliance monitoring' and 'diagnostic monitoring' (see Box 3). Professor Charles Sabel, of Columbia University, worked closely with the Secretariat to develop the questions and also participated in the four days work with the 170 members of the Consultative Panel.

The members of the Consultative Panel were asked to describe approaches to review, monitoring, diagnosis and learning that they had used or seen in the course of their work. They asked whether existing systems of review and evaluation were sometimes used as a means to avoid or delay action. Finally, we posed a number of questions were posed about the capabilities, roles and responsibilities involved in their approach to review, distinguishing between organizational, inter-personal and intra-personal levels.

Mapping and Discussing the Evidence

As noted above, a key way in which the FuturesIreland project sought to add value and make sense of the evidence being produced by the deliberations was by exploring ways in which three spheres of public governance, wealth creation and society interact, since this is identified as critical in existing futures studies. The work with the members of the Consultative Panel highlighted a second dimension, namely the interplay between personal experience and identity, inter-personal relations and institutions in creating the context for innovation and learning.

Mika Aaltonen, Riel Miller, Larry O'Connell, Rory O'Donnell & Stefan Bergheim

In order to explore these two dimensions we adopted a simple framework, represented in Table 7. This provided a useful way to catalogue, discuss and analyze the stories told by the participants.

	Social Integration	Public Governance	Business/ Wealth Creation
Institutional			
Interpersonal			
Intrapersonal			

Table 7 *Framework for Mapping and Discussing the Evidence*

Although the visual presentation of the analytical framework distinguishes between societal factors, public governance and wealth creation, it is not intended to suggest that they are separate spheres. There is a significant sense in which markets and parts of public governance are embedded in society (Granovetter, 1985). As the project proceeded the focus was increasingly on the nature of the interaction between the three spheres—a form of interaction that we labelled cross-fertilization. The lines between the spheres are deliberately broken in order to focus attention on what flows between them. In the diagram public governance is placed in the centre of framework, reflecting the importance for FuturesIreland of *exploring* whether changes in society and business can help us rethink the challenges facing public governance.

On the vertical axis scale the identification of three levels: institutional, inter-personal and intra-personal reflects the content of the stories told within the Consultative Panel. Almost invariably, the stories of innovation included reference to personal factors (e.g., passion, self belief and self-understanding), inter-personal factors (e.g., relationships and contacts) and institutional factors (e.g., willingness to challenge accepted routines, norms or practices). Indeed, in many of the

---

Box 3

Compliance Monitoring and Diagnostic Monitoring

With compliance monitoring it is assumed, by an individual or an organization that a good understanding of the process exists and that, if properly executed, it will produce the desired goal. It is also assumed that this goal actually serves the purpose to which it is dedicated. Under those circumstances monitoring occurs by checking what is expected at each step in the process, and ensuring people do what their instructions prescribe. Typically, an incentive system is created that rewards people for fulfilling their instructions and penalizes them from deviating from it. Hence the term compliance monitoring.

Diagnostic monitoring is used when there is less certainty about the process on how to achieve outcomes and/or when even the eventual outcomes are not always clear at the beginning of a project. It requires monitoring on an ongoing basis to ensure that review and learning, which can be described and demonstrated, are a constant feature of what people at a local service delivery level do. This form of diagnostic monitoring and review is increasingly prevalent. Business firms have found that they cannot ensure quality and safety purely by writing rules; instead they insert quality and safety in the design of products and processes and monitor closely their achievements and failures in each phase of production and marketing. As a result business makes extensive use of range of tools that support diagnostic monitoring: benchmarking, simultaneous engineering, six sigma and lean, back to basics reviews, stage gates. These tools in various ways allow business to probe for the root cause of what works and does not work, both in the context of existing processes and new product, service or process development.

In simultaneous engineering, all parts of new design are discussed concurrently so that the connections between the parts are adequately understood and changes

---

made to one part are immediately examined for their affect on others. In problem solving a technique called 5 whys is often employed to understand or diagnose the underlying causes of failure of under-performance. For example:

- *Why* is machine A broken? Because no preventative maintenance was performed.
- *Why* was the maintenance crew derelict in its duty? Because it is always repairing machine B.
- *Why* is machine B always broken? Because the part it machines always jams.
- *Why* does the jam recur? Because the part warps from heat stress.
- *Why* does the part overheat? There is a design flaw in this part.

To fix the broken machine it is necessary to redesign the part in another part of the factory, so that the repair people will be able to allocate their time in a way that allows them to perform the preventive maintenance necessary to keep the system going. It would have been impossible to have anticipated this, even with considerable engineering expertise. It is likely that more than one person would be necessary to solve this problem to get to the root cause. It might, for example, require a team that searches through the possible explanations.

stories the dynamic combination of capabilities at these three levels, and between social patterns, public governance and value creation was cited as critical in achieving innovation and learning. In addition, where these connections were absent, or ineffective, this often emerged as a key factor inhibiting innovation and learning.

The central argument to emerge from FuturesIreland was that Irish people in business, society and public service are ready for much greater innovation, more widespread learning and richer accountability; but the capabilities and practices that support these are inhibited by some features of our organizational system. This argument has significant implications for how Ireland addresses the current acute crisis and how it lays the foundations for future prosperity and social cohesion. The work highlighted, that as in the 1950s and 1980s, Ireland is once again at a turning point. While there are, of course, reasons to fear that Ireland is moving to a more uncertain and less benign context economically, socially and in public policy, the FuturesIreland work lends support to a more positive view of the turning point we are in and the transition we might experience.

This perspective on Ireland's ability to create a learning society is derived from the four main findings of the project.

Finding 1: New forms of cross-fertilization between the economy, society and public governance are increasingly evident and enhancing the ability to learn and innovate;

Finding 2: Innovation and learning are systematic, almost always combining initiative, disciplined review and a willingness to confront challenges at three levels: institutional, interpersonal and personal;

Finding 3: A systematic review provides the basis for both innovation and accountability, allowing us to combine stability and radical change which is particularly relevant in a period when we seek both stability and radical change;

Finding 4: The kind of innovation and learning we have found cannot flourish, and cannot yield a full harvest, without profound change to our organizational systems, particularly our systems of control and accountability.

These findings are based on evidence gathered from 160 innovators from business, social and cultural organizations and the public service. One-hundred and sixty people told their story in the course of the project. They included doctors, business people, parents, teachers, university professors, inventors, students, care workers, community volunteers and farmers.

The evidence documented in the FuturesIreland work shows people from all sectors of Irish life innovating in practical ways and solving problems despite numerous difficulties. The breadth of evidence heard demonstrates that operating in this manner is possible within many different sectors. In summarizing the evidence, the FuturesIreland work illustrates that common assumptions—about the flexible business world versus the rigid public sector, or rigorous public organizations versus flaky NGOs—are confounded. There were exemplar cases in business and industry, but also among people working in education, health, planning and the arts.

Conclusion: What Does FuturesIreland Tell Us?

Can we infer from FuturesIreland? This is an incisive and valid question. Amongst the many answers, perhaps the most telling is about innovation and learning. As was made clear above, the group of 170 innovative actors in the Consultative panel was not a *random* sample. They were selected precisely because they were people who had achieved change and improvement in the sphere of their work. The sample selection was based, not on drawing from across the population, but *among innovators*, drawing from across the spheres of business, technology, voluntary work, culture, social organization and, importantly, care and public service. The hypothesis to be tested was not *that everyone is innovating and learning.* In the first instance, the hypothesis was the innovation in business and technology differed from improvement in NGOs and the public system. More generally, the null hypothesis was that innovation, learning, autonomy and quality of the kind achieved by modern *firms are impossible,* especially in Ireland's public system and among community and voluntary organizations. Against such an hypothesis—swans cannot be black—finding one black swan is a real surprise and telling refutation.

Irish development is a story of black swans disproving prevailing beliefs about things being impossible in Ireland. Nineteenth century history seemed to prove that it was impossible to imagine Ireland being industrialized. An earlier generation of developmentalists proved that wrong. There was good reason to think that the voluntarist and adversarial system of industrial relations made it impossible to stabilize the economy and handle distributional conflict. Social partnership proved that wrong. Even in the 1980s, there was reason to believe that, while Ireland's people are a creative and fun-loving, it is impossible to imagine them running high technology industries. Yet a generation of Irish engineers and agencies, working with leading firms, made Ireland a significant centre of software and process engineering.

The current generation of impossibility beliefs are very much centered on the public system. It is impossible to imagine Irish regulation ensuring standards and constraining bad behavior; or it could only do so if it severely limited discretion and innovation. It is impossible for Irish public services to tailor what is offered to the diverse needs of citizens. It is impossible to imagine public sector organizations undertaking intense review of day-to-day work with a view to continuous improvement. It is impossible for voluntary providers and local social organizations to conduct themselves in a way that bears any resemblance to how good firms are run. The black swans who participated in the Futures Ireland have proven each of these beliefs to be wrong.

Of course there is still the over-arching belief that, while the Irish have surprised themselves by being capable of using high technology, and confirmed a self-image by continuing to create culture, the same cannot be true of organizing a decent, devolved, public system. In today's Ireland the most prevalent hypothesis may be that it is impossible for the centre to do what even the Government wants: to move from input control to outcome monitoring. Although FuturesIreland does not offer definitive evidence to the contrary, everything in the project, and indeed the world in recent years, tells us to expect to be surprised.

Stefan Bergheim has worked with topics concerning long-term growth, forecasts, predictions and decision-making. In his article *"The breadth of societal progress"* Stefan Bergheim pushes the traditional boundary further and takes a wider look at the issues of importance for societal progress.

Around the world, many initiatives are currently working on new ways to measure the amount of progress that societies are making. The OECD is hosting a global project on "measuring the progress of societies" with a large number of promising activities. The European Commission published a communication to the Council and the European Parliament in September 2009, calling for "indicators that do what people really want them to do, namely measure progress in delivering social, economic and environmental goals in a sustainable manner." In France, a commission set up by President Sarkozy and led by prominent economists Joseph Stiglitz and Amartya Sen released a comprehensive report in September 2009 on what indicators societies should look at beyond GDP. And in Canada, a private research institute is preparing the Canadian Index of Wellbeing.

These initiatives are important and should be supported or followed by many countries in order for them to be able to choose better policies that address the truly important is-sues for their citizens. However, these initiatives tend to pay only little attention to the strong linkages among the many aspects of societal progress. Robust and sustainable societal progress is taking place when all aspects develop hand in hand. Otherwise, specific weaknesses in some aspects may sooner or later cause severe problems in the whole system—in particular after some large unexpected shock hits a country. The United States after the recent financial crisis can be seen as an example of a country suffering from system-wide prob-lems caused by weaknesses in some areas: primarily trust and democracy.

This chapter will first show that theories of societal progress indicate high correlations among item such as in-come, education, trust, freedom, life satisfaction and many others. These correlations can be found in data even for a set of relatively homogenous developed countries. The chapter ends with some country-specific examples.

Theories of Progress

A number of thinkers in different disciplines—most notably from economics, political sciences and sociology—have for-mulated theories of societal progress. The focus here will be on Richard Nelson and Sidney Winter, Friedrich August von Hayek, Amartya Sen as well as Ronald Inglehart and Christian Welzel. These researchers build on previous work by great names such as David Hume, Adam Smith, Karl Marx and Josef Schumpeter.

The first important insight is that different theories of societal development tend to use the same variables although they each emphasise particular elements more strongly. A second common thread across all theories is that they high-light the complementarities between the different aspects of development: All the relevant variables tend to develop hand in hand. However, the theories focus on different levels of the society: on the individual (Sen), firms (Nelson & Winter) and society as a whole.

Mika Aaltonen, Riel Miller, Larry O'Connell,
Rory O'Donnell & Stefan Bergheim

Economists have looked at theories of economic progress for decades. Richard Nelson and Sidney Winter[31] made a valuable contribution in their 1982 book "An evolutionary theory of economic change". Since their approach is difficult to test with empirical models, it did not receive the attention it may have deserved. Nelson and Winter define evolution as the self-transformation of a system over time, usually from a low to a higher level of complexity.

Building on the work of Josef Schumpeter they model an economy where companies tend to follow existing routines and rules of thumb that were developed in the past and so do not maximize profit at every instance. When low profits force them to change or when their environment offers easy opportunities, firms imitate the techniques of a more successful competitor or even completely abandon old routines by innovating. As more companies apply better technology (routines) than before, their productivity and profits rise but so does the pressure on those companies that continue to use the relatively more outdated routines. However, the overall economy has reached a higher state of development.

Change, economic development and progress are the key concerns of evolutionary theories. So how can societies foster progress? Through more and smarter competition and selection, and better education and innovation that leads to higher income and wealth. What Nelson and Winter do not address are the deeper societal conditions for this progress.

Friedrich August von Hayek (1899-1992) looked closely at how societies develop. His theory of cultural evolution as outlined in his 1988 book "The fatal conceit" goes well beyond the purely economic aspects emphasized by Nelson and Winter—whom he does not quote. Hayek developed his theory in the 1970s and 80s against the backdrop of competition between the capitalist and socialist systems. Hayek's main thesis is that economic and social systems cannot be rationally created or designed using reason. The best we can do is to try and develop an existing system gradually further over time.

---

31. Nelson & Winter 1982.

Change and development are possible, but not easy.

Hayek builds on the ideas of David Hume, Adam Smith and Charles Darwin and says societies that prosper are able to change their rules and institutions to enable them better to adjust to an ever-changing environment. The processes and abilities that prove successful in everyday competition will prevail: they are robust.

In contrast to biological evolution, cultural evolution does not rely purely on the inheritance of successful genes (or on mutation).The transmission of habits and information comes not only from the individual's natural parents, but from an indefinite number of "ancestors". In the 21st century, modern information and communication technologies even allow us to learn from societies farther away.

What are the characteristics of a successful and prosperous society according to Hayek? He mentions private property, legal security (trust), honesty, truthfulness, individual freedom, cooperation (networking), innovation, high income, population growth and, finally, happiness.

While Nelson and Winter focus on companies and Hayek on society as a whole, Nobel Laureate Amartya Sen[32] who quotes Hayek intensively in his book "Development as freedom" is mostly concerned with the individual. For him, a high level of development is synonymous with a high level of freedom and individual capabilities. Social, economic and political opportunities as well as social and environmental protection produce conditions under which individuals can make full use of their potential. Freedom in all its dimensions is both "the primary end and the principal means of development"[33].

With his five freedoms, Sen covers a wide spectrum of variables:

- Economic facilities: Material resources and income as well as companies' access to finance;

---

32. Sen 1999.
33. Sen 1999.

- Political freedom: Political expression and freedom to choose between different parties;
- Social opportunities: Education, healthcare and other institutions are important in themselves but also facilitate participation in economic and political activities;
- Transparency: Openness that allows trust and prevents corruption, and;
- Protective security: A social safety net that prevents people from falling into abject misery if material changes adversely affect their lives on a massive scale.

Sen admits that there is no ideal approach with which to evaluate economic and social policies. Due to the mutually reinforcing connections between freedoms of different kinds, Sen sees a "need to develop and support a plurality of institutions, including democratic systems, legal mechanisms, market structures, educational and health provisions, media and other communication facilities and so on".

In their theory of human development, Ronald Inglehart[34] and Christian Welzel use ideas similar to those of Hayek, although their 2003 and 2005 publications do not quote his work or that of Nelson and Winter. In contrast, the link to Sen's capabilities approach is explicit. Inglehart and Welzel's insights bare also based on empirical analysis and make considerable use of data from the World Values Survey which they manage.

According to Inglehart and Welzel, three closely intertwined components characterize human development or societal progress: socioeconomic development, emancipative cultural value change and democratization. These three elements broaden human choices through more individual resources (income), expanded priorities and more freedom of action. This definition of progress also encompasses Sen's key concern, human capabilities.

Inglehart and Welzel also see the possibility of societal progress. Their analysis shows a causality running from in-

---

34. Inglehart & Welzel 2005.

creased income to emancipative value change and eventually to more civil and political liberties. Elites with a high degree of integrity enable and support this progress. Inglehart und Welzel see corruption as an indication that elites are depriving citizens of their rights, thereby hampering progress.

This theory is quite comprehensive and uses a large number of variables in three areas:

i. Socioeconomic development: income, education, innovation, health and so on;

ii. Emancipative cultural change: traditional conformity values tend to give way to more emancipative values that emphasize freedom and individual human choice. Tolerance and trust grow, and;

iii. Democratization: more civic participation, direct democracy and less corruption lead to ever more effective democracy.

Strong correlations across countries

The data used to assess societal progress at the national level covers a wide spectrum of variables and comes from a large number of sources. Several empirical methods can be applied to these data, ranging from simple correlation analysis, factor models and cluster analysis to panel co-integration analysis. This section will sketch some of the results and indicate how the insights can be used for an assessment of the level and robustness of a country's societal development.

The approach presented here differs from most academic work in growth empirics, happiness research, social capital research and related areas, that tends to still mostly employ cross-section regression methods. In this work the variable of interest—GDP, life satisfaction, trust etc.—is treated as the dependent variable on the left-hand side of a regression, while all other variables are seen as the independent variables on the right-hand side. The correlations among the usually many "independent" variables are rarely examined and there are few cross-references to neighboring literatures, where the variables are used on different sides of the regression.

The data comes from a wide range of different sources and was gathered in different ways. Relatively hard data such as gross domestic product is set in relation to "softer" survey results. Added to this are composite indicators consisting of more than one sub-indicator. The sources are the World Values Survey, the OECD, the Fraser Institute, Eurostat, the Groningen Growth and Development Centre, the World Bank, the Economist Intelligence Unit, Transparency International, the European Commission, Johns Hopkins University and the Milken Institute.

Sixteen variables are used for 20 countries. The variables are 1. Life satisfaction, 2. Freedom 3. Control, 4. Interpersonal trust, 5. Tertiary education, 6. Income, 7. Employment of older people, 8. Birth rates, 9. Government effectiveness, 10. Quality of democracy, 11. Corruption perception, 12. Tolerance, 13. Commitment and participation, 14. Broadband access, 15. Innovative capacity and 16. Capital access. Not all of these variables will be discussed here in detail. East Asian countries are not considered, because some of them have rather different economic and social structures. In Japan and Korea, for example, a large proportion of underemployment is kept within companies, resulting in low official unemployment rates but also low productivity. Including the Central and East European countries in the dataset does not alter the general statements: All the variables tend to be lower there than in the 20 countries analyzed.

The analysis of economic data over time supports the view that the most important variables develop hand in hand. And the analysis of different societies at a certain point in time shows that highly developed countries with satisfied people have much in common. This makes it difficult to identify causalities and suggests that analyzing the correlations is necessary. For example, it is assumed that theories tend to be more helpful and quantitative results more robust if based on such a range of data instead of explaining only gross domestic product, for example. Moreover, individual statistics or observations that may otherwise be problematic (such as Canada's ratio of university graduates, which stands out as unusually high in the charts) are less important under such a broad approach.

Correlations, Factors, Clusters and Co-integration

First, a simple correlation analysis can be conducted. The 16 by 16 matrix with simple correlations of the variables shows many high values although only a small group of relatively highly developed and hence similar countries is analyzed here. Particularly high is the relationship between, for instance, life satisfaction and the ratio of university graduates, government effectiveness and corruption, with correlation coefficients of 0.8 and higher. Interpersonal trust is especially closely related to the quality of democracy and tolerance in societies.

In addition to the simple correlation analysis, more complex methods can be applied to the data. A factor analysis (or principal components analysis) examines the 16 variables for commonalities and reduces them where appropriate to a lower number of dimensions and factors. This analysis with the data discussed produces one dimension that can be described as the level of societal development. It explains 57% of the total variance between the 16 variables (eigenvalue 9.1). All variables load extremely positively on this factor. The second factor calculated explains only 12% of the total variance and can thus be disregarded. The result that all variables can be depicted with one dimension confirms the theoretical insight that the variables go hand in hand and can be considered in total as the level of societal development.

A cluster analysis combines elements with similar characteristics with new elements that have the average characteristics of its components. We can treat the 20 countries as separate elements and calculate the distance between the countries on the basis of the variables seen as important for life satisfaction. Denmark and Sweden are rather similar to each other, as are Canada and Australia. The Netherlands then are similar to the Denmark-Sweden combination and Switzerland is similar to the Canada-Australia combination. Eventually we have to stop combining elements at some stage. Reducing the 16 countries to three groups, we can distinguish a "Happy variety of capitalism", a "Less happy variety" and an "Unhappy variety"—using terms from the debate about the varieties of capitalism led by Peter Hall and David Soskice. Members of the "Happy variety" include Sweden, Denmark, Finland, Switzerland, Australia, Canada, the Netherlands and with a few reservations the USA and the UK. Less happy are Germany, France, Belgium, Austria and Spain. And the "Less happy variety" consists of Italy, Greece and Portugal.

So far, all empirical analysis has been applied to a single point in time across different countries. However, progress is a dynamic phenomenon that should be discussed with the use of time series. Unfortunately, many of the variables presented so far can not be examined in a useful manner as time series. Some of them are only available for one or two years, so immediately drop out. Others might be available over a longer time span, but their construction limits them to a certain range, for example between 0 and 10. In some cases (e.g., the corruption index) an improvement in one country may not show up as such if the average of countries improves even more. In other cases, the construction of surveys (e.g., life satisfaction) with a fixed scale for the answers prevents any significant change over time in the aggregate. Yet other cases such as the unemployment rate have a natural lower or upper limit.

Therefore, only a few series are non-stationary and can be used in a panel co-integration analysis where data for different countries over a long time span are combined: GDP, physical capital stock, human capital stock (years of education) and trade openness. Panel co-integration analysis shows that these variables are pair-wise co-integrated. For example, GDP and physical capital move exactly in step: over the long run, a 10% increase in one variable is matched by a 10% increase in the other. Similarly, human capital and physical capital tend to go hand in hand over time. One additional year of average education is associated with a 20% increase in the physical capital stock, and so on. These results are in line with the idea that the key variables are complements.

Even More Variables of Possible Importance

In addition to the variables analyzed above, there is a large number of other factors that may be important to people's well-being and a country's progress. Here we examine variables that (a) fit into the scheme described above but were not considered in greater detail for lack of space or owing to the uncertainty of the data basis, (b) that are presumably very important but do not fit into the scheme and (c) that are often discussed but exhibit no empirical and/or theoretical connection.

In the first group we find job protection, which is regularly calculated by the OECD, and also fits into the system. In advanced countries it tends to be low, enabling flexible adjustment and a low unemployment rate. Also, the World Economic Forum's Global Gender Gap Index suggests that women play a greater part in advanced countries than in others. However, there is considerable uncertainty here about the quality of the data. In advanced countries the transaction costs for purchasing real estate are low, which increases flexibility and could be a sign of openness and competition on the real estate market.

In the second group, life expectancy is without doubt enormously important to people, but the data for 20 countries shows no correlation with other variables presented in this study. Life expectancy presumably depends on eating habits and the climate of the country and less on the quality of state regulation. Measures such as Ruut Veenhoven's Happy Life Years or the Human Development Index are therefore good ways of combining life expectancy with other relevant variables.

The quality of environmental protection is also important to people. However, Yale University's Environmental Performance Index reveals no significant correlation with the other variables. It is up to sustainability strategies to ensure environmental protection and thereby support an even broader definition of well-being over the long term.

In the third group, a large number of variables exhibit no systematic correlation with people's life satisfaction in happiness and development research. They are not significant either in micro or macro studies, nor in the set of data presented here:

- The government spending ratio (leading to the conclusion that it is not how much a government spends, but what it spends it on that matters);
- The population size;
- National pride (from surveys asking "How proud are you to be a citizen of your country?");
- The proportion of immigrants in a population (homogeneous societies are no easier to govern than heterogeneous), and;
- Present-day religiosity (in contrast to historical roots, which are partly determined by religion).

Changes are Possible

The main focus of this chapter has been a comparison of different countries at a given point in time: What did advanced countries have in common in 2005? However, the ultimate aim has to be to suggest changes towards progress over time. For this, examples from countries that have actually achieved measurable progress are helpful. As far as the data pool permits, we can compare the values from 2005 with values from 1995.

Although changes are possible, the origins of some present-day structures reach back centuries. Max Weber stressed how strongly a society is shaped by its cultural heritage. Path dependencies are important and powerful. Robert Putnam's famous illustration examines administrative reform in Italy in the 1970s. This was more successful in those regions that had already built up a civil society in the Renaissance period featuring guilds, cooperatives, good neighborliness etc.

Hayek likewise pointed to the importance of traditions, which crucially determine societal development. Present-day institutions are the heritage passed down by our ancestors, and changes are possible only on a limited scale. For example, German history abounds in events which even today shape its institutions and structures. Sabine Bode points to the experiences of the baby boom cohort of the 1930s, who formed the Federal Republic in the 1970s and 1980s. Their childhood was one of war, hunger and poverty; many of their fathers had been killed or were taken captive. Understandably, they were later at pains to promote institutions that would offer the guarantee of "never again". The big German welfare state was one consequence. (It can be argued that the backdrop of rivalry with the socialist German Democratic Republic also helped the German welfare state develop as they argued over which one had the best social system.) That way the experiences of their childhood were institutionalized and passed on to the following generations.

Recognizing this path dependence does not imply that change is impossible, however. Deep historical roots do not rule out the possibility of change. Some countries (or regions) are capable of developing faster than others. This can happen partly by learning from success stories elsewhere, although a basic willingness to embark on this learning process must always be present.

Comparing the values from 2005 with those from 1995 (approximately and where data is available) reveals that all countries show a marked increase in gross domestic product, the level of education and employment of older people. Other variables do not enable identification of any general improvement, owing to their construction as mentioned above, although, some countries have advanced considerably more than the average.

In many, but not all, areas Spain registered marked improvement between 1995 and 2005. Life satisfaction, for one, increased 1.2 times faster than the standard deviation across all 20 countries. The ratio of university graduates, the birth rate and corruption also posted exceptionally strong improvements. However, people say they have relatively less control over their lives, and according to the World Bank the quality of government has deteriorated. In the Netherlands, Australia, Denmark and Finland some variables also improved exceptionally strongly.

The example of the USA shows that change can also mean relative regression. Across the variables analyzed here, the US is losing ground on the other countries. Its decline is particularly severe in terms of education, life satisfaction and interpersonal trust. So it is hardly surprising that social capital research has been developing exceptionally dynamically in the USA.

A Robustness Check for Sweden and the USA

Based on the theoretical framework sketched at the beginning and on the empirical analysis across the 20 OECD countries, we can now examine individual countries for the level and robustness of their societal development. Sweden and the USA are examples of interest.

Sweden stands out as a country with high readings on most of the relevant indicators: life satisfaction, trust, tolerance, absence of corruption, democracy, innovative capacity, capital access, government effectiveness and employment of older people rank among the highest in the world. However, there are a few relative weaknesses that could possibly become a focus of attention over the coming years: First, unemployment is higher than in the best countries such as Denmark and the Netherlands that use the so-called flexicurity approach to achieving low unemployment. Second, the level of freedom is lower than in the best-performing countries. There is a difficult balancing act between high trust and high individual and economic freedom, where Sweden might want to focus somewhat more on the issue of freedom. Overall, Sweden is showing one of the highest and at the same time most balanced and therefore robust levels of societal development.

On the other hand, the USA shows extremely high readings in some indicators, but quite poor ones on others. The USA is one of the leaders in rankings on per capita incomes or GDP. It also shows high levels of tertiary education and high fertility rates. The level of economic and individual freedom in "the land of the free" is among the highest in the world. However, these strengths have to be seen against a number of serious weaknesses in other areas. In particular, there are concerns regarding the quality of the US democracy as indicated by low scores on the Democracy Index published by the Economist Intelligence Unit as well as on the Voice and Accountability Index published by the World Bank. In addition, corruption appears to be more widespread than in many other developed countries and interpersonal trust is relatively low. The election of Barack Obama as President of the USA might have its root in the public discontent with these weaknesses and is therefore something that needs to be addressed for societal development to resume.

How to Foster Progress

When a society wants to improve the level or pace of progress, it may use the following four filters to identify areas for action: (1) What are the really important and relevant aspects of progress and life satisfaction? (2) In what areas does a country perform comparatively poorly when it is compared to other countries? (3) Which aspects can be changed by specific action? (4) Given the close connections between the different variables, where might changes have particularly pronounced long-term effects that could lead to improvements in other areas? Country-specific recommendations can be derived using this approach. However, it is clear that sustainable progress is possible only if many areas are addressed simultaneously and consistently at several levels: Federal, state and local government, businesses and individuals all need to be involved.

Mika Aaltonen, Riel Miller, Larry O'Connell, Rory O'Donnell & Stefan Bergheim

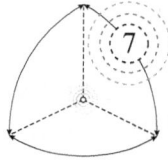

7. Probing Futures

Grant an idea to be true. What concrete difference will its being true make to anyone's actual life? What experiences will be different from those which would be obtained if the belief was false? What, in short, is the truth's cask-value in experimental terms?

William James, *Pragmatism* 1907

If we describe what we know as a sphere that has been continuously expanding, the area of contact with the unknown will grow out of proportion.[1] The traditional scientific and industrial strategies we use to project, predict, and program the future by using our knowledge of the past as the basis for which the future can be known and forged, are often bypassed. As are those on which the innovation is justified and safety established.

The French sociologist Paul Virilio[2] argues that a society, an organization or a company that privileges the present, real time, to the detriment of the past and future, privileges risks and accidents. At the same time, the distances of the life-size scale of the globe are shrinking, time ratios, lags and scales are being eliminated. The nations and the people of the planet are pushed together, without expanse and without temporal extension. As a result everything is telescoped, rammed into everything else, distances reduced to nothing by the instantaneous synchronization of exchanges.

Two conclusions follow. First, there is a need for new theories, approaches and models that are better equipped to

1. Le Journal du Dimanche 2002.
2. Virilio 2007.

deal with the unknown and uncertainty. Naturally, *Robustness* represents one such theory. Secondly, there is a loss of the sense of reality—no one knows anymore what will be true and real for people. It will be harder to tell the difference between truth and lie.

Philips Design Strategic Director Josephine Green[3] has some ideas on how to work within these boundaries, within this context, she advises us to:

- Cultivate opportunities and projects where we can work together as equals;
- Explore more partnerships, including public-private opportunities;
- Help, facilitate, enable and incubate experiments;
- Scale up those successful, and first of all, and;
- Create a more open and experimental mindset.

In the following chapter *Riel Miller* asks an ever more relevant question *"to experiment or not to experiment"* in his input.

We are living a moment when the swirling clouds of evolutionary complexity part, offering a glimpse of a landscape where three features stand out and what needs to be done becomes clear. It is time to embrace experimentalism.

The Shocking

The first feature is that the emperor has no clothes. The financial system's detachment from the "real economy" is evident for everyone to see. This is not an artificial divide due to malice of forethought or some particular form of pernicious greed. It is a common event in the history of firms and sectors that get

---

3. Green 2007.

drawn away, initially by innovation and the good profits that go with it, to a point where the core role of what they produce is forgotten. There are famous examples of firms and indeed even whole nations that lose sight of the essential, focusing on doing things that end up being peripheral and ultimately non-resilient.

The Routine

The second feature is that every morning, when each of us wakes up and starts about our own day, the "real economy" is still there. This is the continuity of human activity that creates wealth in the form of useful output. It is important, very important and not easy in these queasy days at the end of the industrial era, to admit that wealth creating activity includes not just the familiar physical objects that come off automobile assembly lines or the "white collar" services offered by Wall Street brokerages but also the "unique creation" that defines peer production, the experience of the market events, "do-it-yourself" craft, and coproduced relationships arising in fluid networked communities.

The Jackpot

The third feature is a jackpot of riches waiting to be created by reconnecting the "real economy" with the financial system. We face a historically rare opportunity. The emergent "learning intensive society" requires a financial system that can do the traditional things a financial system does: That is specialize in both the allocation of capital and the management of liquidity in ways that correspond to the present nature of what is being produced and accumulated in the form of assets (capital). Without this essential system the new types of output and the new ways of producing this output and including the emergence of new business models on a viable basis, cannot happen.

Time to Experiment

In this time of crisis the reflex of retrenchment, consolidation and refuge in familiar routines is understandable. But it should also be self-evident that financial system innovation is essential for developing the potential of the present. History is replete with examples.

The invention during the Renaissance, over four centuries ago, of such primordial ingredients of the financial system as double entry bookkeeping and the then exotic financial instrument called a "bill-of-exchange" were critical for enabling new business models and new markets to emerge. It is easy to forget that instruments and institutions that we take for granted today like bonds, stock markets and even central banks did not always exist but had to be invented and refined through experimentation.

What to Experiment On

Past experience shows that finding the right fit between the emergent system of wealth creation and an appropriate financial system requires experimentation in at least four underlying socio-economic sub-systems—identity, property rights, transaction systems, and shared meaning. One take[4] on today's context suggests experimentation along the following lines:

Identity. The emergent "learning intensive society" is characterized by "unique creation" in highly fluid and diverse networks. If there is no easy way to prove and own your identity in a practically useable form then there are very high costs and low incentives to opening an account, making an investment, accumulating assets or taking responsibility (recognizing liability). Citizenship, birth certificates, social security cards and the panoply of rights that we take for granted now need to be extended into cyberspace—it is time to establish the infrastructure of cyber-citizenship.[5]

---

4. Miller 2006, Miller & Bentley 2003.
5. Miller 1997-99.

Property rights. The new relationship between property rights and finance needs to be based on accounting systems that rest on clear and operational property rights systems that validate and valorize two key asset classes: i. Creativity in all its cumulative and composite richness (copyleft), and ii. Human capital as the verified acquisition of competences—things you know how to do—that can be deposited in a "knowbank".[6] A willingness to undertake creative experiments equivalent to those of the 19th century, like the daring decision to introduce universal compulsory schooling, could easily establish the accounting and assessment methods needed to bring property rights and accounting systems back into realignment with the emergent systems of wealth creation.

Transaction systems. Composite creative works that are formed from a collage of accumulated inputs and spontaneous teams that coalesce for joint activities/joint production of utility (social, business, personal) can only work if there is an easy way to measure value and make payments. For a variety of reasons, including inadequate identity and property rights systems as noted above, the development of a state backed token that can be used for peer-to-peer payments has not emerged. The problems are not technological but institutional.[7] Central banks did not take initiatives in this direction at the time of the dot.com boom for fear of destabilizing financial sector business models. Now that the sector has to be rebuilt anyhow will there be a better moment to experiment with new forms of payment that can help create new valuation markets and facilitate the viability of new business models in a broad, global-local transaction economy?

Shared meaning. Language is an obvious enabler of networking but it is the kind of standard that takes centuries and innovations like nation states and compulsory public schooling to become ubiquitous. The equivalent challenge today is to es-

---

6. Miller 1996.
7. Miller, Michalski & Stevens 2002.

tablish a more rapid, task and context specific ability to arrive at shared meanings. This is a key enabler of a learning intensive networked society. Already much grass roots experimentation is happening with what some are calling the "semantic web", a glimmer of what might be imagined as Web 3.0. Now is the time to be more explicit in encouraging experiments in achieving transparency (finding what you need not just what you already know).

Resistance to Experimentation

Collective action to introduce experimentation along these lines provokes resolute and often nasty defensive reactions. This is a normal reaction since the emergence of new systems that function on the basis of different logics reshuffles the stocks and flows of capital and power.

A recent rather low key but costly example of this resistance to change happened during the dot.com boom. This explosion of creative and risky ideas both inflated too fast and collapsed because powerful interests not only protected existing systems of property rights, payment, valuation, and accounting but also, maybe more importantly, stymied experimentation with alternatives. During the dot.com boom experimentation was fenced in to a narrow range of "wild entrepreneurialism" that left institutions, accounting practices and power untouched.

Some might say that the current context is different. Given the breadth and depth of the failure of the existing systems the choice of experimentalism may seem like a "no brainer". Turning to experimentalism could even appear like a good way to show some regret over how things turned out and a willingness to try something new. "Hey, let's run a few pilot projects to see if they work. What have we got to lose?"

Fear of Experimentalism

Plenty. Embracing experimentalism, as defined here, means abandoning administration. This is a huge and frightening loss. Administrative systems use simplification in conjunction with command and control to achieve planned outcomes and manage risk. Administration has been brilliantly, wildly successful, but at a price.

Using administrative methods to address the reality of complex evolving systems entails a loss of information and freedom.[8] By resting on the "Newtonian" world-view that the universe can be explained, predicted and planned, the administrative approach even in its most reflective mode contains two insurmountable limitations: first the premise of predictability means that failure is due to inadequate planning and hence logically failure is avoidable, failure is someone's fault, and fear of failure inhibits learning through experimentation[9]; and second the presumption that the future of complex systems can be explained undercuts the modesty and imagination needed to question the assumptions that limit our perceptions of the potential of the present.[10]

To embrace experimentalism is to let go of the organizational forms and practices of planning and administration that are logically at odds with failure and hence, fundamentally at odds with learning. It is to take another, more spontaneous, diversified, fluid and open path to achieving our goals and managing risk.

The Courage to Do It

Today we look back at the crash of 1929, the immense costs of the Great Depression, and denounce what now seem like pointless political conflicts, obvious policy blunders and the excruciatingly slow pace of institutional innovation.

Will history repeat itself? What will our epitaph be? Will hindsight's verdict in fifty years be that we systematically and

---

8. Miller 2006.
9. In an administrative system the verdict of success or failure, hence the dynamics of experimentation occurs most tellingly through the birth and death of organizations. This is too "lumpy", too limited by the administrative form, for unique, networked, co-creation activities.
10. Miller 2007.

purposefully sought out experimentalism as a new way to take advantage of the opportunities created by the complex evolutionary processes within which we live? Or will they once again lament our inability to imagine changes in the conditions of change and do something about it?

At least our choice is simple—will we embrace experimentalism or not?

We can discuss the knowable when we use the concept of horizon. Horizons are neither crossable nor reachable. They outline the fragments of the specific spaces of potentialities in which conditions are maturing, and as conditions are mature, the horizons move ahead.

Our outlook shifts the focus on potentialities whether they are opportunities waiting to be triggered or properties still immature. Without horizons we are dead. We may still continue along our trajectories, but real novelties and innovations rarely appear: things are forever fixed.[11]

Horizons push knowledge, habits and prejudices, to the limits where new ideas have to be put forward. Try imagining a project ambitious enough to match building the pyramids in Egypt or what would be your opinion on working on a challenge as big as organizing and training thieves and murderers into Roman legions, or an equivalent leadership act to execute the great maneuvers of Charlemagne today?

Dream Company's Chief Imagination Officer *Rolf Jensen* creates notional worlds, small narratives, to discuss how some of the vital social markers that have constructed and constrained our lives have moved—and throws people into them in order to learn about possible developments. Here is one of them. *From the Few to the Many, from Them to You.*

---

11. C.f. Poli 2009b.

The traditional value chain: from creator to producer to retailer to consumer is about to disappear, not tomorrow, but soon. The trend has started already and it will gain momentum in the years to come. The consumer is becoming the creator, the producer and retailer as well. Talent, ingenuity, skills and the desire by more and more people have to take part is one reason for this trend, the other is the Internet. The many are wrestling power from the few, they become empowered, from passive to active, from watching to playing.

From consumer to consumer, C2C is the new market place. The classic examples are Wikipedia and other wikis. Wiki asked people to provide the content for an encyclopaedia—for free—and they responded enthusiastically. Let us call them the amaproffs, amateurs working professionally. This is, however, only a small part of the trend that affects knowledge, information, entertainment and products.

Information. The internet is loaded with information on any subject. From the teenager recommending a café to the CIA fact book, it is available for free. Can we rely on information from private or unofficial sources? Well, be critical—that is a rule that applies to all information. Thanks to the e-books and soon the e-newspapers, production and distribution costs will be reduced to a few dollars. Furthermore, the tools for reading will be available on the mobile phone, on TV, on e-readers and on computers—anywhere. The cost of publishing will be reduced dramatically. This is what opens up the "long tail", enabling all people with talent—and even some without—to become authors and publishers. The market for niche subjects will soar, which is exactly the idea of the long tail. Blockbusters will count for less and publications that sell perhaps 100 copies will become a bigger part of the revenue and profits for publishers like Amazon. We can all become authors. We can also sell our e-books directly from our homepage, too. The number of bloggers will soon reach 100 million and from person-to-person dialogue will continue to rise through You Tube and other social networking media. Visibility in the public domain is democratized. From the few to the many.

Entertainment. The same is happening with fiction, with books, movies, music, photos and games. The equipment is becoming cheaper and distribution costs are disappearing. The hardware and software for producing a movie or music is coming down and soon we will see software being offered for producing our own computer animated movies and games. The market place will no longer be reserved for a few experts and artists anointed by the big companies. The door will soon become wide open to any person with talent and a good story to tell.

Products. The traditional assembly line is being challenged by the demand for mass-customization, yes, but that is only part of what will happen. The 3D printer is on its way to a shop near you. You can print in 2 dimensions on you traditional printer, but it cannot print objects, products, like a vase or a Barbie doll. The 3D printer is currently in professional use in a lot of companies and as prices come down due to mass production, it will become available in you computer shop for a thousand dollars. You will as a consumer become creator, producer and consumer—all three things in one. Philip Starck is a famous designer, but he will receive fierce competition in a few years from now. When you are the designer, you can demonstrate your talent, your creativity, the market place will change— again from the few to the many. The 3D printer will be put close to the old printer, but first you will have to go to the corner store with your design and let them produce it, although not for long. This is likely be the biggest IT revolution happening in the second decade of this century.

The implications for companies are vast. The challenge is obvious: companies must learn to listen a lot more to their consumers. Companies may choose to deliver equipment to consumers and may invite their consumers to take part in creation and production, but ultimately, the end of the hierarchical value chain as we know it is just over the horizon.

Using novel methods and imagination to make sense of the changing world is one thing. Another thing is to manage perceptions, to process and incorporate new information into a social system for our own purposes. According to Paul Virilio[12] in the winter of 2001 the US Defense Department announced the quiet creation of a new Office of Strategic Influence (OSI) under the control of the Under-Secretary of Defense to diffuse false information to influence the hearts and minds of a terrorist enemy. Very swiftly, the Secretary of Defense, Donald Rumsfeld, denounced this project, which was designed to manipulate public opinion in enemy or allied states indiscriminately. By the end of February 2002, the OSI was officially canned.

Perhaps the above example is an extreme one, but for some time there have been discussions that the Ministry of War should change its name to the Ministry of Fear and be run by the movie industry and the mass media as integral parts of the audiovisual continuum in our daily lives. The screen has become a substitute for the battlefield of the great past wars.[13]

In every society the production of discourse is somehow controlled, selected and redistributed according to a certain number of procedures, which role is to avert its powers and its dangers, to cope with chance events, and to evade its ponderous, awesome materiality.[14]

In contradiction to a top-down, linear and one-directional change where the director introduces change while staff are changed, a capability to invade the imaginary of people is an indirect strategy to affect people's behavior to create novel ideas (for innovative purposes), to influence people's emotions (for psychopolitical ends) or people's perceptions (for decision-making).

---

12. Virilio 2007.
13. Virilio 2007.
14. Foucault 1976.

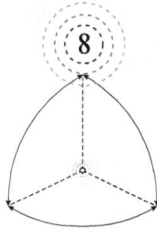

8. Leadership—
Impact as Strategy

Prime Minister's Office
Helsinki

The Senate Square is a concentration of power in Finland. Opposite to the offices of Prime Minister and the Cabinet is the main building of Helsinki University, and in the Northern edge the Helsinki Cathedral. Not to forget the statue of Alexander II, located in the center of the square, which became a symbol of quiet resistance during the attempted Russification of Finland.

The Secretary of State Vesa Vihriälä from the PM's office coordinates the inter-ministry foresight network and smoothly presents the Finnish approach. Twice a season the ministers coordinate their views of the most important topics, phenomena and challenges and the potential responses to them. The time period considered is relatively long from 10 to 30 years but that helps us to adapt to the changes. Towards the end of a parliamentary season the Finnish government expresses its opinion on a significant long-range issue, last time the issue was aging, at the moment it is sustainability.

According to Vihriälä the distinctive features of the Finnish approach are the will to get concrete results quickly, the ability to network and involve any Finnish person, a flexible organization and training people to take a position with regard to difficult situations. Three methods are preferred: the official view, scenarios, and uncertainty analysis. There is an explicit tendency to search for reflexivity by returning to previous topics by asking are the drawn policies at place, have they been turned into practices, is the situation still the same or has it changed, and have we received novel information.

"We cannot rely on any single approach, we need several approaches to foresight", says TEKES Foresight Director Pirjo Kyläkoski. In below Figure 21 present some of the main actors and the respective focus areas in which their foresight is embedded.

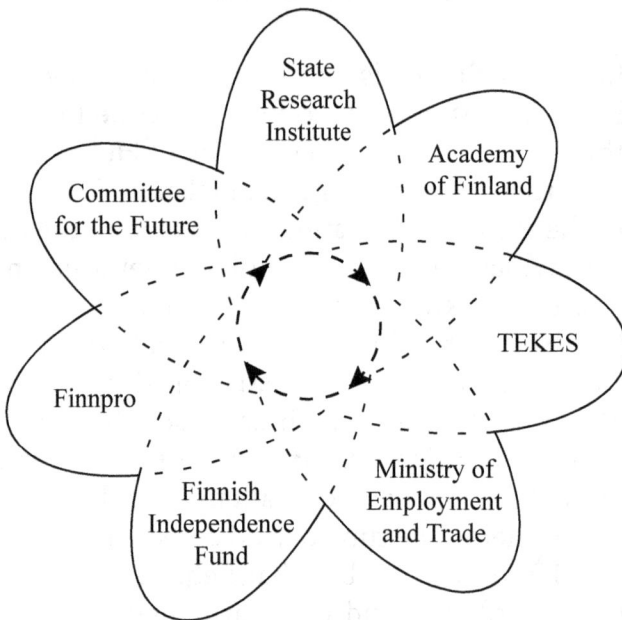

Figure 21 *The Finnish foresight system*

Some of the actors have a longer history like the Committee for the Future that deliberates parliamentary documents referred to it, and when requested to do so; FINNPRO's Bats instead is a brand new initiative to use collective intelligence to map new opportunities for Finnish industries. Even if the general tendency is towards networking between Finnish actors and with relevant actors outside Finland, some of the actors are naturally closely interconnected,e.g., TEKES strategic competence concentrations should work with Academy of Finland top research units.

Now I am in a hurry. I am meeting Professor Karl-Erik Sveiby in a nice restaurant by the old market place at the harbor. Karl-Erik earned his reputation as a first generation knowledge management expert. His renowned papers and books are covered by boxes and diagrams, much like European or American academics' works do. Today he is a changed man, he has worked 18 months with Australian Aboriginals, especially with their storyteller, whose role is to pass on the traditions of one of the oldest peoples on the earth[1]. Now he talks and writes about shared leadership consisting of temporary leaders and temporary followers as well as horizontal leadership with a strong code of conduct for both.

Approximately fifteen years ago *Uffe Elbäk* thought the Danish schools were not teaching what people really needed in their lives and decided to do something about it. Now, the founder of KaosPilots, an alternative education curricula, he has received the Knight of Danneborg for his educational services for Denmark. He feels close to previous thoughts when he writes about his recent experiences as CEO of World Outgames in Copenhagen in the *event as an entrepreneurial and attitude-forming strategy.*

Just under a month after the rainbow flags were taken down from Copenhagen City Hall, the University and the Cathedral, we begun finalizing the accounts for the World Outgames 2009. What has Copenhagen got out of the significant financial and political investment? Yes, what does such an international sport, cultural and human rights event mean for the participants, the city and the local LGBT (lesbian, gay, bisexual

---

1. Sveiby & Skuthorpe 2006.

and transgender) community?

Before I answer those questions, here are some key facts about World Outgames in Copenhagen (referred to as WO from now on).

Firstly, it was important for both the secretariat and the board not just to attach equal importance to the three program elements of sport, culture and human rights, but also to prioritize them as follows:

Human rights was the core and fundamental premise for the whole event. It could not have been otherwise, when a third of the world's countries still criminalise love between two people of the same sex, and when in seven of those countries homosexual love is tantamount to the death penalty.

The cultural program was crucial as a dynamic bridge builder, both internally within the LGBT community and between the LGBT community and the rest of the city. Because it was crucial for the board, the secretariat and the politicians in City Hall that WO not be a closed festival for few but an open festival for all.

The sports program was prioritized as a unique social framework for thousand of LGBT sports-people from abroad (who made up largest amount of the paying participants). But as well as being a social framework, the sports program was also a visible and therefore very important political point with regard to the homophobia which unfortunately—especially within men's team sports—still characterizes many sports environments. Both in and outside Denmark.

A "Business as Unusual" Event

As well as the prioritization of the program as mentioned above, the project stood for some clearly-worded values, meaning that we wanted WO to be characterized by aspects such as:

- Cultural diversity (within the organization and with regard to the program);

- Social innovation (new working relationships between the public, private and voluntary sectors);
- Transparency (everyone should be able to see and understand our decisions), and;
- Generosity anyone could be part of the event, and everyone who wanted to could have access to the event.

Finally, there was a mutual understanding that WO should not just be an event for the participants to identify with, but also one for Copenhagen as a city to identify with. Because by being the host for WO, Copenhagen sent out a clear message, both to the local and the international communities, that in Copenhagen we want to bang the drum for diversity, tolerance and personal freedom. In the LGBT community as well.

Purely because of its program prioritization, value base and the project's primary target group, WO was not therefore a "business as usual" event. On the contrary, it was a "business as unusual" event.

Which also meant that simply because of its purpose and identity, the event put occupied a contentious political seat. And of course, there was a debate. Anything else would have been strange. But interestingly enough, it was not a debate among politicians inside City Hall. Because before, during and after the event, there was broad political support for WO in that building from the far left to the far right.

No, the debate about the event was first set in motion rather dramatically by the local newspaper Nyhedsavisen. When the newspaper subsequently went bankrupt, the debate moved sporadically over to BT, another newspaper, because the journalist and the editor who had written the articles and leaders in Nyhedsavisen found employment there.

But apart from these very few deliberately negatively-angled stories in the newspapers, the overall media coverage of and about WO was generally positive.

Pockets of Intolerance

It goes without saying that this was only with regard to professional journalistic coverage. Because if you look at the many private and professional blogs that have been on the Internet before and during WO, you can often be very shaken by the intolerance which still exits in certain parts of Danish society towards homosexuals. Not so much because of the content of the columns and blogs even though these themselves can be noteworthy enough. But more because of the violent reactions they generated among lots of ordinary Danes. Reactions that clearly showed a picture of fear, hate and aversion towards homosexuals.

Just one single entry from the conservative-liberal blogger Michael Jalving headlined "Spare us from the Gay Olympics" resulted in 275 particularly emotive comments, most of which supported in very unambiguous terms Michael Jalving's distaste and lack of understanding of WO as an event and a political priority.

This intolerance unfortunately progressed from being a democratically legitimate verbal expression on the Internet to actual physical violence, as right after the opening event at City Hall Square on the Saturday evening, July 25th, three WO participants were kicked and attacked by two aggressive and homophobic young men (to quote the words of the police). Fortunately, both were arrested immediately after the attack. The same was the case when a man threw powerful fireworks onto the track at Österbro Stadium during WO. He was also arrested and subsequently charged under aggravated hate crime laws.

As well as these episodes reported in public, the secretariat is also aware of a large number of situations where participants were verbally abused, had things thrown at them, as well as one other serious case where a young lesbian was attacked by a group of young male right-wing exterminists. Unfortunately, this case was not reported to the police because the young woman did not want to do so alone because the witnesses who had seen the attack declined to give statements to the police.

These unfortunate situations prove unambiguously that events such as WO are not just relevant in an international perspective but also relevant to us in Denmark.

Success from the Point of View of the Program, the Organization and the Finances

After two and a half years preparatory work, WO opened on July 25th with a large public event on City Hall Square in Copenhagen. It marked the start of the WO week. Nine days with the focus on LGBT sport, culture, art and human rights.

WO was in every way a significant event but also an event for ordinary people. Just a few key figures: 5518 paying participants came from 91 countries. In addition, 7500 LGBT tourists (the secretariat's estimate) chose to come to Copenhagen purely because of WO. During the course of the week, more than 2000 different program activities spread across the three program pillars were held. Sport had the most (1800 competitions in 34 disciplines), followed by culture with 3030 separate items on its agenda—from exhibitions to choir concerts and the numerous cultural events on the six OutCities stages: Melbourne, Rio de Janeiro, Mexico City, Tel Aviv, Antwerp and Aarhus. And finally, the international LGBT Human Rights Conference in the Danish Broadcasting Corporation's new concert hall and at the IT University. More than 24 key note speeches and more than 110 work shops were held there.

In total, more than 200 000 local Copenhagers and tourists took part in an enormous number of free events during WO. From the official opening in City Hall Square where more than 25 000 people took part, to the Run for Love race and the official closing ceremony held in conjunction with Copenhagen Pride.

It should also be noted that more than 300 journalists covered the event, of which around half came from foreign media. And as the backbone of the organization, we had 1800 people who chose to use their summer holidays to do voluntary work for WO. Without volunteers, WO would never have been the success it was.

At the time of writing, we have generally only received positive feedback about the vent. From ordinary Copenhagen people and public authorities)police, fire service and city institutions) to the participants themselves. For example, the participants stayed an average of eight days in Copenhagen rather than the five anticipated. So they must have liked what they saw. In short, it was successful from the point of view of the program, the organization and the finances. The latter resulting because budgets were kept to, and because it can be seen that the grant of DKK 30M from the city gave a good return on investment. Participants spent between DKK 50M and 60M in the city on hotels, transport and general consumption (Wonderful Copenhagen's calculations).

But as well as the city being able to look back on a successful event, is it also possible to say something more in principle about what WO meant for Copenhagen? Has the event, consisting of nine interesting and intense days, left more permanent marks on the city's social, political and cultural life? Has the city been affected and therefore actually changed its opinions and ways to act—has there been social and cultural growth? These questions are relevant, and are just as interesting to ask as the question whether the event has contributed on the plus side to the local economy.

Financial, Social and Cultural Growth

When the secretariat was established in the beginning of 2007 to take on the task the City of Copenhagen had given us of developing, planning and running WO the management was also in agreement that "just" delivering a one-off event was not itself a success criterion. Of course we also had to do just that. However, we decided to look at the job of holding WO as a potential entrepreneurial and attitude-forming strategy for the city.

In other words, we wanted the city's various players to be able to use the event as a strategic springboard to move forward organizationally, culturally and from a business point of view in their own development processes. So, how did these players use WO as a testing ground for new ideas, new products, new partnerships and new communication strategies?

But just as important as it was for WO to be understood and thought of as an entrepreneurial strategy for the city (financial growth), it was important that WO should be seen as a attitude-forming strategy for Copenhagen (social and cultural growth). This twin focus had a lot of influence on the way the event was organized, communicated and run. Or as we said it to each other in the secretariat: "WO must be consciously used to upgrade Copenhagen: financially, socially and politically."

So was the strategy successful? It would appear so. Because if you take the following few selected "upgrade items", you can see WO as a good example of how politics can use an event as an "upgrade engine" for the local community that resides where the event is to be held. In this case, it started with the city's LGBT community.

Upgrading the Infrastructure

Politically, hosting WO was used both as an argument and an indicator for renovating Österbro Stadium and for building a new swimming arena at Bellahöj. Investments in facilities which will be of benefit to the local community for many years to come. But there was also another and perhaps just as important upgrade to the infrastructure, namely the experience of making more proactive use of public spaces for a large international event.

Not only were the official opening and closing ceremonies held at City Hall Square, but most of the free cultural programs were also held in public spaces, to the delight of local people and tourists alike. That applied to the whole OutCities route, which ran from Vor Frueplads by the Cathedral, to Gammeltorv and Nytorv squares and Sören Kierkegaard Plads, ending at Islands Brygge across the harbor. A number of the sports activities also tested out the potential for using public space. For example the Run for Love race, Open Air Milonga and synchronized swimming in the harbor.

Upgrading Organizations

The local LGBT community in Copenhagen was neither especially prominent nor especially well organized at the time that Copenhagen City Council decided to host WO 2009. The Council was also conscious of the fact that WO could not be held without the support and contribution of that very same local LGBT community.

So it has been very important for the staff at the secretariat that an additional benefit of the city hosting WO was that the local LGBT community would be strengthened both culturally and organizationally as a result. Indeed this happened and to an extent we did not expect to see, but not just because thousands of LGBT people in Copenhagen were involved in holding the event. People are now confident about their own strengths and purpose, which can be seen in new, promising projects that have already been launched. Projects which are characterized by a new openness toward the already numerous existing players in the LGBT community and an openness and readiness to take on board new talent that has not yet proven itself on the stage.

WO also meant that completely new working relationships were created. A good example was the anti-hate campaign which was developed in the run-up to and during the WO. A campaign conceived and implemented in close cooperation between the Copenhagen Police, the City of Copenhagen, the Danish Institute of Human Rights, the National Association of Gays and Lesbians and WO. This partnership is just one of the many new inter-organizational links which have come about between LGBT and mainstream organizations as a result of WO.

Upgrading Businesses

For the first time, a number of Danish companies have actively sought the financial growth potential of the LGBT target group. A good example is Scandinavian Airlnes, which as part of its sponsorship of WO was the first airline to set up a special website for LGBT customers wanting to fly to and from

Scandinavia and Copenhagen. On the airline's LGBT website, customers could also find all the general information about Scandinavia as a region and more specifically LGBT news from Oslo, Stockholm and Copenhagen.

But SAS was not alone. Because the tourist organizations Wonderful Copenhagen and Visit Denmark as well as a number of local companies also used WO to build on an already existing partnership, the purpose of which was to attract even more international LGBT tourists to the city.

Upgrading Knowledge

Before WO, there were more assumptions than facts in debates about LGBT issues. Set against the other countries Denmark normally compares itself to, we had no systematic knowledge and documentation about the lives of our LGBT citizens and how they actually lived and felt. No public authority in Denmark, either locally or nationally, had any official or professionally-collated information about the current living conditions for LGBT people—either for the present day or historically. We did not know whether there were more or fewer hate crime attacks this year than last, whether LGBT citizens have more or less confidence in public institutions than their heterosexual counterparts, or whether there were more or fewer social problems in the LGBT group than among heterosexuals, etc.

The National Association of Gays and Lesbians has for many years sought a national survey of LGBT living conditions as seen in for example in Norway, Sweden, the Netherlands or the UK. Only with the arrival of WO was it possible with the support of the City of Copenhagen and the Tryg Foundation to undertake Denmark's first national living conditions survey.

The results from the survey were presented at the human rights conference during WO and are a contributing factor to both local and national politicians for the first time having a serious basis for decision-making about potential new legislation in the area.

In addition, Copenhagen Police have decided that in the future all attacks on lesbians and gays and transgender people will be documented systematically. This is partly a consequence of the survey and partly because of the hate crimes committed during the actual WO week.

Upgrading Language

When the WO secretariat was first established, a number of articles in national newspapers appeared—and with good reason. Articles with headlines such as "The gays are coming" and "Gay Olympics". At the time, homosexuals were regarded as only being gay men. In any event according to the print and electronic media. In other words: lesbians were pretty much invisible and transgender people did not exist.

Now the language and terms used have become more nuanced and open. Lesbians are acknowledged both culturally and in the media. As one newspaper wrote "lesbians are the new gays". In the same way, the challenges faced by transgender people have risen in the political agenda. This includes the notable fact that the Socialist People's Party has become the first party to select a transgender person as a candidate for the forthcoming local elections.

From homosexuals only meaning gay men, the term "LGBT" is now used assiduously by both journalists and politicians. Which shows that a mainstreaming of the term has occurred. This language nuance and precision have wide-ranging consequences. This is because as we know, words create reality. Or in other words, what is invisible, does not exist. And anything that does not exist, does not have any rights! So for WO, making lesbians and transgender people visible in the media was a success.

Upgrading Culture

For the first time ever in the history of Denmark, an established cultural history museum included LGBT cultural life in ts program as part of WO. It was the Museum of Copenhagen, which produced the "Som jeg er/As I am" exhibition. An exhibition about more than 200 years of LGBT life in the Danish capital, and a chapter of the city's history never previously covered or therefore presented to a wider audience. The project consisted partly of a special exhibition of newly-collected contemporary and historical material and partly of exhibits the museum already had in its collection.

An interesting challenge for the Museum of Copenhagen was that throughout its history, LGBT issues and people have been either undesirable, rendered invisible or made illegal. Which again has meant that museums could not to any significant degree collect material which could document LGBT people and the community's existence and development either in Copenhagen or anywhere else in the country.

The museum therefore decided to do something about this as part of WO, and gave itself the goal of being the first cultural history museum in Denmark to be able to present a broad-based exhibition of LGBT history. The "Som jeg er/As I am" exhibition has not just been a big success with the public, it was also the reason why the Museum of Copenhagen has decided to collect and thus document the living conditions and lives of LGBT people more systematically in the future.

But it was not just the Museum of Copenhagen which used WO as a reason to hone cultural attention and thus focus on the artistic production which has its roots and therefore its basis in the city's creative queer community. The Nikolaj Copenhagen Contemporary Art Center and a large number of the city's other galleries did the same. Teater Rio Rose, a theater group, also used WO as a motive to further develop an already existing play, "Battlefield", so that the play not only covered the dynamics of a heterosexual couple's relationship, but also included gay and a lesbian relationships too.

Upgrading Identity

The sum of all the above-mentioned upgrades in infrastructure, organizational, business, knowledge, language and cultural upgrading are all part of the final upgrade: which is the upgrading of the city's cultural identity.

At least that is how the large amount of feedback the secretary received during the actual WO week and in the weeks after from the city's own citizens can be interpreted. Feedback such as "I am proud of Copenhagen again", "great that the city is supporting diversity", "people smiled more during Outgames", "why can't we have the OutCities cultural program again next year?" or "can the Aarhus stage not stay a little longer? All these words were pieces in the puzzle, which, at the end of the day paints a picture of a more self-aware and culturally alive capital city.

The large amount of positive feedback from local peole was like an echo of the "reviews" which the numerous foreign journalists, participants and artists gave Copenhagen during the WO week. They were unanimous in being impressed by the city's hospitality, openness and tolerance. Not least the way the city made its squares, streets, canals, harbor and beaches available for an event such as WO. In fact the way the whole city supported WO, from the Lord Mayor to ordinary people in the street, made a big impression on the numerous visitors from abroad. This very much strengthened the identity both within the city and outward to the surrounding world. The people of Copenhagen became happier and prouder of living here. And the many thousands of visitors from abroad could be convinced about the high quality of life the city actually has by being able to experience it for themselves.

Sources of Anticipation and Adaptation

As an opposite to Immanuel Kant's *Critique of Pure Reason*, which concentrates strictly on epistemological issues, I have aimed at re-establishing the connection between the spatio-temporal context, or the ontology of the situation, and knowledge, methods and leadership interventions, by arguing that in everyday sense-making and decision-making the classical idea of fixed and absolute knowledge seldom works.

I take my argument even further and claim that the major problems of our times whether we refer to social, economic and environmental sustainability cannot be resolved in a vacuum, atemporally and acontextually.

Throughout *Robustness* we have concentrated on how leadership can be exercised in various spatio-temporal contexts. My approach can be described as *polynomial*: every chapter of the book is situated in a specific context and uses particular terms, theories and examples.

I believe that effective, sustainable and timely interventions become possible when:

1. The locus of isolated actions by individual leaders is expanded to contextual interactions that occur across entire social systems;
2. The context, the properties of the strategic landscape and the time frame at stake, is explicitly considered, and;
3. Our understanding of how leadership gets enacted and received is enriched.

We have claimed that several basic assumptions in the traditional leadership theory are inappropriate (if not mistaken) and instead of fostering anticipation and adaptation they are perhaps partly hindering them. Traditional leadership theories are based on top-down thinking, and assume that the leadership rests within the character or the characteristic behavior of leaders, and they note that a leader acts on organizations in order to achieve his objectives.

According to Dave Snowden[2] there are three silently shared presumptions in traditional leadership. The first one is the *presumption of order* according to which it is believed that there are underlying relationships between cause and effect regarding human interaction and the market and that we are capable of discovering and verifying them. It is

2. C.f. Snowden & Boone 2007.

then presumed that we are capable of designing models and intervening and altering our lives in order to achieve our goals. The *presumption of rational choice* is the second one. It presumes that when faced with a choice between one or more alternatives, people will make a rational decision to minimize pain or maximize pleasure, consequently they can be managed. And the third one is the *presumption of intentionality*: It presumes that every act in organizational life is intentional. To quote an American contemporary philosopher Alicia Juarrero "we assume every blink we see is in effect a wink, and act accordingly".[3]

If these presumptions do depict and guide our current thinking, then it follows that this kind of thinking will lead to certain ways of acting. We have wanted to complement this rational picture of a human being with a flesh and blood perspective, the vertical top-down view with horizontal and bottom-up perspectives, and linear approaches with complex and disruptive ones.

Often the systems we deal with, like organizations, markets or economies, consist of a large number of agents, each of which behaves according to its own principles, values and ideas. No individual actor, not a leader nor a president, can totally understand or determine the patterns of behavior a system displays. This is because emergent patterns result from the consequence of local interaction between actors.[4]

Furthermore, we need to comprehend and be explicate with the properties of the appropriate systems. Viewing all the systems as something in constant flux and susceptible to rapid change neglects stability and the structures necessary for the existence of a system. This means that from time to time it is indeed correct to prefer linearity to nonlinearity, continuity to discontinuity and stability to novelty. Above all this means that issues concerning robustness must be viewed actor by actor, level by level, or-

---

3. Juarrero 1999.
4. Aaltonen 2007.

ganization by organization, system by system.

To rethink the nature of the leadership landscape we must learn from the nature.[5] Not everything is ordered there. Let us look at the two best-known examples of phase transition that demonstrate the existence of different systems in which different causal assumptions apply: the freezing of water and the emergence of a magnet. They both represent phase transitions from chaos to order. Liquid water is relatively disorganized. At freezing point it gives up this disordered state and chooses instead a state of symmetry and order. Similarly, the randomly oriented spins in a ferromagnetic metal are in a state of chaos, but they take up a highly ordered orientation once cooled under a critical temperature. Certainly, human systems are not identical to those found in nature. Human beings have multiple identities and they can shift between them, they make decisions based on past patterns of success and failure, and they intentionally pursue the changing of systems for their own benefit. Due to these properties it can be stated that distinguishing between social systems is always approximate and socially constructed.

Figure 22 shows an ordered, linear system where cause and effect relationships are discoverable and repeatable on the left. On the right there is a chaotic, disruptive system where cause and effect relationships can be made sense of only afterwards or not at all. The complex system is an ordered one too, but the order cannot be top-down imposed on the system instead it stems from the local interaction between the actors involved. Furthermore, the shape of the figure is motivated because as long as people are alive and organizations exist, the leadership landscape is not stable. It will always undergo and set in motion continuous change created by actors and their actions, which subsequently affects all other actors and their actions.

---

5. For an important and clear argument see Stuart Kauffman's *At Home in the Universe. The Search for the Laws of Self-Organization and Complexity.*

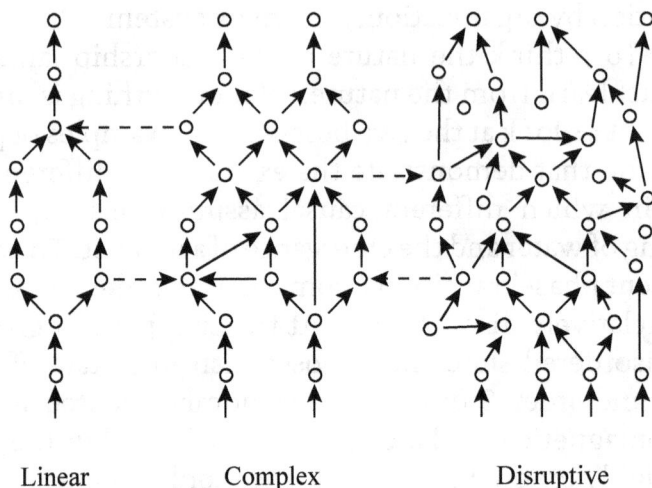

| Linear | Complex | Disruptive |

Figure 22 *Different systems and emergence of futures*

Over time not only do the actors shift position, but the landscape in which the action takes place alters too. This is how we see *the nature of living systems*. The systems unfold over time, they have a history that influences their present behavior, and that they anticipate the future. In brief, *in an anticipatory and adaptive human system the past, present and future states may influence the present changes in that system*. It follows naturally that our understanding of time is multi-leveled. The various conceptions of pasts as well as the different time horizons of the futures can turn into causal forces to determine present and future social realities.

Figure 22 provides clear strategies for leadership. Firstly, as Chuan Lam Leong states, human systems are complex systems, even if many of the things in our lives work according to linear logic. Secondly, in the long run the best place for an ant or a human being or a system to survive in evolution is not in the ordered, linear system, because it cannot renew itself fast enough with respect to the changing landscape. Nor is the best place to survive in chaotic system, in the most disruptive system, because in that system far too much energy is consumed in order to make sense of what can be done. The best place to survive is in between in the complex system. Here we find the two innovation strategies: if you are in the ordered, linear system, push the actors towards a chaotic system, then new ideas, new actions can emerge; if you are in a chaotic system, introduce order to the actors, then they can act more efficiently. Thirdly and polynomially, certain ideas and methods work best within certain systems and contexts.

Impact as Strategy

From the start we have considered the Newtonian tradition partly misleading. The legacy of focusing on efficient cause, in science and economics, is the reason why many everyday problems are difficult to make sense of and hard to resolve, and why we, human beings, have trouble dealing with complex chains of causality.

In a system each emergent outcome, at any level, is part of the overall process of interaction. Thus improving the relationships between the different actors and different levels is itself part of the broader context of creating an anticipatory and adaptive system. If leadership is seen as part of that emergent process, then it may be thought about in terms of multiple non-linear inter-related influences at different levels. Thus enabling the success of any or many actors benefits the whole system; and because there are dynamic inter-level relationships, both bottom-up and top-down leadership interventions are necessary.[6]

My aim has been to provide a fuller futures context for consideration; to expand thought levels, concerns, and planning so that we recognize a whole web of interrelated causes that can influence our respective futures.

In *Robustness*, the leadership interventions gain their impact not from tools, techniques and methods alone but from the fit between the tools, techniques and methods and the appropriate ontology of the situation.

In Table 8 the situational context is depicted by linear, complex and disruptive systems and the temporal con-

---

6. Mitleton-Kelly 2007.

text by tactical, strategic and visionary time horizons. The tactical time horizon is the immediate future, the strategic to medium-distance, and visionary to long or very long time horizons. This is a general contemporary description; it uses some of the well-known ideas and approaches as representations. It is also open for more specific definitions that are made case by case, and for new futures contents.

I often think that, because of the rational outlook we have taken, the leadership interventions are those on the left side of Table 8. The focus is on linear interventions forming hierarchical and structured management procedures when it is necessary, and when they exist to improving and re-engineering them, and that this occurs mostly on the tactical and strategic time horizons (see Chapter 2). Hence the visionary time horizon is rarely considered. When it comes to visionary leadership, the habit is to produce visions, missions and values; and to prepare for the future (see Chapter 5). It is additionally important to introduce new environments and experiments that allow new patterns to emerge, and identify leverage points where the future is emerging inside and outside your organizations and place your resources there (see Chapter 7).[7]

I believe that by concentrating only on the above elements, we give up some of our possibilities to lead and are only partly able to fulfill our leadership potentiality.

It has been stated on several occasions that a rich mental toolbox (the use of many methods and concepts; inside teams and outside networks; and multiple sources of information) is a major source of anticipation and adaptation. This is true for a simple reason: an event in the environment of a system, no matter how important, does not have inherent and immediate meaning for the system. Its meaning is established in time as it is enacted in the system and carried over into the future. If an event cannot find a relevant context in the system, it will remain meaningless. A rich mental toolbox provides us with multiple interfaces

7. C.f. Sanders 1998.

	Linear	Complex	Disruptive
Visionary	Evaluates forthcoming changes and prepares the system with new skills, abilities and business frames in order to face them	Creates visions and missions, builds value-based leadership	Manages perceptions, reframes existing contracts and boundaries, introduces new attractors, sets and removes constrains
Strategic	Ensures adherence to a vision, reallocates existing resources, emphasizes problem-solving	Focuses on and leads interactions between actors, groups and organizations	Creates environments and experiments that allow new patterns to emerge
Tactical	Exploits the existing opportunities; e.g., process re-engineering, best practice	Opens up strategic dialogues, builds factual richness and cognitive diversity	Acts and makes fast decisions, looks for what works; e.g., authorative leadership, crisis management

Table 8 *Leader's role in multiple contexts*

for an environment, and thus the chances for an event to be enacted in a system are enhanced.

There are several ways to lead complex environments in tactical and strategic time horizons (see also Chapter 6):

- Promoting timely strategic dialog for creating meaning, direction and energy,
- Keeping a high level of cognitive and factual heterogeneity when hiring graduates, experts and managers,
- Favouring the admission of actors and companies outside the appropriate system, and

- Fostering coevolution by managing direct and indirect feedback loops on markets, customers, new technologies, products and services worldwide, and increasing the motives for connecting with others.

When a situation and the system is in a disruptive state, it is better to make your move, act and take a position, and see what follows (Chapter 4). The disruptive futures at strategic time horizon cannot be led in a similar fashion to those of more linear contexts. In fact, I believe the linear leadership interventions prevent us from succeeding in these contexts. Instead we need to create enabling economical, cultural and technological structures, support the developments of joint projects, and increase the ability to undertake easy and low-cost joint ventures (see Chapter 7). There are a few organizations that explicitly concentrate on leading the disruptive visionary time horizon by perception management, reframing existing contracts and boundaries, introducing new attractors or setting and removing constraints.

Fostering anticipation and adaptation requires the use of multiple contextually motivated leadership interventions. Furthermore, by making the current states and behavior of a system dependent on its past, present and future states; feedback not only incorporates the effects of time into a system's states and behavior patterns, but it also relates the system closely to its environment. The whole evolutionary process depends on and is in fact enabled by direct and indirect feedback loops.

There is a need to shift and expand the locus of how we perceive leadership. Instead of separating and classifying it so that it belongs to certain people or a certain class of people we should include it as a natural way of behaving for all the people and see it as an essential element of every-day life. This definition has significant practical implications for the public sector as well as for businesses, because it changes the way we comprehend the emergence of futures whether we refer to the move from a government-centric approaches to more citizen-centric ones or democratizing of innovation by helping the millions of Einsteins outside big corporations to present their ideas and have their voices heard.

The shift and expansion of locus makes it necessary for us to move beyond the present mono-causal approach that is based on the predominance of efficient cause. *Robustness* suggests that the notion of causality needs to be rethought of as multiple non-linear inter-related influences situated on different levels; that vision and intention may contribute towards shaping or guiding final cause, although they do not determine it; and in which emergence needs to be thought of both as a top-down and a bottom-up reciprocal *process*, as well as an *outcome*.[8]

There are also many differing margins for improvement in our ability to assist people to resolve some of the major challenges around them. Seeing these margins results from considering the situational and temporal contexts explicitly. There are different systems in which different cause and effect relationships apply. The challenges that people face have their natural time scales, which are essential to consider. When the properties of systems and the natural time scales of events are highlighted more appropriate leadership interventions in a system become achievable. These interventions together form a net of causes that influence the emergence of the future.

---

8. C.f. Mitleton-Kelly 2007.

Bibliography

Aaltonen, M. and Wilenius, M. (2002). *Osaamisen Ennakointi - Pidemmälle Tulevaisuuteen, Syvemmälle Osaamiseen*, ISBN 9513736504.

Aaltonen, M. and Heikkilä, T. (2003). *Tarinoiden voima. Miten yritykset hyödyntävät tarinoita?* ISBN 9521407085.

Aaltonen, M., Barth, T., Casti, J.L. and Mitleton-Kelly, E. (2005). *Complexity as a Sense-making Framework*, ISBN 9515642868.

Aaltonen, M. (2007a). *The Third Lens. Multi-ontology Sense-making and Strategic Decision-making*, ISBN 0754647986.

Aaltonen, M. (2007b). "Chronotope space: Managing time and the properties of strategic landscape," *Foresight*, ISSN 1463-6689, 9(4): 58-62.

Aaltonen, M. (2007c). "The return to multi-causality," *Journal of Futures Studies*, ISSN 1027-6084, 12(1): 81-86.

Aaltonen, M. (2007d). "Circular cause, time and narrativity," *Int. J. Management Concepts and Philosophy*, ISSN 1478-1484, 2(3): 183-193.

Aaltonen, M. (2009). "Multi-ontology, sense-making and the emergence of the future," *Futures* 41, ISSN 0016-3287, 279-283.

Adam, B. (1990). *Time & Social Theory*, ISBN 0745607403.

Adam, B. (1998). *Timescapes of Modernity: The Environment and Visible Hazards*, ISBN 0415162742.

Adam, B. (2004). *Time*, ISBN 0745627773.

Akin, R. (2002). "Out of despair: Reconceptualizing teaching through narrative practice," in N. Lyons and V. LaBoskey (eds.), *Narrative Inquiry in Practice: Advancing the Knowledge of Teaching*, ISBN 0807742473, pp. 63-75.

Albertrazzi, L. (1996). "From Kant to Brentano," in L. Albertrazzi, M. Libardi and R. Poli, *The School of Franz Brentano*, ISBN 0792337662.

Alker, H.R. (1996). *Rediscoveries and Reformulations: Humanistic Methodologies for International Studies*, ISBN 0521466954.

Atwood, G. and Stolorow, R.D. (1984). *Structures of Subjectivity: Explorations in Psychoanalytic Phenomenology*, ISBN 0881630128.

Baianu, I.C. and Poli, R. (2010). *From Simple to Super- and Ultra-Complex-Systems: A Paradigm Shift Towards Non-Abelian Emergent System Dynamics*, Unpublished manuscript.

Barbalet, J. (ed.) (2002). *Emotions and Sociology*, ISBN 1405105577.

Bearman, P. Moody, J. and Faris, R. (2003). "Networks and hHistory," *Complexity*, ISSN 1076-2787, 8(1): 61-71.

Bergheim, S. (2007). "The happy variety of capitalism," *Deutsche Bank Research: Current Issues*, ISSN 1612-314X, April 2007.

Bergheim, S. (2008). "The broad basis of societal progress," *Deutsche Bank Research: Current Issues*, ISSN 1612-314X, October 2008.

Bergheim, S. (2008). *Long-Run Growth Forecasting*, ISBN13 9783540776796.

Bourdieu, P. (1963) "The attitude of the Algerian peasant towards time," in J. Pitt-Rivers (ed.), *Mediterranean Countrymen*, Paris: Recherches Mediterranéennes 1.

Buehler, K. (1934). *Sprachtheorie: Die Darstellungsfunktion der Sprache*, Jena: Fischer.

Burke, K. (1954). *Performance and Change*, Hermes: Los Altos.

Burke, K. (1955). *A Rhetoric of Motives*, George Braziller: New York.

Burke, K. (1957). *Philosophy of Literary Form*, Vintage Books: New York.

Burke, K. (1968). *Language as Symbolic Action*, University of California Press. London.

Calhoun, C., Rojek, C. and Turner, B. (eds.) (2005). *The Sage Handbook of Sociology*, ISBN13 9780761968214.

Campbell, D.T. (1974). "Downward causation in hierarchically organized biological systems," in F.J. Ayala and T. Dobzhansky (eds.), *Studies in the Philosophy of Biology*, Macmillan: London, pp. 179-186.

Campbell, D.T. (1990). "Levels of organization, downward causation, and the selection-theory approach to evolutionary epistemology," in G. Greenberg and E. Tobach (eds.), *Theories of the Evolution of Knowing*, ISBN 0805807551, pp. 1-17.

Campbell, V. (2004). "How RAND Invented the Postwar World: Satellites, systems analysis, computing, the internet - almost all the defining features of the information are were shaped in part at the RAND Corporation," *Invention & Technology*, ISSN 8756-7296, Summer.

Castells, M. (1996). *The Rise of the Network Society*, ISBN 1557866171.

Casti, J.L. (1989). "Newton, Aristotle, and the modeling of living systems," in J.L. Casti and A. Karlqvist (eds.), *Newton to Aristotle*, ISBN 0817634355.

Chateaubriand (1861). *Essai Historique, Politique et Moral sur Les Révolutions Anciennes et Modernes*, Paris.

Clandinin, J. (2005). *Handbook of Narrative Inquiry: Mapping A Methodology*, ISBN13 9781412915625 (2006).

Clark, C.M. (ed.) (2001). *Taking Shop: Authentic Conversation and Teacher Learning*, ISBN13 9780807740309.

Czarniawska, B. (1997). *Narrating the Organization: Dramas of Institutional Identity*, ISBN 0226132293.

Czarniawska, B. (1998). *A Narrative Approach in Organization Studies*, ISBN13 9780761906636.

Czarniawska, B. (1999). *Writing Management. Organization Theory as a Literary Genre*, ISBN 0198296142.

Davies, B. (1982). *Life in the Classroom and Playground*, London: Routledge and Kegan Paul.

Deegan, J., Devine, D. and Lodge, A. (eds.) (2004). *Primary Voices: Equality, Diversity and Childhood in Irish Primary Schools*, ISBN 1904541178.

Denzin, N. (1984). *On Understanding Emotion*, ISBN 0875895883.

Denzin, N. (1989). *Interpretive Interactionism*, ISBN 080393002X.

Denzin, N. (1992). "The many faces of emotionality: Reading persona." in C. Ellis and M. Flaherty (eds.), *Investigating Subjectivity: Research on Lived Experience*, ISBN 0803944977, pp. 17-30.

Dewey, J. (1915). *Democracy and Education*, New York: The Macmillan Company.

Dewey, J. (1933). *How We Think*, (rev. ed.), Lexington, MA: Heath Publishing.

Diderot (1781). Encyclopédie 12.

Ditto, W.L. and Pecora, L.M. (1993). "Mastering chaos," *Scientific American*, ISSN 0036-8733, 269: 78-84.

Durkheim, E. (1971). *The Elementary Forms of Religious Life: A Study in Religious Sociology* (1912), J.W. Swain (trans.), London: George Allen & Unwin.

Eisenhardt, K.M. (1989). "Building theories from case study research," *Academy of Management Review,* ISSN 0001-4273, 14(4): 532-550.

Ellis, C. and Flaherty, M. (eds.) (1992). *Investigating Subjectivity: Research on Lived Experience,* ISBN 0803944977.

Evans, K., Fraser, P. and Taylor, I. (1996). *A Tale of Two Cities: Global Change, Local Feeling and Everyday Life in the North of England,* ISBN 0415138280.

Fitzmaurice, G. (ed.) (2005). *The World of Bryan MacMahon,* ISBN 1856354679.

Florio-Ruane, S. (2001). *Teacher Education and the Cultural Imagination: Autobiography, Conversation, and Narrative,* ISBN 0805823751.

Foucault, M. (1976). *The Archeology of Knowledge,* New York: Colphon Books.

Foucault, M. (1978). *History of Sexuality,* ISBN 0713910941.

Gadamer, H.-G. (1994). "What is truth?" in B.R. Wachterhauser (ed.), *Hermeneutics and Truth,* ISBN 0810111438.

Gell, A. (1992). *The Anthropology of Time: Cultural Constructions of Temporal Maps and Images,* ISBN 0854967176.

Gitlin, A. (2005). "Inquiry, imagination, and the search for a deep politic," *Educational Researcher,* ISSN 0013-189X, 34(3): 15-24.

Glaser, B. and Strauss, A. (1967). *The Discovery of Grounded Theory: Strategies for Qualitative Research,* ISBN 0202302601.

Godet, M. (2006). *Creating Futures: Scenario Planning as a Strategic Management Tool,* ISBN 2717852441.

Goleman, D. (1995). *Emotional Intelligence: Why It Can Matter More Than IQ?* ISBN 055309503X.

Goodson, I. (1988). "Teachers life histories and studies of curriculum and schooling," in I.F. Goodson (ed.), *The Making of Curriculum: Collected Essays,* ISBN 1850001847, pp. 71-92.

Gordon, T. J. (2008). "Management of systems in chaos," *Futures,* ISSN 0016-3287, Summer.

Gordon, T. J. (2009). "Uses of chaos analysis in forecasting," in *Futures Research Methodology 3.0,* ISBN13 9780981894119.

Graham, L. (1992). "Archival research in intertextual analysis: Four representations of the life of Dr. Lillian Moller Gilbreth," in C. Ellis and M. Flaherty (eds.), *Investigating Subjectivity: Research on Lived Experience,* ISBN 0803944977, pp. 71-92.

Green, J. (2007). *Democratizing the Future: Towards a New Era of Creativity and Growth*, Koninklijke Philips Electronics N.V.

Guicciardi (1935). Ricordi. Bari.

Hargreaves, A. and Fullan, M. (1992*). Understanding Teacher Development*, ISBN 0807731889.

Hargreaves, A. (2002). "Teaching in a box: Emotional geographies of teaching," in C. Sugrue and C. Day (eds.), *Developing teachers and Teaching Practice: International Research Perspectives,* ISBN 0415262542, pp. 3-25.

Hayek, Friedrich August von (1988). *The Fatal Conceit. The Errors of Socialism*, ISBN 0226320685.

Heidegger, M. (1962). *Being and Time*, ISBN 0060638508.

Herder, J.G. (1955). *Metakritik zur Kritik der reinen Vernunft*, Berlin.

Ho, P. (2008). "The RAHS Story," in E. Tan and B. Hoo (eds.), *Thinking About the Future: Strategic Anticipation and RAHS*, National Security Coordination Secretariat & S. Rajatnam School of International Studies Publication: Singapore.

Hochschild, A. (1983*). The Managed Heart: Commercialization of the Human Feeling*, Berkeley, CA: University of California Press.

Husserl, E. (1970). *The Crisis of European Sciences and Trasncendental Phenomenology*, ISBN 081010458X.

Huxley, A. (1932). *A Brave New World*, London: Penguin.

Hämäläinen, R.P. and Saarinen, E. (2007). *Systems Intelligence in Leadership and Everyday Life*, ISBN13 9789512288373.

Hämäläinen, R.P. and Saarinen, E. (2008). *Systems Intelligence. A New Lens on Human Engagement and Action*, ISBN13 9789512295272.

Inglehart, R. and Welzel, C. (2005*). Modernization, Cultural Change and Democracy*, ISBN 0521846951.

James, W. (1907). *Pragmatism: A New Name for Some Old Ways of Thinking*.

Jaques, E. (1982). *The Form of Time*, ISBN 084481394X.

Juarrero, A. (1999). *Dynamics in Action: Intentional Behavior as a Complex System*, ISBN 0262100819.

Kaminska-Labbe, R. and McKelvey, B.T.C. (2006). On the co-evolution of causality: A study of Aristotelian causes and other entangled influences," presented in the Academy of Management Meeting, August 14, Atlanta.

Kant, I. *Anthropology from a Pragmatic Point of View*, ISBN 9024715857.

Kelley, K. (1994). *Out of Control*, ISBN 0201483408.

Kemper, T. (ed.) (1990). *Research Agendas in the Sociology of Emotions*, ISBN 079140269X.

Kern, S. (1983). *The Culture of Time and Space 1880-1919*, ISBN 0674179730.

Keuck, K (1934). *Historia Geschichte des Wortes und seiner Bedeutungen in der Antike und in den Romantischen Sprachen*, Munster.

Koselleck, R. (2002). *The Practice of Conceptual History: Timing History, Spacing Concepts*, ISBN 0804743053.

Koselleck, R. (2004). *Futures Past: On the Semantics of Historical Time*, ISBN 0231127715.

La CIA au service de Hollywood (2002). *Le Journal de Dimanche*, ISSN 0242-3065, 16 June 2002.

Loescher, M.S., Schoeder, C. and Thomas, C.W. (2000). *Proteus: Insights from 2020*, ISBN 0970688504.

Loughran, J., Hamilton, M. LaBoskey, V. and Russell, T. (2004). *International Handbook of Self-Study of Teaching and Teacher Education Practices*, ISBN 1402018126.

Louie, A.H. (2006). "(M, R)-systems and their realizations," *Axiomathes*, ISSN 1122-1151, 35-64.

Louie, A.H. (2008). "Functional entailment and immanent causation in relational biology," *Axiomathes*, ISSN 1122-1151, 289-302.

Louie, A.H. and Kercel, S.W. (2007). "Topology and life redux: Robert Rosen's relational diagrams of living systems," *Axiomathes*, ISSN 1122-1151, 109-136.

Luhmann, N. (1986). "The autopoeisis of social systems." in E. Geyer and J. Van Der Zouwen, *Sociocybernet Paradoxes: Observation, Control and Evolution of Self-steering Systems*, ISBN 0803997353, pp. 172-192.

Luhmann, N. (1995). *Social Systems*, ISBN 0804726256.

Luhmann. N. (1997). *Die Gesellschaft der Gesellschaft*, ISBN 351858247X.

Luhmann, N. (2000). *Organization und Entscheidung*. Opladen und Wiesbaden. Westdeutscher Verlag, ISBN 3531134515.

Lupton, D. (1998). *The Emotional Self: A Sociocultural Exploration*, ISBN 0761956026.

Lyons, N. and LaBoskey, V. (eds.) (2002). *Narrative Inquiry in Practice: Advancing the Knowledge of Teaching*, ISBN 0807742473.

MacIntyre, A. (1981). *After Virtue*, ISBN 0715609335.

MacMahon, B. (1992). *The Master*, Dublin: Poolbeg.

Martela, M. and Saarinen, E. (2008). "The nature of social systems in systems intelligence: Insights from intersubjective theory," in R. Hämäläinen and E. Saarinen (eds.), *Systems Intelligence: A New Lens on Human Engagement and Action*, ISBN13 9789512288373.

Maturana, H. (1981). "Autopoeisis." in M. Zeleny, *Autopoeisis: A Theory of Living Organization*, New York: North Holland, pp. 21-33.

Maturana, H. and Varela, F. (1980). *Autopoeisis and Cognition*, ISBN 9027710155.

McGahern, J. (2005). *Memoir*, ISBN 0571230393.

Merleau-Ponty, M. (1962). *The Phenomenology of Human Perception*, New York: Humanities Press.

Miller, R. (1996). *Measuring What People Know: Human Capital Accounting for the Knowledge Economy*, ISBN 9264147780.

Miller, R. (1997-99). "Rules for radicals," Monthly column for ezine, intellectualcapital.com.

Miller, R., Michalski, W. & Stevens, B. (2002). *The Future of Money*, ISBN 0712699910.

Miller, R. and Bentley, T. (2003). *Unique Creation*, National College for School Leadership, UK.

Miller, R. (2006). "From trends to futures literacy: Reclaiming the future," *Centre for Strategic Education, Seminar Series Paper No. 160*, December 2006.

Miller, R. (2007). "Futures literacy: A hybrid strategic scenario method," *Futures,* ISSN 0016-3287, 39: 341-362.

Miller, R. *et al.* (2010). *The World and Europe in 2025: Imagining the Potential of the Present*, draft proposal.

Miles, M.B. and Huberman, A.M. (1994). *Qualitative Data Analysis: An Expended Sourcebook*, ISBN 0803946538.

Mills, C.W. (1959). *The Sociological Imagination,* London: Oxford University Press.

Mitleton-Kelly, E. (2007). "The emergence of final cause," in M. Aaltonen (ed.), *The Third Lens: Multi-ontology Sense-making and Strategic Decision-Making,* ISBN 0754647986, pp. 111-122.

Muller, J. Von (1830). *Vier und Zwanzig Bucher allgemeiner Geschichten besonders der europäischen Menscheit*, Suttgart.

Nelson, R.R. and Sidney G.W. (1982). *An Evolutionary Theory of Economic Change*, ISBN 0674272285.

OECD (Organization for Economic Co-operation and Development) (2005). *Teachers Matter: Attracting, Developing and Retaining Effective Teachers*, ISBN 9264018026.

Orange, D., Atwood, G. and Stolorow, R. (1997). *Working Intersubjectivity: Contextualism in Psychoanalytic Practice*, ISBN 0881632295.

Parsons, T. (1951). *The Social System*, New York: Free Press.

Perla, P.P. and Markowitz, M.C. (2009). *Wargaming Strategic Linkage*, CNA Publication CRM DOO19256.A2.

Perthes, C.T. (1872). *Friedrich Perthes´ Leben*. Gotha.

Pirsig, R.M. (1979). *Zen and the Art of Motorcycle Maintenance*, ISBN 0688052304.

Primary School Curriculum (1999). Dublin: Government Publications.

Poli, R. (2006). "Ontology: The categorical stance." in R. Poli and J. Seibt, *TAO: Theory and Applications of Ontology*, ISSN 1520-8583, Dordrect: Springer.

Poli, R. (2007). "Three obstructions: Forms of causation, chronotopoids, and the levels of reality," *Axiomathes*, ISSN 1122-1151, 1-18.

Poli, R. (2009a). "An introduction to the ontology of anticipation," *Futures*, ISSN 0016-3287.

Poli, R. (2009b). "The complexity of anticipation," *Balkan Journal of Philosophy*, ISSN 1313-888X ,1(1): 19-29.

Poli, R. (2010). "The many aspects of anticipation," *Foresight*, ISSN 1463-6689, forthcoming.

Prigogine, I. and Stengers, I. (1984). *From Being to Becoming. Time and Complexity in the Physical Sciences*, San Fransisco: W. H. Freeman.

Rashevsky, N. (1958). "Topology and life: In search of general mathematical principles in biology and sociology," *Bulletin of Mathematical Biophysics*, ISSN 0007-4985, 317-348.

Richelieu (1947). *Testametn politique*, L. Ándre and L. Noel. Paris (eds.).

Richert, A. (2005). "Narratives that teach: Learning about teaching from the stories teachers tell," in N. Lyons and V. LaBoskey (eds.), *Narrative Inquiry in Practice: Advancing the Knowledge Of Teaching*, ISBN 0807742473, pp. 48-62.

Rifkin, J. (1987). *Time Wars*, ISBN 0805003770.

Rosen, R. (1958). "A relational theory of biological systems," *Bulletin of Mathematical Biophysics*, ISSN 0007-4985, 245-260.

Rosen, R. (1972). "Some relational cell models: The metabolism-repair systems," in R. Rosen, *Foundations of Mathematical Biology*, Vol 2, New York: Academic Press, pp 217-253.

Rosen, R. (1972). *Planning, Management, Policies and Strategies: Four Fuzzy Concepts*, Unpublished typescript.

Rosen, R. (1978). *Fundamentals of Measurement and Representation of Natural Systems*, ISBN 0444002618.

Rosen, R. (1985). *Anticipatory Systems: Philosophical, Mathematical and Methodological Foundations*, ISBN 008031158X.

Rosen, R. (2000). *Essays on Life Itself*, ISBN 023110510X.

Rosengeil, S. and Seymour, J. (1999). *Practising Identities: Power and Resistance*, ISBN 0312222270.

Ross, W.D. (1955). *Aristotle Selections*, ISBN 0684146991.

Sanders, T.I. (1998). *Strategic Thinking and the New Science: Planning in the Midst of Chaos, Complexity, and Change*, ISBN 0684842688.

Schieder, T. (1940). *Deutscher Geist und ständische Freiheit*, Königsberg.

Schutz, A. (1967). *The Phenomenology of the Social World*, ISBN 0810103907.

Shavelson, R., Phillips, D., Towne, L. and Feuer, M. (2002). "On the science of education design studies," *Educational Researcher*, ISSN 0013-189X, 32(1): 25-28.

Shotter, J. (2006). "Understanding process from within: An argument for 'withness'-thinking," *Organizational Studies*, ISSN 0170-8406, 27(4): 585-604.

Shutz, A. (1973). "On multiple realities," in *Collected Papers I. The Problem of Social Reality*, ISBN 9024715024, pp. 207-259.

Seidl, D. (2005). "The basic concepts of Luhmann's theory of social systems," in D. Seidl and K.H Becker, *Niklas Luhmann and Organization Studies*, ISBN 9147702095, pp 21-53.

Sen, A. (1999). *Development as Freedom*, ISBN 0198297580.

Sieyés (1791) "Histoire," in *Nouveau dictionnaire historique.*

Snowden, D. and Boone, M. (2007). "A leader's framework for decision making," *Harward Business Review*, ISSN 0017-8012 , November 2007.

Von Stein, L. (1959). *Geschichte der sozialen Bewegung in Frankreich von 1789 bis auf unsere Tage.*

Stolorow, R.D. (2002). "Impasse, affectivity, and intersubjective systems," *Psychoanalytic Review*, ISSN 0033-2836, 89(3): 329-337.

Stolorow, R.D. (2004). "Autobiographical reflections on the intersubjective history of an intersubjective perspective in psychoanalysis," *Psychoanalytic Inquiry*, ISSN 0735-1690, 24: 524-557.

Strong-Wilson, T. (2006). "Re-visioning one's narratives: Exploring the relationship between researcher self-study and teacher research," *Studying Teacher Education: A Journal of Self-study of Teacher Education Practices*, ISSN 1742-5972, 2(1): 59-76.

Sveiby, K-E. (2006). *Treading Lightly: The Hidden Wisdom of the World's Oldest People*, ISBN 174114874X.

Tan Hong Ngoh, E. and Hoo Tiang, B. (2008). *Thinking about the Future: Strategic Anticipation and RAHS*, National Security Coordination Secretariat & S. Rajatnam School of International Studies Publication, Singapore.

Tocqueville, A. De (1889). *Democracy in America*, London.

Ulmer, G. (1989). *Teletheory: Grammatology in the Age of Video*, ISBN 0415901200.

Virilio, P. (1991). *La Vitesse*, Paris: Flammarion.

Virilio, P. (1995). *The Art of the Motor*, J. Rose (trans.), ISBN 0816625719.

Virilio, P. (2000). *Open Sky*, J. Rose (trans.), ISBN 1859841813.

Virilio, P. (2007). *The Original Accident*, ISBN 0745636136.

Waldron, J.C. (2000). "Cultural identity and civic responsibility," in W. Kymlicka and W. Norman (eds.), *Citizenship in Diverse Societies*, ISBN 019829770X, pp. 155-174.

Waller, W. (1932). *The Sociology of Teaching*, New York: Russell and Russell.

Waters, R. (2009). "Search complete," *Financial Times*, ISSN 0307-1766, August 1/August 2, 2009.

Welzel, C., Inglehart, R. and Klingemann, H.D. (2003). "The theory of human development: A cross-cultural analysis," *European Journal of Political Research*, ISSN 0304-4130, 42: 341-379.

White, H. (2002). "Foreword," in R. Koselleck, *The Practice of Conceptual History. Timing History, Spacing Concepts*, ISBN 0804740224, pp. ix-xiv.

Wittgenstein, L. (1953). *Philosophical Investigations*, New York: MacMillan.

Wittgenstein, L. (1958). *The Blue and Brown Books: Preliminary Studies for the "Philosophical Investigations"*, New York: Harper and Row.

Wittgenstein, L. (1961). *Tractatus Logico-Philosophicus*, Atlantic Highlands: Humanities Press.

Yin, R.K. (1994). *Case Study Research: Design and Methods*, ISBN 080395662.

Zedler, J.H. (1732). *Universal-Lexicon*, Halle and Leipzig.

Zerubavel, E. (1985). *The Seven Day Cycle: The History and Meaning of the Week*, Chicago, IL: University of Chicago Press.

Index

A

accountability 174, 176, 181-2
accounts, historical 33, 57
actions, corresponding 74, 78
actors 24, 31, 59, 62-4, 99, 118-19, 131, 138, 156, 165, 175,
    212-13, 226-7, 229, 231
agencies 63, 85-6, 109-10, 183
alternative futures 88-9, 94, 96
ambiguity 161, 163, 165, 174, 176
analysis, correlation 189, 191
antibiotics 44, 46
assumptions, causal 28-9, 31, 227
autopoietic systems 20-1, 23

B

becoming 71, 73, 80-1, 85, 98, 162, 207
behavior 8, 76, 86, 101, 153, 226, 232
boundaries, open 130
business 15, 55, 93, 105-6, 124, 155, 163, 165, 172, 175-9,
    181-3, 197, 203, 223, 232
business models, new 201-3

C

capacities 8, 20, 23, 43, 81-2, 102, 156-8, 161, 170
capital 190, 201, 204
categories 4, 27, 73
causality 10, 15, 21, 23-4, 156, 188, 190, 233
chronotope 9, 25, 31-2, 101
chronotope space 31-3
clock time 41, 43
collective intelligence 158, 212
communications 6, 23, 61, 67, 157, 159, 173, 184
communities 76, 79-80, 109, 131, 138, 156, 160, 171, 183,
    214

complex systems 87-9, 94, 156, 205, 227-9
complexity 1, 11, 49, 59, 86, 95, 105, 154, 156-8, 160, 174,
    186, 227
concepts 6, 9, 15-16, 18, 24-5, 58-9, 75, 79, 85, 100, 137, 206,
    230
conditions 33, 55, 60-1, 63, 86, 119-20, 128, 157, 165-6, 168,
    187, 206
conformity 64, 74-6, 78-80, 82
contexts 5, 8-9, 11, 15, 17, 19, 21, 23, 25, 27, 159-60, 163,
    176-7, 204, 225, 229
  linear 10-11, 33, 232
control 41, 43, 47, 101-2, 118, 175, 182, 190, 196, 205, 209
controllers 25-7
  feedforward 25-6
Copenhagen 13, 213, 215, 217-24
correlations 185, 189-91, 193
corruption 188-9, 191, 196-7
crises 11, 63, 87-9, 95, 174, 202
cultures 30, 42, 77, 81, 182, 184, 214, 217

D

degrees 10, 18, 20, 41, 81, 90, 96, 103, 163
design 44, 71, 138, 140, 144-5, 154, 156, 172, 176, 179, 208
diagnostic monitoring 177, 179
digital era 161-2
dimensions 24-5, 45, 75, 77-8, 117, 126, 178, 187, 191, 208
discourse 53, 64, 70-1, 81, 209
discovery 85, 114, 156-7, 170-1
disruptive system 29, 227-9
drivers 40, 125, 145, 163-4

E

economy 23, 59, 87-8, 125, 162, 181, 183, 186, 226
education 51, 65, 68-9, 81, 172, 175, 182, 185, 188-9, 192-3,
195-6
effect relationships 3, 29, 32, 55, 118, 227, 233
emergence 10, 15-17, 19, 21, 23, 25, 27, 29, 31, 33, 35, 49, 54,
    95, 158, 233

emergent behaviors 95
emotions 11, 31, 64-5, 69, 71-3, 78, 81, 152
environment 8, 20-1, 23, 25-7, 31, 67, 77, 86, 91, 97, 99, 124,
        130, 135-7, 140, 230-2
events, historical 33, 52-3, 59
evidence 74, 79, 144, 157, 168, 171, 174-8, 182
expectations 7, 30, 60, 80, 120-1, 158, 168, 170
experience 4, 11, 54-5, 58, 60, 62-3, 70, 75, 78, 80, 105,
        119-20, 126, 151, 174-5, 195
experimentalism 12, 200, 204-6
experimentation 157, 176, 202, 204-5
experiments 12, 66, 158, 200, 202-4, 230-1
experts 1, 70, 123, 137-8, 140, 144, 149, 231

F

failure 98, 105, 166, 179-80, 204-5, 227
feedback 26, 86, 102, 224, 232
feedback controllers 25-6
financial system 201-2
foresight exercise 123, 125, 160, 166, 168
framework 8-9, 29, 49, 61, 88, 137, 167, 178
  analytical 108, 174, 178
freedom 16, 59, 76-7, 82, 131, 142, 185, 187-90, 196, 205
  individual 64, 74-6, 78, 80, 187, 197
functional activities 19-20, 24
functions 7-8, 17, 26, 52, 55, 107, 110-11, 156, 204
futures 2-3, 6, 12, 44, 46, 60, 117, 119, 121, 123, 125, 127-9,
        137-9, 143, 153-4, 169-70
futures studies 161, 163-4
FuturesIreland 149, 154-60, 163, 165, 167-74, 178, 181-2

G

GDP 184, 189, 192, 197
generations 21, 30, 54, 66, 77, 183, 195
globalization 41, 125-6
goal congruence 97-8
government 1, 85-6, 107, 117, 122, 124, 131, 137-8, 140,
        155, 162, 184, 194, 196

groups 3, 53, 104, 108, 115, 123, 138, 174, 182, 191-2, 194, 216, 231

H

history 6, 11, 33, 43, 52-63, 65, 90, 121, 130, 153, 157, 200, 202, 205, 212, 222-3
horizon scanning 85, 92-3, 96
human beings 6-10, 43, 47, 55, 60, 62, 102, 120, 129, 150-2, 227, 229
human rights 142, 214, 217, 220
human systems 18, 39, 102, 129-30, 150, 227-8
  adaptive 3, 6, 19, 25, 53, 121, 150, 228
hypothesis 159, 173, 182-3

I

identities 6, 52, 65, 69-71, 74-6, 78-81, 177, 202, 215, 224
  elaborated 74-5
identity processes 74-5, 78
imagination 69, 72, 133, 157, 159-60, 170, 205, 209
imagining 138, 145, 158-9, 168, 206
  rigorous 158-9, 170
improvement 125, 136, 182-3, 192, 195, 197, 233
individuals 3, 6, 64, 66-7, 97, 160, 163, 174, 187, 197
information 3, 21, 23, 52, 66, 100-2, 104, 106, 187, 205, 207, 221, 230
initiatives 143, 181, 184-5, 203
innovation 12, 44-5, 105-6, 109-10, 122, 142, 158, 163, 165, 174, 176-8, 181-3, 186-7, 189, 199, 201
  process of 95, 107
innovation system 107, 109-10
  appropriate 104, 108
innovators 155, 169, 182
institutions 1, 3, 48, 63, 177, 187-8, 195, 202
intelligence 103-6, 149
interaction 2, 21, 24, 34, 70, 143, 152, 163, 172, 178, 229, 231
Internet 43, 66, 102, 207, 216
inventions 43, 47, 158, 160, 166, 202

investments 67, 134, 202, 218-19
Ireland   71-2, 81, 154-5, 157, 160-1, 163-5, 167-75, 181, 183-4

K

knowledge 3, 8-9, 11-12, 27, 34, 48, 51, 70, 105-7, 119, 128, 154, 156, 160, 172-3, 223-4

L

landscape, strategic 28, 31, 225
language 11, 33-4, 51, 53, 58-9, 61, 71, 77, 159, 203, 222-3
leaders 170-2, 197, 215, 225-6
leadership 2, 10, 13, 27-8, 34, 175, 211, 213, 215, 217, 219, 221, 223, 225, 227-9, 231-3
learning 11, 39, 41, 52, 64, 66-7, 72, 81, 121, 162-3, 165, 175-7, 179, 181-3, 195, 204-5
lesbians 213, 220-2
levels 3, 6, 23-4, 31, 49, 64, 70, 93, 158-9, 168-70, 176, 181, 185-6, 195-7, 226, 229
life satisfaction 185, 189-92, 195-7
life stories 57-8

M

management 11, 28, 38-9, 86-7, 122, 201, 218
managers 29, 39, 89, 97, 99, 231
markets, labour 67-8
memory 6-7, 18-19, 25-6, 64, 69-70
mind 7, 23-4, 56, 98, 149-50, 209
models 13, 18, 21-2, 26, 30, 45, 91, 99, 108, 142, 166, 168, 186, 199
motion 8, 37-8, 215, 227

N

narrators 57-8
natural time scales 5, 233
Newtonian physics 8, 37-8, 40

O

ontological universals 4-6
operations analysis 11, 47, 103, 111
organizations 5-7, 19, 30, 44-5, 47, 54, 87, 89, 96-7, 107, 129,
    152-3, 160-3, 217-18, 225-7, 230-1

P

participants 64, 72, 74, 81, 94-5, 119, 136, 144-5, 150, 154,
    158, 166-8, 171, 174-5, 215-16, 218
partnerships 104, 142, 144, 200, 220
past experience 26, 95, 202
patterns 16, 22, 53, 65, 90, 93, 159, 165
performance 88, 91-2, 98
perspectives 22, 30, 53-4, 76, 79, 120, 134, 145, 152-3,
    158-9, 181, 226
phases 102, 138, 168-70, 179
planning, spatial 124, 136-7, 145
policy 47, 67, 70, 111, 124, 128, 137, 162, 165-6, 168-70,
    176, 212
politics 4, 81, 120, 123, 125, 219
possible futures 12, 85-6, 117, 128, 138, 143, 145, 158
potentialities 7, 63, 127, 206
predictions 118, 120-1, 125, 184
principles 31, 39-40, 91, 119, 131, 218, 226
probabilities 88-90, 96, 121, 129, 158
process 1, 3-4, 16-17, 38, 42, 69, 85, 100-1, 121-2, 138, 145,
    152-3, 155-8, 167-8, 170-4, 179
progress 53, 78, 184-6, 188-9, 192, 194, 197
public governance 163, 165, 177-8, 181

Q

quality 28, 31-2, 162, 174-6, 179, 183, 191, 193, 196-7

R

reason 15, 33, 51, 53, 87, 89, 111, 121, 123, 134, 176, 183,
        186, 207, 222-3, 229-30
received identities 74, 78, 80
recognition 24, 27, 29, 53, 81-2, 156
responsibilities 6, 38, 66-7, 70, 76, 81, 131, 136, 162, 177,
        202
reward system 87, 92, 97, 99
rewards 88, 91-2, 95, 98
rights, property 202-4
risk assessments 90, 92, 98
risks 11, 66-7, 88-9, 91-5, 97-9, 110, 205
robustness 2, 7, 9-11, 13, 28, 34, 120, 189, 196, 200, 225-6,
        229, 233

S

scenario planning 92-4, 96
scenarios 85, 94, 122-5, 137, 163-4, 166, 168-70, 212
sciences 2, 4, 9, 15, 23, 52, 87, 90, 105, 122, 127, 229
sectors 98, 110, 125, 182, 200, 203
service 106-10, 174, 179, 218, 232
  public 164, 181-2
signifier 33-4
social markers 42, 206
social structures 58, 190
social systems 21-3, 149, 186, 209, 225, 227
societal development 185, 189, 195-7
societal progress 184-5, 188-9
societies 42-3, 66, 72, 121-2, 125, 127, 160, 162-3, 165, 167,
        171, 176, 178, 181, 184-7, 190-1
spatial planning processes 132, 138, 145-6
spatio-temporal contexts 2-3, 5, 8-11, 27-8, 30-2, 34, 53, 149,
        224-5

spontaneity 39, 157-8
stakeholders 123-4, 136, 138, 143, 162-3
stories 57, 62-3, 65, 157, 159-60, 166, 169-70, 173-4, 178, 181-3, 208
Strategy 13, 211, 213, 215, 217, 219, 221, 223, 225, 227, 229, 231, 233
structural vision 131-2, 135-8, 142-5
structures 21, 58, 62-4, 86, 121, 135, 137, 195, 226
student teachers 69, 73-6, 78-81
subsystems 23, 40
support 80, 108-10, 143, 162, 175, 177, 181, 188-9, 194, 220-1, 232
system-model relationship 21, 26, 38
systems
  accounting 203
  adaptive 19, 22, 25, 229
  chaotic 101, 228-9
  closed 20-1
  economic 20, 98
  emergent 156, 202-3
  global 87, 98
  individual 47, 103
  inter-subjective 151-3
  linear 29, 32, 87, 227-9
  living 19, 39, 228
  organizational 181-2
  public 163, 176, 183-4
  self-referential 21-2
  transaction 202-3
  visionary 29, 31-2
systems theory, inter-subjective 150-2

T

teachers 66, 68, 70-3, 75-82, 121, 182
teaching 11, 64, 66, 68, 70-3, 75-6, 78-9, 81-2, 213
  cultures of 72-3, 78
technology 40, 45, 48, 85-6, 102-3, 105, 115, 125, 127, 149, 172, 182-3
themes 73-4, 78-9, 140, 144, 160, 163

theory 2-3, 19, 27, 62, 105, 150, 156, 186, 188-9, 200
thinking 1-3, 15, 21-2, 28, 30, 49, 52, 73, 79, 85-6, 89-91,
        117, 150, 155-8, 168-9, 226
time-frame 5, 30-1
time horizon 88, 93, 97, 134, 145, 154, 228
  relevant 33, 88
time-scales, natural 30
timelessness 43
tolerance 189-91, 196, 215, 224
tools 18, 27-9, 93, 107, 155, 179, 207, 229
traditions 51-2, 61, 195, 213
transformations 1, 4, 156-7
trends 88-9, 124-5, 145, 163, 166, 207
trust, interpersonal 190-1, 196-7

U

uncertainties 1, 11, 32, 66, 86, 88, 90, 92, 94-9, 105, 149, 161,
        163, 193, 200
understanding 3, 6-8, 10, 23, 25, 48, 66, 150, 152-3, 157, 174,
        179, 216, 225, 228

V

values 22, 25, 31, 59, 61, 64, 66, 68, 75, 81, 89, 94, 98, 104,
        170, 194-5
variables 22, 27, 74, 118, 185, 189-97
visionary 29, 31-2, 230-1
visioning exercises 135-6, 138, 144
visions 52, 70, 85, 122, 136, 138, 145, 175, 230-1, 233

W

water management 136-7, 140, 142
wealth creation 163, 175, 177-8, 202-3
well-being 68, 115, 175, 193-4
WO 214-24

www.ingramcontent.com/pod-product-compliance
Lightning Source LLC
Chambersburg PA
CBHW061146220326
41599CB00025B/4369